MIMESIS, GENRES AND POST-COLONIAL DISCOURSE

Mimesis, Genres and Post-Colonial Discourse

Deconstructing Magic Realism

Jean-Pierre Durix
Professor of English
Université de Bourgogne
Dijon, France

palgrave
macmillan

Published by PALGRAVE MACMILLAN
Houndmills, Basingstoke, Hampshire RG21 6XS and
175 Fifth Avenue, New York, N.Y. 10010
Companies and representatives throughout the world

PALGRAVE MACMILLAN is the global academic imprint of the Palgrave Macmillan division of St. Martin's Press, LLC and of Palgrave Macmillan Ltd. Macmillan® is a registered trademark in the United States, United Kingdom and other countries. Palgrave is a registered trademark in the European Union and other countries.

Outside North America
ISBN 0–333–73224–3

In North America
ISBN 0–312–21585–1

This book is printed on paper suitable for recycling and made from fully managed and sustained forest sources.

A catalogue record for this book is available from the British Library.

Library of Congress Catalog Card Number: 98–3656

Transferred to digital printing 2002

Printed and bound in Great Britain by
Antony Rowe Ltd, Chippenham and Eastbourne

For Carole
and to Catherine and Jean-François

This book was initially started during a sabbatical granted by the Université de Bourgogne. Its composition has benefitted greatly from discussions with students in my classes, with many colleagues and members of the 'Centre de Recherches Image/Texte/Langage' in Dijon, amongst whom Michel Baridon and Jean-Michel Rabaté have always been most helpful. Some of my initial reflexions on 'magic realism' were nurtured by the works of Jeanne Delbaere (Université Libre de Bruxelles). Among friends all over the world to whom this work owes a great deal, may I thank in particular the writers Patricia Grace, Wilson Harris, Isabel Huggan, Witi Ihimaera and Albert Wendt, the academics Jacqueline Bardolph (Université de Nice), Michel Fabre (Université Sorbonne Nouvelle), Christiane Fioupou (Université de Toulouse), Gareth Griffiths (University of Western Australia), Hartwig Isernhagen (University of Basel), Hena Maes-Jelinek (Université de Liège), Luigi Sampietro (University of Milan), Paul Sharrad (University of Wollongong) and Terry Sturm (University of Auckland).

CONTENTS

GENERAL INTRODUCTION

Many innovative experiments in literature have been made by writers from areas of the world which, half a century ago, did not produce much literature, or which were ignored by the main centres of culture because they were considered peripheral or unsophisticated. This prejudice has affected most colonized countries, even when, as was the case with Canada, Australia or New Zealand, the inhabitants' cultural references were predominantly European. This bias has generated a number of attitudes which, for a long time, largely tainted the relationships between metropolises and colonies. Undoubtedly the systems of government which varied from indirect rule to assimilation created specific local situations. However an examination of post-colonial literatures across the language divide reveals disturbing similarities in themes, structures and in attitudes to language. So it may not be totally incongruous to suggest that common features exist between the literatures of South America, of the French-speaking Caribbean and of the 'Commonwealth', a much criticized term whose main merit is to include most of the former British colonies. I personally favour the term 'New Literatures' which, for me, groups under one heading all the countries that underwent a process of colonization, including South Africa which, though technically outside the Commonwealth, shares many features with other former colonies. The present trend however is to use the adjective 'post-colonial' which suffers from the ambiguities related to the idea of 'posteriority', though Homi Bhabha[1] argues that this prefix need not be taken only in its historical sense but rather in the meaning of 'beyond'. 'Post-colonial' however has no alternative as an adjective referring to the theories so well illustrated by Edward Said,[2] Homi Bhabha, Stephen Slemon, Bill Ashcroft, Gareth Griffiths, Helen Tiffin[3]... to mention just some of the most prominent authors in the field. All these terms presuppose characteristics shared by countries which, at some point in their history,

---

[1] In *The Location of Culture*, Bhabha reflects on the relevance of the trope of the *beyond* to relate to our end of the century: 'At the century's edge, we are less exercised by annihilation — the death of the author — or epiphany — the birth of the 'subject'. Our existence today is marked by a tenebrous sense of survival, living on the borderlines of the 'present', for which there seems to be no proper name other than the current and controversial shiftiness of the prefix 'post': *postmodernism, post-colonialism, postfeminism....*' (p. 1)

[2] In particular in his *Orientalism*.

[3] See Bill Ashcroft, Gareth Griffiths and Helen Tiffin, *The Empire Writes Back: Theory and Practice in Post-Colonial Literatures*. See also by the same authors, eds., *The Post-Colonial Studies Reader*.

suffered the imposition of an alien culture presented as an absolute model.

Grouping together under the heading 'post-colonial' people who are members of the settler group and those whose land and sovereignty were alienated by the former has also raised legitimate objections. Erasing differences between these basically different cultures may lead to a banalization of the phenomenon of colonization and to a blurring of the divergent interests of mainly European-based colonial civilizations which made little of native interests in the early stages of their settlement and of those who were victimized and underwent spoliation of land, sovereignty and culture at the hands of imperialists. When talking of the written literature of these countries, one should be careful to contextualize the production, not to deny its participation in the wider network of world artistic productions but simply to render justice to its complex anchoring and involvement in its particular cultures and historical setting.

In a previous book,[1] I have developed more fully the major issues at stake in the New Literatures in English. Some scholars have suggested that one should distinguish between those writers who have continued to work from their original homelands and the migrants. Though these objections contain some truth, there are enough resemblances between the aims and the achievements of writers from the former colonies to justify a term which, like all classifications, has only limited contextual value but can serve to highlight important features.

One must also be careful of enclosing the New Literatures within strict limits which are just as artificial as the notion of the Orient as a unified body is to Edward Said.[2] The New Literatures do have specificities but they are part of the wider field of world literatures with which they maintain a constant dialogue, even if, at times, it is one enlivened by discordant voices or shrieks.

It would be exaggerated to fight against the dominance of the Western canon through insisting on a new canon, this time situated in the margins, which would be suddenly essentialized, endowed with all merits after having been ignored for centuries. Overevaluation presents as many dangers as ignorance of their value. Quasi-metaphysical glorification of 'otherness' leads to a new binary hierarchic scale in which everything

---

[1] *The Writer Written.* See also C. and J.P. Durix, *An Introduction to the New Literatures in English.*

[2] '... never has there been such a thing as a pure, or unconditional, Orient; similarly never has there been a nonmaterial form of Orientalism, much less something as innocent as an "idea" of the Orient' (*Orientalism*, Penguin edition, pp. 22-3 [all further references will be to this edition]).

that does not fit in is rejected into a cultural and literary limbo. Edward Said has demonstrated with enough pertinence the sterile division inherent in Orientalist discourse between 'us' and 'them'[1] for critics to be cautious of creating another mental ghetto. Our common experience in this multimedia, 'Internet' world is more of interrelation and interdependence of the different cultures than of strict separate national entities, even if this means that those who have predominant access to or control of these new instruments of communication may well become the new 'information colonizers'. Questions concerning the identity of individual cultures are too complex to be summed up in simplistic dichotomies.

The cultures of the world are now intertwined, involved in a possibly unprecedented power struggle, but also in an accelerated process of hybridization. This situation may lead to a new form of cultural and economic colonization, this time extending around the globe. But it also contains the seeds of cross-fertilization, provided other people's right to their specificities is respected. Such a process requires an acknowledgement of the dangers inherent in 'pure' national cultures, a major problem not only in Western nations threatened by the resurgence of neo-fascist ideologies but also in recently decolonized states struggling for an original sense of self-definition or simply attempting to solve through authoritarian means the problem of the artificial boundaries imposed by colonization. The historical factor of conquest and foreign occupation initiated a dynamic of domination, of appropriation, an attempt at times to eradicate the other. But it also paradoxically reactivated the potential for those 'marginalized' to strike back at the 'centre'.

Despite the great differences generally acknowledged between the various forms of imperialism, the colonial process has engendered ideological and imaginary representations which are often comparable throughout the colonized territories. The weight of history and the dominance of western culture have created a special climate favourable to the emergence of certain artistic forms which are more widely represented in formerly colonized countries than in the metropolitan centres.

---

[1] 'Can one divide human reality ... into clearly different cultures, histories, traditions, societies, even races and survive the consequences humanly?.... I mean to ask whether there is any way of avoiding the hostility expressed by the division, say, of men into 'us' (Westerners) and 'they' (Orientals).' (*Orientalism*, p. 45)

Though writers from the New Literatures suffered for a long time from an inferiority complex and often needed to be consecrated in the metropolises before having some confidence in their own worth, the situation has now changed. Salman Rushdie's celebrated phrase 'the empire writes back' sums up this new-found assurance which is beginning to be rewarded by some of the most prestigious literary awards. One only needs to think of the major contribution to world literature made by Salman Rushdie from India, Gabriel García Márquez from Colombia or Tahar Ben Jelloun from Morocco to realize that the former colonial territories, which used to depend on the 'mother-countries' for their cultural nourishment, are now beginning to invert the process.

There are historical reasons which account for the former colonies' reversal of the cultural pattern prevalent until the last few decades: the 1950s and 60s saw most former British colonies become independent and strive to create a sense of national identity which became even more urgent after the creation of sovereign states. Before literature produced in the new independent states could have a wide readership, some obstacles had to be overcome: people who had always been taught that greatness in art could only be found in metropolitan models, that an African equivalent to Tolstoy was unthinkable, had to be convinced that their own writers were as worthy of consideration as the 'Great Masters'. In an intermediary period, the inclusion of local authors in school curricula was encouraged and developed. Still, initially, 'serious literature' was read mostly by educated people living in the richer countries of the world or by a tiny elite in the Third World.[1] The first public for such writers was to be found among left-wing or liberal intellectuals with a personal or theoretical interest in the world outside and a concern for human rights and equal opportunities. Yet the changed political situation did not immediately remove all prejudices; the former colonies continued to be considered as 'exotic' places, areas where the West's dreams of otherness could materialize, where their wildest fantasies could come true. Some of the early settler literature had encouraged such visions.[2] After the

---

[1] I use this term in the sense of those countries which have not yet been in a position to benefit from the standard of living common in most developed countries. The merit of this label is that most readers agree with this definition although, strictly speaking, the world is no longer divided into three worlds since the virtual disappearance of communism. In his study *In Theory*, Aijaz Ahmad rightly underlines this as well as the tendency for 'first-world' intellectuals to globalize the 'third world' irrespective of the infinite variations and differences within and between the countries concerned. I hope that the care with which I attempt to contextualize my examination of different literary works shows that I do not forget the essential link between literature, culture and history.

[2] See, for example, Rolf Boldrewood or 'Banjo' Paterson in Australia.

eighteenth century's craze for orientalism and the nineteenth century's fascination for India and China, a new frontier was offered to escapist appetites. In *Orientalism*, Edward Said shows how the West has for a long time reduced the East to manageable and understandable representations which often betrayed the very originality of the different cultures studied:

> The Orientalist, poet and scholar, makes the Orient speak, describes the Orient, renders its mysteries plain for and to the West. He is never concerned with the Orient except as the first cause of what he says.... as early as Aeschylus's play *The Persians* the Orient is transformed from a very far distant and often threatening Otherness into figures that are relatively familiar.... The dramatic immediacy of representation in *The Persians* obscures the fact that the audience is watching a highly artificial enactment of what a non-Oriental has made into a symbol for the whole Orient (pp. 20-1).

What Edward Said was saying about the Orient could broadly apply to many parts of the 'Third World', though, in this case, the fascination for 'exotic' places developed later, mostly from the second half of the nineteenth century on. India in the nineteenth century focalized many of these fantasies in England. But the craze had started with the crusades and the ensuing image of the Moors or the Muslims as the archetypal infidels or foes. The Africa represented in the travellers' tales of the time of imperialism mostly corresponds to a europeanized rationalization of images belonging to the colonizers. The basic structures are similar though the shapes assumed by fantasized images differ. The Orientalist visions of carnal pleasures in harems were replaced by nightmares of cannibalism as one can see in the 'unspeakable rites' evoked by Joseph Conrad in *Heart of Darkness*. For the early conquerors of New Zealand, once the Land Wars were finished in the 1870s, representations of the bloodthirsty Maori soon gave way to another form of Pakeha[1] appropriation in the form of the 'noble Maori', usually a chief or a princess, who was, after all, not so different from 'us' and whose qualities of nobility could almost be compared with those of 'Ye Olde England'. In all these examples, the identity of the other was confiscated by the colonizer, tamed and made acceptable to Western tastes.

This prejudice has not completely disappeared, even among well-informed readers. Rather than affront the radically new perspectives offered by the major writers from the New Literatures, some still prefer to approach distant literary shores in the company of professional Western travelling writers (Graham Greene, Somerset Maugham, Paul Theroux...)

---

[1] A term used by Maori to refer to New Zealanders of European origin.

who offer apparently more alluring packages. These new interpreters 'pre-digest' the 'other' and make it more accessible. Said[1] quotes Marx in *The Eighteenth Brumaire of Louis Bonaparte* to exemplify this tendency: 'Sie können sich nicht vertreten, sie müssen vertreten werden'. They cannot represent themselves, they have to be represented. The Western eye in this case is the necessary mediator of perception.

In a fitting demonstration of this reduction of a culture to the status of an exotic object, literature from the former colonies was first considered as anthropologically interesting. *Things Fall Apart* and *Arrow of God*, Chinua Achebe's early novels, were published at an appropriate time to comfort this feeling. Novels are considered as little more than the presentation of strange customs among queer savages, whose habits can only be understood by specialists and which are of little interest to mere lovers of 'good literature'. Pressure is even applied by some publishers on post-colonial writers to produce books that will fit into that category because of the demand for such exotic artefacts. The success of Chinua Achebe's early novels may be linked with such readers' expectations. The Samoan novelist Albert Wendt was more popular with *Leaves of the Banyan Tree* or *Pouliuli*, both set in Samoa, than for his more recent *Ola* or *Black Rainbow* which cannot so easily be fitted into the 'anthropological' category. In the 1970s and 80s, the classification of post-colonial books in major British bookshops was a good indication of this state of affairs. Universities do not always show more discernment: when Wole Soyinka, who was later to win the Nobel Prize for literature, was offered a fellowship at Cambridge, he was attached to a department of anthropology. Writers in general protest against this reduction of their literature to the status of a social document. They object to this implicit hierarchy which classifies European or North American works as 'literature' and the rest as sources of fantasy, magic or escapism, but rarely as sophisticated artistic creations. The reduction of literature to its supposed anthropological content presupposes that the West has a monopoly on 'pure fiction'. Literary criticism concerns 'our' culture whereas 'theirs' is best approached from another angle. In this sense ethnology is rarely envisaged as an instrument to observe Western cultures which implicitly lie in a sort of absolute existence outside the scope of the relativist assessment of the anthropologist's eye. A French anthropologist is perfectly justified in studying the Dogons but a Dogon anthropologist would surprise Parisians if he/she came to enquire into their strange living habits or kinship system. Such a distinction between

---

[1] *Orientalism*, p. 21.

'us' and 'them'[1] presupposes a hierarchy of cultures in which the central point of reference is inevitably the West.

Another persistent stereotype, which is the corollary of the previous one, is that the New Literatures abound in ploddingly realistic descriptions of culture clashes and labouring treatises on Third-World liberation theories. The New Literatures are supposed to lack in post-structuralist and deconstructionist subtleties and to be ignorant of the most sophisticated *avant-garde*. Adepts of post-modernism[2] and deconstruction tend to look down on realistic forms as signs of artistic backwardness, forgetting that realism is probably more varied than any other fictional mode of representation. There is more to it than the brief interlude of 'socialist realism', an artistic dead end because the 'reality' presented was non-problematic and art merely served to provide recipes for successful social behaviour, an intention which is incompatible with any profound artistic enterprise. The fashion for absolutely narcissistic narrative has sometimes led to excessive admiration for aesthetic objects cut off from any social relevance. Delight in the author's manipulation of various codes has become the main criterion for greatness. This has diverted attention from the almost inexhaustible source of creativity which lies in the imaginative dialogue between several cultural codes. Where post-modernists have indulged in the firework displays of linguistic virtuosity, in the shimmering brocades of intertextuality, in the dizzying spiral of echoing signifiers, post-colonial writers have tapped the plentiful source of cultural variety which, for the first time, was not envisaged from an Orientalist standpoint but through the eyes of insiders personally involved in the cross-cultural experience.

Though initially published mostly in the West and largely with a Western readership in mind, post-colonial texts present a number of specific problems. The status of enunciation and its reference or non-reference to 'reality'[3] is a major preliminary question. The relative

---

[1] This division of the world into 'them' and 'us', with the latter being considered inevitably superior to the former is a characteristic feature of imperialistic discourse according to Edward Said (in *Culture and Imperialism*).

[2] For a discussion of the difference between postmodernism and post-colonialism, see Simon During, 'Postmodernism or Post-Colonialism Today' in Ashcroft, et al. eds., *The Post-Colonial Studies Reader*, pp. 125-129.

[3] We do not use the word 'reality' in the positivist sense of that which can be defined absolutely and with any 'scientific' accuracy but rather as the infinitely varied representations of this 'reality' presented in literary works. Reality in a work of fiction is always *represented*, organized through a particular '*parole*' (in the acceptation of Ferdinand de Saussure), an individual appropriation of language which gives meaning to a particular experience. Therefore it is closely dependent on varied cultural codes and on personal reactions to these codes.

proportion of narration and representation may also reveal much about the relationship between writer and reader. Which potential public are the writers aiming at? One often hears contemporary novelists half-seriously boasting that they are only really writing for themselves. Does the same tendency apply to the New Literatures in English? Certain illocutionary modes - to use Searle's terminology - appear more frequently in some areas of the New Literatures: the directive and the declarative modes are particularly common. In the latter, the enunciator is trying to provoke changes in the world with his enunciation. This perlocutory function characterizes modes in which works are written from a strong moral standpoint and aim at modifying the behaviour or beliefs of the public. Such a purpose is limited by the realities of the relationship between writer and reader: in practice, works with a strong perlocutory content are mostly read by people who share similar ideas. Because a book can be easily dropped when interest flags, the potentially revolutionary contents of a novel will often reach only the already convinced.

But perhaps, before examining such obvious questions, it might be wise to take into account some characteristics concerning the publishing of literature, particularly when this comes from countries which, traditionally, relied on orality for the transmission of knowledge and culture.

A masterpiece cannot be appreciated without the presence of readers and therefore without the intervention of efficient publishers and distributors. Whether one likes it or not, the existence of a cultivated, liberal middle-class also conditions the success of the enterprise. One may wish for major fiction or poetry to reach the common people; unfortunately, in most cases, it only falls into the hands of readers with enough leisure time to reflect in peace on essential psychological, political or personal issues. Social conditioning also predetermines people's attitudes towards reading. For all these various reasons and until the last century, fiction and poetry were produced mainly in the large cities of the major nations economically and technologically speaking. In the last fifty years or so, the USA has developed into the foremost world power in terms of financial prosperity (though this predominant position is now threatened by the economic boom in Japan and the Far East). This hegemony has been reflected in the influence of American fiction on modern taste. Yet America has not acquired the same importance as the old colonial powers in terms of literary canon, perhaps because it was the last frontier to be explored before the empire began to 'write back'. The literary supremacy which the USA has failed to secure up to now has been widely compensated for by their dominance of world cinema, a medium which some see as better adapted to the tastes of our contemporaries.

Initially expatriates and new settlers steeped in the values of the old metropolises produced the first literary works in colonial territories. Then they were relayed by local elites who, though widely influenced by the colonial ethos, began to voice their preoccupations and grievances as dominated subjects. Even in the fifties, a decade which saw a tremendous burgeoning of exceptional talents, writers who wanted to reach a wide reading public had to send their manuscripts to metropolitan publishers who, in turn, could only take the financial risk involved if, as was the case with Heinemann in London, they had the security of a well-established school market in the writer's country of origin. The abundance of novels from Africa probably reflects this state of affairs. But the uneven quality of this corpus - which has been detrimental to the image of post-colonial literatures in general - possibly stems from the confusion between a flawed conception of didactic requirements and art. This raises another question: could the Western intelligentsia appreciate such radically different works? V.S. Naipaul provides a fairly pessimistic analysis of the situation affecting his first novels set in the Trinidadian context of his childhood:

> The social comedies I write can be fully appreciated only by someone who knows the region I write about. Without that knowledge it is easy for my books to be dismissed as farces and my characters as eccentrics.... It isn't easy for the exotic writer to get his work accepted as being more than something exotic, something to be judged on its own merits. The very originality of the material makes it suspect.[1]

Other reasons, besides this economic factor, account for the particular pattern of development in the New Literatures in English. It is often argued that a first novel is generally autobiographical. One also forgets that writers usually start by re-writing or writing against other texts which, to them, have acquired canonical value. In the colonies, and even after independence, these mostly belonged to the 'classics' or to British, Russian, French or German nineteenth-century or twentieth-century fiction. Some critics have argued that this has resulted in a feeling of alienation in the new writers who could only express themselves through colonial or foreign media, ideological representations, images and character typologies. Initially this may have been true. Yet, as soon as the foreign models no longer appeared as the only references, a fruitful

---

[1] Naipaul's essay first came out in *The Times Literary Supplement*, 15 August 1958 and was republished in Robert D. Hamner, ed., *Critical Perspectives on V.S. Naipaul*, p. 7.

dialogue between different traditions started to emerge and enriched the inspiration of the artists concerned.

Some critics have articulated the specificity of the New Literatures in terms of a problematic relationship between two different traditions: British values, which were inculcated as part and parcel of the imported language, were opposed to native inspiration. For some readers eager to find a post-colonial alternative, the second strand of inspiration was idealized to the detriment of the first. In their opinion, the New Literatures in English were great because they provided a tradition thanks to which the people could reject the tyranny of British culture. Many early critical responses carried this argument, which, despite its basic relevance, may have been over-emphasized and thus perhaps contributed to maintaining the New Literatures in a 'Third-World ideology' ghetto. During that stage, the degree of opposition to the 'mother culture' was frequently mistaken for a sign of artistic achievement. It was inevitable - and even desirable - that a measure of positive discrimination should counterbalance the decades and, in some cases, centuries of colonial prejudice. But this factor was only useful in the pragmatics of reversing priorities. Once the phase of decolonization was completed, other criteria had to be taken into account.

What has been called the 'native' tradition is often the result of a long process of cross-cultural exchanges going back to the first contacts between invaders and native people. Even earlier, the history of each social group was generally one of hybridization through contacts with neighbouring groups of population. So there is no 'pure' or 'authentic' native tradition.[1] This notion is just as much an ideological representation as the werewolf of the 'English tradition', which does not mean that both have not had their part to play in the evolution of post-colonial literatures.

Much had been made - especially by the Negritudinists - of the conflict between two cultures, a dichotomy which clearly separates elements accounting for the individual's supposed cultural 'schizophrenia'. This may have had some relevance in some French colonies where the native people suddenly discovered that their ancestors were not the Gauls, as they had been taught in colonial schools. But this can in no way be generalized as a comprehensive description of the post-colonial situation. It would also be a mistake to replace the colonial dichotomy of the split personality (native v. metropolitan), the 'conflict

---

[1] Gareth Griffiths rightly denounces the 'myth of authenticity' in *De-Scribing Empire* edited by Chris Tiffin and Alan Lawson (pp. 70-85).

between two cultures', by the conflict of two discourses. This topology can only remain relevant if one remains aware of its limitations.

Still what does appear as a new phenomenon is the emergence of a strong and assertive body of literature, which sometimes even overshadows, with its innovative power, the more established metropolitan literatures. The so-called 'Rushdie affair' has given new significance to a reality which has progressively come to the forefront: the renewal of literary forms now largely depends on original syntheses produced by what, up to that point, had remained the margins of empire or its latest avatars. The tragic developments surrounding the publication of *The Satanic Verses* have shifted public attention to the sociological or political oversimplifications of the literary 'message'. But at least the existence of literature as a force with direct influence on contemporary society has been re-asserted with particular vigour, even if the whole controversy was also an occasion for people to judge a novel without having read it, on the faith of 'authorities' who had no first-hand familiarity with the book or were too biassed to understand the subtle richness of a masterpiece. Under the guise of defending orthodoxy or authenticity, many commentators hastily moulded their argument into the old dichotomy (colonial v. native) and branded Rushdie as an Indian who tried to be more British than the British and to prove that he could outdo them at their own game. This stereotyping barred any problematic reading of the work with its multiple and complex layers of meaning concerning the issues of faith, religious doubt, immigration, the relationship with one's various roots and cultural references and the use of a multiple and fragmented form of narration.

Because of their particular origins and of the historical conditions in which they have been produced, the New Literatures have imposed a new vision of reality which is beginning to have its effects not only on the post-colonials themselves but also on the former metropolises. After the 'nouveau roman' and the different deconstructionists, the writers from the 'margins of empire' are beginning to revolutionize literature in ways which are anything but peripheral. From their still peripheral position, they sap and renew cultures largely based on metropolitan models and in danger of turning into monoliths. They offer their diverse appropriations of languages originally imposed from the outside. They sometimes pretend to mimic[1] the colonizer's values and representations while

---

[1] We do not use the term in the reductive sense of V.S. Naipaul's 'mimic men' or hollow men. Homi Bhabha shows in *The Location of Culture* that mimicry can be a subversive mode of appropriation: 'Under cover of camouflage, mimicry, like the fetish, is a part-object that radically revalues the normative knowledges of the priority of race, writing,

introducing their differences which undermine the pretended self-sufficiency of these established systems. They gradually impose as alternatives their different visions of reality which originate in completely new syntheses.

Every artist writes partly out of a desire to complete himself/herself through the creation of his/her imagination and sometimes in order to foster changes in the society around. The creative work arises out of an attempt at constructing with words this structure which is felt to be sorely absent in the world. Language can also be a way of taking possession of a reality which is perceived as particularly elusive. In the contemporary period, with the erosion undergone by major ideologies and the increasing looseness of the social fabric - especially in urban societies - this need to build private fictions is more urgent. Yet, even in this context, writers from the New Literatures are placed in a particular position: they share with other writers the task of writing against ready-made representations of the present world. But, unlike people with the backing of a more stable tradition, their own history has often been confiscated by other powers.[1] Even those few centuries, at best, are not really theirs in the sense that external patterns of representation have been imposed on them by the colonizing power. Often their own past has been eclipsed or devalued and they need to reclaim[2] their personal image of it before they can be comfortable in their fictional world.

The particular conditions which predominate in the postcolonial field have led the writers to use accepted genres in unusual manners. Salman Rushdie's mixture of fantasy and historical fiction comes to mind as a striking example. Wilson Harris has conflated the novel, poetry and philosophy into one new 'macro-genre'. Derek Walcott and Albert Wendt have given a new allegorical dimension to verse. Faced with such innovative structures, the critic has difficulty fitting these works of art into recognizable genres.

---

history. For the fetish mimes the forms of authority at the point at which it deauthorizes them. Similarly mimicry rearticulates presence in terms of its 'otherness', that which it disavows' (p. 91).

[1] This feature is much truer of slave societies than of more established and age-old cultures such as those of India.

[2] The word 'reclaim' may well be an ideological construct in the sense that what one seeks to reclaim is a representation which is always structured and conditioned by the rules of language and in terms of prevailing ideological models. The past does not hang in the air like an object waiting to be recuperated. What one seeks to revivify is an image, not the 'real' thing, which anyhow only existed through the multiple perceptions that the different people experiencing it fashioned in their minds.

The preoccupation with labelling and taxonomy may appear futile if one envisages it only as originating in a desire to put order into what basically represents the richness of human productions. But perhaps the concept of genre might be a fruitful ground for the definition of some essential specificities of the New Literatures, in which case the enterprise might seem less gratuitous. Most commentators have remarked on the close link between literature and the society which inspires its production in the New Literatures. Jean-Marie Schaeffer[1] outlines the relationship between generic classification and the institutional dimension of literature. So, unsurprisingly, such preoccupations have special relevance in the examination of post-colonial texts.

---

[1] In *La Licorne* 22, p. 247: 'La problématique des genres force le poéticien à prendre en compte la dimension institutionnelle de la littérature: en effet, si le destin des traditions génériques est *inscrit dans* les textes, il se *décide entre* les textes, dans le passage d'une oeuvre à l'autre — donc, dans la tête de l'écrivain, et par là-même (le paradoxe n'est qu'apparent) dans l'espace public de la littérature comme pratique créative socialisée.'

I - ARE DISTINCTIONS BETWEEN GENRES STILL RELEVANT?

A- A Compulsive Search for Taxonomy?

Why do readers - and especially literary critics - feel the need to classify works of art into categories which one often calls genres? On the one hand fashionable ideas lead some commentators to argue that, in this infinitely innovative world, genres have become irrelevant because traditional rules have been subverted. The ineffable *text* (sacralized in italics) is all that counts. Yet, on the other, their description of works of literature inevitably resorts to such terms as 'fantasy', 'allegory', 'realism', 'tragedy', even if they carefully place these in inverted commas. As the 'reception' school of criticism has convincingly shown, a novel, poem or play takes on its full meaning when it is integrated in the framework of the reader's or spectator's generic expectations.[1]

But is the reader alone in this compulsive search for taxonomy? Though less explicitly concerned with knowing to which category his/her work belongs, the writer usually creates with certain traditions and works in mind. In the same way as the exploration of the contradictions surrounding the question of filiation forms an essential part in the constitution of the individual, the writer's acceptance or rejection of certain literary codes fashions his/her identity as an artist.

In *Genres in Discourse*, Todorov writes that genres exist as an institution and constitute "horizons of expectation' for readers and as 'models of writing' for authors'.[2]

> Like any other institution, genres bring to light the constitutive features of the society to which they belong.... a society chooses and codifies the acts that correspond most closely to its ideology; that is why the existence of certain genres in one society, their absence in another, are revelators of that ideology.... a genre is the historically attested codification of discursives properties.[3]

---

[1] See in particular Hans Robert Jauss's notion of the 'Erwartungshorizont' (horizon of expectation) in his *Towards an Aesthetic of Reception*.

[2] *Genres in Discourse*, pp. 50-51. '... les genres existent... comme des 'horizons d'attente' pour les lecteurs, des 'modèles d'écriture' pour les auteurs' (p. 18)

[3] *Genres in Discourse*, p. 19. 'Comme n'importe quelle institution, les genres mettent en évidence les traits constitutifs de la société à laquelle ils appartiennent.... une société choisit et codifie des actes qui correspondent au plus près à son idéologie; c'est pourquoi l'existence de certains genres dans une société, leur absence dans une autre, sont révélatrices de cette idéologie.... Le genre est la codification historiquement attestée de propriétés discursives' (*Les Genres du discours*, p. 51).

One may question the idea of a society having an ideology. In most cases, and especially in the post-colonial world, there is a criss-crossing of many ideologies. Still Todorov's remark draws an interesting parallel between the history of ideas and that of genres.

In *The Architext: an Introduction*, Gérard Genette also stresses the close relationship between the evolution of genres and historical change: 'all species and all subgenres, genres or supergenres are empirical classes, established by observation of the historical facts'.[1] His definition rightly insists on the fact that our perception of genres is always linked with a pragmatic experience and not with any kind of essence. For Alastair Fowler in *Kinds of Literature*, the evolution of genres depends on extra-literary and literary factors:

> What causes genres to change? There are causes to be found... in extraliterary events: pastoral was obviously affected by urban development.... The external has to do with social change and with changes of sensibility that matter deeply to the literary critic. Nevertheless genre has its own history too. There are literary laws of change.... And individual works play a part too - especially original and paradigmatic ones. (p. 277)

Chinua Achebe's *Things Fall Apart* has greatly contributed to the foundation of the 'village novel' in Africa and in other emerging countries of the world. 'Magic realism' would not have known the fortune it has without García Márquez's *One Hundred Years of Solitude*.

We all think we know what we mean by 'genre' but we inevitably differ in our implicit personal hierarchies. Which are the main forms? Are we to take Aristotle's categories of poetry, tragedy and history as absolutes? Can we still examine the post-colonial literatures only with the help of Hegel's distinction between epic, lyrical and dramatic poetry? Alastair Fowler implicitly establishes a hierarchy between what he calls 'kinds', a sort of generic superstructure which suffers little from historical erosion and subgenres which are described as much more ephemeral and pliable:

> Although genres are notoriously inconsistent, they exhibit at least one regularity. The terms for kind... can always be put in noun forms ('epigram'; 'epic'), whereas modal terms tend to be adjectival. But the adjectival use of generic terms is a little complicated. Consider the expressions 'comedy', 'comic play', 'comic'. 'Comic play' is almost equivalent to 'comedy'. But 'comic' is applied to kinds other than comedy, as when *Emma* is called a 'comic novel'. (p. 107)

---

[1] p. 66. 'Toutes les espèces, tous les sous-genres, genres ou super-genres sont des classes empiriques, établies par l'observation du donné historique' (p. 70).

The limit of Fowler's description is that it applies essentially to English literature and cannot be generalized to all others.

In *Genres in Discourse*, Tzvetan Todorov comments on what some contemporary critics see as the disappearance or irrelevance of the notion of genre:

> ... 'genre' as such has not disappeared; the genres-of-the-past have simply been replaced by others. We no longer speak of poetry and prose, of documentary and fiction, but of novel and narrative, of narrative mode and discursive mode, of dialogue and journal.[1]

New genres are constantly being formed and transformed. Jean-Marie Schaeffer[2] warns against the tendency to postulate an ideal text which might be the absolute prototype for a genre, an attitude which leads the critic to forget that genres are historical artefacts.[3] He insists on the anchoring of genres in 'networks of resemblances' between texts, thus privileging the notion of structure over that of essence. Taking up a similar argument in his *Introduction à la littérature fantastique*, Tzvetan Todorov discusses these rules which operate through several texts and which are commonly called 'genres'. He insists on the essentially metamorphic nature of each genre and on the mutual interchanges between genres and individual works. Unlike scientific objects, 'Every work modifies the sum of possible works, each new example modifies the species'.[4] For Todorov, a text is not only the product of a pre-existing combination; it also transforms this combination.[5] 'A new genre is always

---

[1] p. 14. 'Ce ne sont pas les genres qui ont disparu, mais les genres-du-passé, et ils ont été remplacés par d'autres. On ne parle plus de poésie et de prose, de témoignage et de fiction, mais du roman et du récit, du narratif et du discursif, du dialogue et du journal' (p. 45).
[2] In 'Du texte au genre' in Gérard Genette et al., *Théorie des Genres*, pp. 179-205.
[3] Schaeffer criticizes the notion of 'generic exteriority': 'c'est la procédure qui consiste à 'produire' la notion d'un genre non à partir d'un réseau de ressemblances existant entre un ensemble de textes, mais en postulant un texte idéal dont les textes réels ne seraient que des dérivés plus ou moins conformes, de même que selon Platon les objets empiriques ne sont que des copies imparfaites des Idées éternelles.' (in Genette et al, *Théorie des genres*, p. 190)
[4] See T. Todorov, *The Fantastic: a Structural Approach to a Literary Genre*, p. 6. 'Toute oeuvre modifie l'ensemble des possibles, chaque nouvel exemple change l'espèce' (p. 10).
[5] See Todorov: 'a text is not only the product of a pre-existing combinatorial system... it is also the transformation of that system' (p. 7). 'un texte n'est pas seulement le produit d'une combinatoire préexistante.... il est aussi une transformation de cette combinatoire' (p. 11).

the transformation of an earlier one, or of several: by inversion, by displacement, by combination.... There has never been a literature without genres; it is a system in constant transformation'.[1] Jean-Marie Schaeffer also insists on this dual nature of the notion of genre which includes an element of reduplication and another one of transformation.[2] So genres are situated at a meeting point between the singular work and the rest of literature. They are 'these relay points by which the work assumes a relation with the universe of literature'.[3]

The rest of literature is primarily made up of the series of works anchored in a similar tradition loosely conforming to the same rules. But these rules can be more or less binding depending on whether the writer feels part of a 'closed' or of an 'open network'.[4] These conventions are clear in the context of the French classical distinction between tragedy and comedy. Corneille and Molière wrote in a period when generic distinctions obeyed strict rules. When dealing with the novel, especially at the present time, when the genre includes so many sub-genres and can offer almost infinite possibilities of variations and modifications, it seems much more difficult to find strict guidelines. Because of the worldwide circulation of texts, an unlimited number of implicit models becomes available, thus making the task of generic classification almost impossible. And yet some paradigms do tend to emerge. The question is whether they exist *per se* or whether they correspond to certain expectations or strategies on the part of the critics and publishers who play a major part in the definition of such categories. Similarly the frequent use of terms such as 'allegory' or 'magic realism' does not guarantee that they correspond to clearly defined entities.

In post-colonial literatures, the networks in which writers work are very 'open'.[5] For Jean-Marie Schaeffer,[6] Shakespearean theatre, with its

---

[1] Todorov, *Genres in Discourse*, p. 15. 'Un nouveau genre est toujours la transformation d'un ou de plusieurs genres anciens: par inversion, par déplacement, par combinaison.... Il n'y a jamais eu de littérature sans genres, c'est un système en continuelle transformation' (*Les Genres du discours*, p. 47).

[2] 'On a trop souvent tendance à identifier la généricité à un de ses régimes, à savoir le régime de la réduplication, alors que le régime de la transformation générique (donc de l'écart générique) est tout aussi important pour comprendre le fonctionnement de la généricité textuelle' (Schaeffer in Genette et al., *Théorie des genres*, pp. 202-3).

[3] See Todorov, *The Fantastic*, p. 8. 'Les genres sont ... ces relais par lesquels l'oeuvre se met en rapport avec le reste de la littérature' (*Introduction à la littérature fantastique*, p. 12).

[4] Notions of sociolinguistics used by Jean-Marie Schaeffer. See *La Licorne* 22, 1992, p. 255.

[5] Some would argue that they are so open that the term 'New Literatures' ceases to have any meaning.

variety of audiences, its plots and subplots, its mixture of comedy and tragedy, is an example of a very 'open' genre. Contemporary literature in general also partakes of this 'openness'. In his study *Les Genres littéraires*, Vincent Combe comments on Joyce's *Ulysses* and on other contemporary works of art in which polyphony, intertextuality and *métissage* play a major part. He remarks on the deliberately 'mixed' nature of important modern literary works whereas those classified as 'paraliterature', for example fiction in the 'Arlequin' series, scrupulously respect generic definitions and distinctions.[1] This tendency to escape generic classification applies even more to the New Literatures which have a potentially much wider and more diversified audience. How will a Chinese implicitly classify a novel by Okara or Rushdie which does not fit accepted categories in his/her country? Does the extreme complexity of generic classification render such a task irrelevant?

This difficulty does not mean that one should give up trying to describe the new genres or modes of writing to be found in post-colonial literatures. These offer interesting examples of innovative possibilities in the treatment of language, in the relation between the narrator or characters on the one hand and different levels of reality or codes of reference on the other. They can serve as the indicators of the mutual influences at work in pluricultural areas of the world and they indicate the possibility of new canonical references.

In *Kinds of Literature*, Alastair Fowler argues a little polemically that generic belonging is not concerned primarily with classification but that it is essential in the readers' individual interpretation of a work of art. Taking up the metaphor of weaving with its vertical and horizontal component threads, he writes that meaning cannot be constituted without this personal experience of each book seen in terms of a combination between 'warp' and 'weft'.[2] Admittedly one's implicit inclusion of a book within the framework of a certain genre, especially when this operation is almost automatic or 'natural', conditions one's 'suspension of disbelief' and one's acceptance of the unspoken 'pact' between writer and reader. One's adherence to the particular 'reality' of the text depends on the proper functioning of this process.

---

[6] See *La Licorne* 22, pp. 253-7.

[1] 'C'est peut-être aujourd'hui le propre des oeuvres littéraires importantes, ambitieuses, que d'être mixtes par nature, tandis que la paralittérature, elle, respecte fidèlement les définitions et les cloisonnements génériques' (*Les Genres littéraires*, p. 151).

[2] 'Generic statements... serve to make an individual effect apprehended as a warp across their *trama* or weft... Genre theory... is properly concerned, in the main with interpretation. It deals with principles of reconstruction.... It does not deal much with classification' (p. 38).

In his essay on Malcolm Bradbury,[1] Ronald Shusterman writes that the search for generic classification is often a particular form of the quest for a theory of reality.[2] For him, this corresponds to a need to base literature on biological or historical necessity. His examination of Malcolm Bradbury's practice as a novelist leads him to think that the theory of genres is a devious way of approaching reality.[3] When a genre is defined essentially in relation to its content, it is based on this relationship with reality, since the content is a sum of elements derived directly or indirectly from reality, either through imitation, through a process of inversion or of modification.[4] Shusterman's theory seems based on the belief that there may exist a perfect adequacy between a genre, which is itself inscribed in a particular historical and social context, and the reality to which the work of art refers. What about times when people suggest that reality and art are radically separate? Some genres seem better adapted to certain periods and mentalities but the relationship between art and reference always remains opaque. Even if a mode of writing appears to cling closely to the way the people in this particular locale perceive the world around, even if the optical instrument used to survey the scene around favours illusion, it remains a useful though artificial device to be considered as such. The adherence of genre to reality will necessarily be loose because the gap between the two is impassable. What appears natural to a period becomes unbearably eccentric or artificial to another. In any case the problematic nature of what people refer to as 'reality' should serve as a *caveat* against oversimplification. Still Shusterman's remark has the merit of outlining the link between genres and referentiality, ideologies, imaginary representations situated in a certain context and at a certain period in history.

Some critics have also wondered whether genres are pure intellectual constructs. When commenting on the connection between a work of literature and its 'reference', Todorov argues in *The Fantastic* that a genre has no justification *per se* but only in relation to other works of art. It cannot be founded on any 'natural' link with reality but only on the possibility it provides to relate a work with other works of art that

[1] *La Licorne 22.*
[2] '... la recherche d'une théorie fondationnelle des genres n'est souvent qu'une instance particulière de la recherche d'une théorie de la réalité' [*Ibid.*, p. 139].
[3] 'les genres eux-mêmes sont souvent définis par les liens avec la réalité qui les soustendent' [*Ibid.*, p. 140].
[4] 'qu'est ce qu'un contenu, sinon un ensemble d'éléments dérivés directement ou indirectement du réel, soit par imitation, soit par renversement ou modification' [*Ibid.*, p. 140].

preceded it. For Todorov, 'literature is created from literature, not from reality, whether that reality is material or psychic'.[1] This formalist viewpoint suggests that, for him, everything is literature; the text has replaced reality. Indeed few realities exist before they have been interpreted, articulated in language, which itself, only knows particular actualizations closely dependent on specific cultures. Still one may go too far in this tendency to reduce reality to texts. Todorov's analysis may well apply to post-modernist Europe or North America where the novel has at times lost all pretension to social relevance. But one only needs to look at the works of Achebe or Soyinka to realize that, in their case, the written work represents a certain vision of reality which may not be essentially intertextual.

he argues against Todorov here!

Many post-colonial writers will agree with V.S. Naipaul that 'fiction hallows its subject'. Artistic representation of an environment gives it an existence, a particular sharpness and relief. Behind the position expressed by Todorov in *The Fantastic*,[2] lies a tendency to avoid anything that smacks too much of the political, or art as involvement of some kind. If all is text, then maybe one can play endlessly with linguistic combinations and forget that some of them have deep resonances in a reality which transcends these words on paper. Unless one considers that the political reality in Third-World countries, that the lack of individual freedom, the corruption and extreme privileges of the upper classes are themselves only texts, how can one deny that certain genres are imposed by the contexts in which the writers who use them live? The abundance of protest poetry in the South African ghettoes of the apartheid era has a direct link with the rage of those who wrote it and the fact that they were too busy with direct action to sit down for months writing novels. There was also a very pragmatic purpose in the reciting of poems in order to arouse consciences and galvanize energies for the sake of the cause of liberation. *Agitprop* theatre was used by Soyinka as a direct response to the emergencies with which the defenders of human rights found themselves confronted in Nigeria. The context cannot automatically determine the genres used by artists but an undeniable relationship between the two exists in many cases.

Which other works of art do the creators in the New Literatures have in mind when they envisage generic anchoring? Knowing how much certain writers from the former British colonies objected to European

---

[1] See Todorov, p. 10: 'la littérature se crée à partir de la littérature, non à partir de la réalité, que celle-ci soit matérielle ou psychique' (p. 14).
[2] In *The Conquest of America: the Question of the Other*, Todorov has corrected what could seem like a tendency to excessive formalism.

models for their own literature, one may wonder whether they could simply turn to the 'oraliture' of their own people to find generic models. Did George Lamming write *In the Castle of my Skin* with the only model of Caribbean oral popular narrations? Even when writers explicitly declared that they were giving up foreign models and were turning instead to the old tales or poems of their own predecessors, the difference between their intentions and their actual achievement may lead us to doubt that these were their only source of inspiration. Should one judge Achebe only in relation to the literature written about the ancient Ibo? In this case, the framing of what knowledge one possesses in anthropological discourse which has its own unspoken presuppositions complicates matters even further. Should one similarly refer Soyinka's *A Dance of the Forests* only to traditional Yoruba theatre? This would lead us to ignore the influence of Shakespearean drama filtered through Wilson Knight as well as that of Brecht or Nietzsche, to mention only the most obvious sources of inspiration.

Theoretical reflections on the notion of genre have not been the object of much discussion among critics of post-colonial literature in English. Writers have had their works published under well-known denominations such as 'novels' or 'short stories'. This does not necessarily reflect their own position but perhaps more those of their publishers who may be desirous to link their production to accepted categories in order to ensure the widest possible reading public. Such labels often escape the writers' control just as much as 'paratextual' details such as the cover illustration or the external appearance of the book.

After all the controversies surrounding the 'nouveau roman' and various experimental or post-modern forms of the novel, some commentators predicted the final disappearance of the 'realistic novel', a mode which had gained importance in the nineteenth century and had been prevalent throughout the first half of the twentieth. Right from the beginning the ambiguities of the term 'realistic' had served various ideological purposes. The appropriation of the label by socialist realism gave it a bad reputation since it became linked with didactic art, with the manipulation of the reader for motivations external to the problematic exploration of reality. After the decline of the involved novel, which, in Europe, took place in the post-Sartrian, post-Malraux period, novels of internal probing concerning the functioning of language and of the unconscious tended to supplant and apparently kill off the realistic mode. Yet, in recent years, there has been a vigorous revival of realism, though not always in its traditional form. Some new varieties such as 'magic realism' have emerged from a post-colonial context. Though not always clearly defined, these experiments have attracted much interest and begun to have an influence on metropolitan cultures, as we see with such works as *L'Exposition coloniale* by Erik Orsenna.[1]

In the novels published by post-colonial writers, realism is to be found, especially at the birth of the national literatures. C.L.R. James' *Minty Alley* in Trinidad, Mulk Raj Anand's *Coolie* in India, Henry Lawson's stories in Australia, Frank Sargeson's early stories in New Zealand all bear witness to this renewed interest. What, to metropolitan readers, may have appeared as the mimicry of a slightly outdated genre was a means for the artists to appropriate a local reality in terms other than those used by the colonizers. The model of the nineteenth-century English novel was thus appropriated and somewhat subverted through the emergence of another voice which, under the guise of adopting the colonizer's, made its difference clearly visible in written form.

Many writers of fiction in the New Literatures in English have a specific approach to 'realism'. There are, among them, a number who deal with more 'intimate' or individual problems; the examples of Jean Rhys, Katherine Mansfield, Christina Stead or Anita Desai witness to this type of inspiration. Less strident but equally incisive, their depiction of fragmented worlds seen from the point of view of individuals do not always strike the reader as much as Rushdie's or García Márquez's firework displays. They do not apparently stage events affecting masses of individuals. They do not seem to tackle 'history' in that their fictional worlds do not encompass crowds, battles, conquests or political disputes as such. Yet the anguish, tragedy and deep human concerns are obviously present in such haunting novels as Anita Desai's *Baumgartner's Bombay*, which tells of the life and death of a Jewish refugee in Bombay, a man forever on the margin of society.

But there is also a significant body of fiction writers who are concerned with interpreting the specific political or historical reality under their eyes in their own terms and in a wider sense (often because they feel it has been misinterpreted by other artists from the metropolises). In the nineteen-thirties, 'social realism' in colonial territories usually involved the articulation of a local idiom, which had been neglected or oversimplified in previous literary representations. A further stage, sometimes called 'magic realism' - especially represented by some of the most famous novels by Gabriel García Márquez - witnesses to the creators' desire to question the naïve 'mirror theory' according to which fiction directly represents reality. They · use

---

[1] Editions du Seuil (Paris, 1988).

metafictional devices to debunk the realistic illusion, while continuing to believe that fiction should have a firm base in reality. The relationship between writer and reader is frequently - and humorously - dramatized in their works. Post-colonial novelists are particularly concerned with the false conceptions vehicled by the colonizer's representation of the reality of their country. When their native tongue is not that imposed by the colonizers, they will be more likely to expose the cultural values inherent in the use of the imposed language. Their increased awareness of the implications of the code switching which accompanies the change from one to the other will often determine attitudes to reality made of familiarity, interest and distance at the same time.

The novel has proved pliable enough to allow practically any variation. Still one may wonder whether this genre, born originally in an age when individual values began to prevail, is really suited to cultures in which art sometimes finds its legitimacy in social use. Taking the example of the old oral tradition in West Africa, tales were meant to educate as well as to entertain. They served to transmit the values of the community to the new generations. What consequences may this role entail for the modern novelist who still cherishes the traditional function of literature and who wishes to find some legitimacy in his role as an educationist? How can the small personal voice so characteristic of many Western novels accommodate a whole range of people whose existence depends basically on their relationship with others rather than on the sophistication of their depiction of a personal universe?

B - Major Themes and Genres

In the novels written during the decades immediately before or after the independence of formerly colonized Third-World countries, the fate of the protagonists frequently serves as an allegory of the major problems of the young nations. Beyond the glorification of the heroes of national liberation which has more to do with propaganda than with serious literature, certain situations are represented too often for it to be purely the result of individual psychology: the novels frequently trace the growth of a young hero whose progression from innocence to experience follows the passage of his/her country from colonial dependence to self-government. Many heroes of Third-World novels are divided between the generation of their grandparents whose roots are still deeply anchored in

[handwritten: NC — Rushdie follows this]

tradition[1] and the modern world with its more individualistic values. The mood darkens once the characters have realized that independence can also bring disillusionment. This is expressed in images of betrayal and of death: women have stillborn children or are struck by sterility. Traitors who pretend to be heroes abound, as one sees in the novels of the Kenyan Ngugi wa Thiong'o.[2] Disappointed ideals in the post-independence period lead to very pessimistic novels peopled by corrupt politicians. The women's inability to produce offspring also frequently represents the new nations' difficulties with their uncertain future. New life cannot be born because the break with old values, the traditional points of reference, has been too radical.

In many post-colonial novels, the rise of the new nation is idealized in epic form and protagonists tend to take on allegorical value. One might also expect to find utopian works in areas where people have fought so hard and so long for their political and social ideals.

1- Repossession of Reality and the Historical Novel

Historical novels abound at times when writers feel concerned about the reinterpretation of their country's history. When their past has long been viewed merely from the point of view of the colonizer, self-assertion must be accompanied by the redefinition of one's relation to the past. The 1980s in New Zealand saw the rise of a very strong drive towards a renaissance of Maori values and of a desire to reclaim land confiscated in the early days of the European settlement and just after the wars between the two communities in the 1860s and early 70s. This particular situation led to the publication of fictional interpretations of that period in Witi Ihimaera's *The Matriarch* and in Maurice Shadbolt's *Season of the Jew*. Ihimaera's Maori viewpoint naturally differs from that of the Pakeha[3] Shadbolt. Yet both are concerned with exploring this uneasy relationship which stems from conquest and confiscation of land by the Europeans.

The repossession of a past overshadowed by European interpretations of the colonial encounter has also led a number of writers to set their novels in traditional communities just before the Europeans came. That was what the Nigerian Chinua Achebe did in *Things Fall Apart*, a

---

[1] A term which should not be reduced to a monolithic idea of unchangeability. Tradition is problematic because it is often used to privilege one strand of the past to the detriment of others, always a political or ideological choice.
[2] See *The River Between*, *A Grain of Wheat* or *Petals of Blood*.
[3] The Maori refer to New Zealanders of European origin as 'Pakeha'.

prototype of the 'village novel', a sub-genre imitated since in many other parts of the Third World.[1] There the explicit aim of the writer is to show that the local past was not one long period of barbarity. Achebe strives hard to put words onto Conrad's dark continent of Africa. He fills the 'blank' spaces of the maps Conrad used in his childhood daydreaming and manages to bring to life a village in pre-European times with its assets and weaknesses. He demonstrates that Kurtz's vision of 'the horror' in *Heart of Darkness* resulted from an inability to view Africa from an African viewpoint. The characters in *Things Fall Apart* speak, reason, organize themselves and possess a 'civilized' culture, all features which contrast with Conrad's outside vision of the black people as threatening and wild practitioners of 'unspeakable rituals'

Writers from the Third World involved in the composition of historical novels extend the notion of historical documents to include the oral tradition which has often been neglected by traditional historiography because it is considered less reliable than texts and written archives. In order to re-evaluate those cultures that had no access to writing until recently, it is urgent that the history handed down from one generation to the next by word of mouth be included in the process of building a collective memory.

2- Relative Scarcity of Utopia and Anti Utopia; the Case of *July's People*

Because post-colonial literatures are produced in regions where the struggle between dominator and dominated has given rise to a hope for a new society freed from the shackles of imperialism, it might seem natural that literature should reflect these ideas. Yet, in the New Literatures in English, very few examples exist of literary utopias. Those that can be found are generally anti-utopias such as C.K. Stead's *Smith's Dream* (1971), a nightmarish vision of New Zealand under a dictatorial and 'big-brother' type government, or Nadine Gordimer's *July's People* (1981),[2] a vision of South Africa after a black revolution which has sent the white population flying for shelter abroad or in the bush.

July's People deserves a longer treatment because it constitutes a valid example of the anti-utopian mode, while proving complex and ambiguous on closer examination. The novel starts after the 'apocalypse' of white South African society. This interpretation is clearly suggested in

---

[1] See for example *Tangi* and *Whanau* by the Maori Witi Ihimaera or *The Crocodile* by the Papua New Guinean Vincent Eri.

[2] All my references are made to the Penguin 1982 edition (original edition 1981) and are included in the text.

the epigraph, a quote from Gramsci: 'the old is dying and the new cannot be born'. The novel articulates white fantasies about a scenario which seemed plausible among the dominant group in the late 1970s.

The threat of a breakdown in the banking system, which actually happens in the Gordimer novel, was also a real fear at a time when international financing companies were pulling out all investments from the country and were refusing to roll over loans. After fleeing their city in a hurry to seek refuge in their black servant's 'homeland', Bam, Maureen Smales and their children are left with nothing but a few movable belongings, a pickup truck, a gun and the (now useless) money they have been able to draw from the bank. They find themselves in the bush at the complete mercy of July, their servant. Seen in the context of the Southern hemisphere, the name of this character probably evokes the 'winter' or eclipse of white civilisation after the black takeover.

The action develops in a sort of limbo, a place where characters belonging to old rural Africa and the survivors of the once triumphant white ruling class are forced together, without really coalescing into anything very hopeful. Time in the European sense seems to have stopped and is only marked by the cycle of women menstruating and of the seasons which punctuate human activities: the thatching of the roofs has to be done when there is grass available. Maureen no longer finds any interest in reading the only novel she has brought along because the pleasure of this activity consists in living for a few hours in another imaginary world. But now 'she *was* in another time, place, consciousness; it pressed in upon her and filled her as someone's breath fills a balloon shape' (p. 29). The implicit opposition between 'timeless', cyclic agrarian temporality and the time of watches is itself symptomatic of a European dream of pristine traditional societies free from the pangs of evolution and in direct contact with the fantasized origins. It is interesting that such a conception also tints the way in which African writers such as Achebe view the society of their ancestors. Still, in Gordimer *July's People*, village society is far from idyllic: the precariousness, dirt and lack of hygiene soon become almost unbearable to the protagonist.

In July's village the roles are reversed: the former servant now rules over the lives of those who used to be his white masters. Bam's family live in fear that the black villagers might spread the news of their presence and thus cause reprisals from black revolutionaries. But this does not happen. July and his friends increasingly take advantage of their situation to show that Bam's material possessions now belong to the whole community. They use his pickup truck without his permission and one day his gun disappears. July calms the Smales' anguish about their car arguing that it has to be kept at a distance so that black planes do not spot the presence of a white settlement. Like the Smales family, the car has now melted into the landscape. From a marvellous intrument of escapism, the pickup truck has become like 'a ship that had docked in a far country' (p. 14).

The tension and incomprehension between black and white in the novel finds a metaphorical representation through two contraptions, Bam's car and gun. The 'bakkie' is initially a vehicle meant for the pleasure of the leisurely whites. Here it has become an emergency vehicle for the Smales family. Once on July's territory, this bakkie is progressively taken over by July, much against the Smales' will. July's possession of the car keys appears as a revenge for the masters' former monopoly on keys. This car also probably becomes an instrument of prestige for July and his friend Daniel. Behaving as 'been-tos', they show off in front of their peasant neighbours, to prove that their going away has enabled them to master instruments of power which the villagers still consider with a measure of awe. Bam's gun used to be merely a weapon for shooting small birds. Bam had never used it for any big game before. Now he has to put it to a more basic use with his shooting of the piglets, an activity after which he re-invents the tribal ceremony of the sharing of the spoils with the rest of the community. Later the gun becomes an object of covetousness among different black people. Daniel eventually runs away with it and will probably use the stolen weapon to shoot white people since it is rumoured that he has joined the rebels.

The 'native' bush which used to be the white people's playground when on safari has now become a detention camp without barbed wire. Their apparent freedom of movement is limited by their fear of being spotted by the rebels. Permission must be granted by their black hosts. Despite these invisible restrictions, the whites, whose government relegated the black people to poorer agricultural districts, later forcing them to take on citizenship of the so-called 'independent nations', are relieved to have been allowed to seek refuge in this 'homeland'.

The terms of the power game have been reversed. But the mentalities have not changed accordingly. Though the Smales are 'liberals' who have always treated their servants well, they discover that the intimacy they believed existed between them and July was based on false premises. They are not received as guests but as July's employers and are still expected to pay their servant, though the situation has changed drastically. July does not dare to burn his 'pass-book' yet. The master-servant relationship perdures despite the balance of power that has shifted in favour of the black population. Perhaps July clings to these white people in their distress because they give him a sense of selfhood in a world where he has somehow become an occasional visitor. Perhaps his identity too has been reduced to his status as a servant, hence the stress he lays on his former masters' assessment of his performance when he asks Maureen what more she could want of him and blurts out: What can you tell? .... That I'm work for you fifteen years. That you satisfy with me. (p. 98).

The Smales' liberal dream of harmonious relationships between the races has been destroyed. Bam can still pretend that he is the providential white man; with his gun he supplies the village with game and he sets up a water tank which will save the women long journeys to and from the river every day. But there is no such satisfaction for Maureen who just resents the sheer discomfort of life in the wilds. Bam has brought a zinc bath. All bathe in it. Yet Mauren cannot bear the bad smell 'between her legs' (p. 9). When she starts menstruating, she has to wash the rags in the river and cannot hide her condition from the other villagers.

Gradually latent conflicts begin to fester: relations between Maureen and her husband lose their spontaneity with the constant presence of the children in the one-room hut. When a quarrel arises between Maureen and July, she threatens to tell July's village wife that her husband has a mistress in town.

One day the white people are requested to present themselves to the chief. The interview starts formally with the Smales showing respect for the old man and half dreading the fact that he might send them away because their presence constitutes a risk to the villagers. Instead of this, they discover an old reactionary of the kind that collaborated with the apartheid regime in the setting up of the 'Bantustans'. July translates the chief's words when he asks why the police did not arrest black rebels in 1976. 'Why the police doesn't shoot' (p. 116). The chief asks Bam to teach them to use guns. Bam finds himself going back to the old romantic rhetoric of the white liberal: 'you're not going to shoot your own people. You wouldn't kill blacks. Mandela's people, Sobukwe's people' (p. 120). In a few minutes with the old man, the Smales realize that their beliefs concerning the unity of the oppressed in the face of apartheid were only a romantic dream. July explains that the old man fears that the Soweto people and all the crowds in the township will surge on the villages and just help themselves to the food and resources that the poor villagers have so much difficulty procuring for themselves. He is just as afraid of changes as the white people are. The meeting is another eye-opener forcing the white to see how ignorant of the reality of life in the homelands they were. They have been deprived of more than their material possessions. They also see the limits of their misguided idealism.

The dystopia presented in *July's People* focalizes fantasies of loss of control by the ruling majority. It dramatizes a situation feared by the white people of South Africa at the time. Yet Nadine Gordimer uses what could have been the pretext for racist hysteria to lay bare the implications of the prejudices entertained by people who thought of themselves as enlightened in terms of their relations to the black people. Far from implicitly condemning the takeover by black nationalists, this novel explores the guilty conscience of white liberals confronted with their barest reactions. The book ends inconclusively on Maureen's wild flight towards a helicopter which could well be flown by white 'saviours' or by black nationalists. Panic leads the heroine to seize any opportunity to escape this unbearable situation.

Perhaps there are relatively few literary utopias in the New Literatures in English because utopias belong to triumphant societies sure of their power and confident in the ideology of 'progress'. Ever since they were 'discovered' by Christopher Columbus and 'civilized' by the missionaries, people from the Third World have generally been at the wrong end of utopias. They were the sufferers when Europeans wanted to start anew on 'empty' territories confiscated from them. They suffered servitude and transportation across the Atlantic in appalling conditions. In the 'New World', their work force made the 'economic miracle' of the sugar cane plantations possible. They were the Calibans whose islands were taken over by Prosperos. They knew the negative effects of utopias on the people who were made to put these into practice, and this might well explain why the genre was not popular among them. Dreams of island paradises were for Europeans, not for Polynesians.

This does not mean that heroic dreams are not represented. But generally post-colonials will search for alternative values in precolonial times. Because they can rarely find objects of admiration in contemporary society, they are wary of any system that promises immediate and easy satisfaction for the oppressed.

3- The Epic and the Oral Tradition

Rather than indulge in utopias, many post-colonial writers use the epic - perhaps at times a disguised form of utopia - either as a traditional genre, as is the case with Mazisi Kunene's *Emperor Shaka the Great* (1979), or as a mode integrated in more conventional poetry or fiction. Traditionally a long narrative poem about the deeds of heroes and warriors, the genre has always represented values of national significance, a particularly important element in the case of post-colonial cultures which had seen their past devalued by the colonizers and their sense of nationhood threatened by centuries of foreign domination.

Epics have also been popular in most other cultures. In *The Epic*, Paul Merchant suggests two basic characteristics to distinguish the genre: it must be 'a work of art surpassing the dimensions of realism' (p. 1). He also adds another feature mentioned by Ezra Pound, who, in his *ABC of Reading*,[1] suggests that 'an epic is a poem including history'. In oral cultures, the epic was indeed the closest equivalent to historical narrations. The genre figures prominently in most great warrior civilizations. This 'vital record of custom and tradition'[2] was also meant to entertain people. The relationship between these narrations and historical 'reality' was one in which the poet's imagination had a major part to play. This did not make them any less 'truthful' or credible to the listeners. Many epics also recounted the mythical origins of the nation turning their representation into some sort of canon which helped the group to distinguish itself from its neighbours. Because these epics were generally told orally to an audience who often knew most of the events and was particularly sensitive to the idiosyncratic specificities of each storyteller, the imaginative reworking of a traditional pattern was inseparable from historical 'truth'. Many such narrations included frequent digressions, which were ways of keeping the audience entertained and of bringing in details which could stress the contemporary relevance of old stories. As a genre, the modern European novel developed from the epic, an inheritance acknowledged by Henry Fielding when he talked of his fiction as being an 'epic poem(s) in prose'. The filiation becomes easily recognizable in the works of pioneers such as Cervantes, Melville or Tolstoy.

The nineteenth-century novel as represented by such writers as George Eliot and Charles Dickens,[3] was often considered by post-colonials to be closely involved in the consolidation of Victorian values associated with imperialism. Consequently a number of writers from the Third World found that the epic was a possible counter-discourse which could counterbalance the weight of the English paradigm.

---

[1] London, 1961, p. 46.

[2] Merchant, p. 1.

[3] The coupling of these two widely different figures is an oversimplification. But the weight of the Victorian literary tradition on colonial mentalities justifies such an odd grouping.

One of the forms of guilt carried by writers who come from basically oral cultures is that they have broken the privileged link between storyteller and audience to replace it by a more distanced one between author and reader. As Ruth Finnegan convincingly demonstrates in her classic study *Oral Literature in Africa*, the oral tale allowed for constant audience participation in the modification of the story. On the contrary, in a printed book, the word is, to some extent, fossilized, or at least contact between teller and 'listener' is more distanced and mediated by the printed page. Many writers such as Salman Rushdie seek to reclaim some of the qualities of the old oral tale by dramatizing the author-reader relationship and by playing the game of 'oral communication' in their novels. Of course this can only be done tongue-in-cheek and the effect is mostly ironical and metafictional. The self-reflective undertone was already present in the performance of many oral tales. So, in a way, under the guise of conforming to post-modernist fashions, the writers concerned also attempt to bridge the gap with their own past. Through the use of the epic, a link was often made between the old stories, which tell of the ancestors of the group, and the more modern genre of the novel.

Critics often distinguish between primary epic - linked with orality and tradition - and literary forms which rely more on the written medium. Most post-colonial works belong to the second category. But, because of historical and ideological reasons, traces of the anchoring in orality generally subsist, sometimes in the form of metafictional elements meant to enrich and subvert the conventional expectations of the novel as a genre. In the West, the assumption is that culture originates in the Roman and Greek societies where the 'cradle of humanity' is supposedly to be found. Thus the archetypal narration is Homer's *Odyssey*. Post-colonial writers do not generally deny the importance of this strand of tradition. But they do object to its universalist pretensions and stress the relevance of their own native traditions.

The epic element is often associated with historical narrations as we see in *The Matriarch* where Witi Ihimaera uses the figure of Te Kooti, the hero of Maori resistance to the confiscation of land by Europeans in nineteenth-century New Zealand. This example illustrates the way in which the epic is used to re-evaluate historical characters who were turned into villains by the colonizers.

Georg Lukács emphasized the epic character inherent in the novel when he said that the novel is the epic of an age in which the extensive totality of life is no longer directly given, in which the immanence of meaning in life has become a problem, yet which still thinks in terms of totality.[1]

Lukács underlines what he sees as a break between an era in which people still believed in the adequacy between the world myths and a supernatural reality and a moment when this communion was no longer possible. He appears to oppose a pre-historical time and the emergence of human beings into change, doubt and historicity. Any close examination of post-colonial cultures does not provide evidence of any such break. Cultures were always submitted to change and to the passage of time. Despite the firm belief in a link between gods and human beings, this did not make the communication between the two any easier. Lukács' vision appears to be that of a nostalgic man who thinks he can isolate a moment close to the paradise of origins when art was simpler because it meant fusion with the supernatural.

The epic has also given rise to a specific form of drama developed by the German Expressionist Erwin Piscator in the 1920s and by Bertold Brecht. The intention was to educate and entertain at the same time. But the audience never forgot that they were in a theatre. A major purpose of this art form was to urge the audience to react and take action to restore justice in their own world after seeing the play. One inevitably thinks of Soyinka and his African plays which, while referring to Yoruba values, are obviously inspired by Brecht (as well as by Greek tragedy). The best examples are his *Agitprop* plays performed on the market place or at street corners.

A fitting illustration of the use of the epic can be found in Ayi Kwei Armah's *Two Thousand Seasons* (1973). Based on the history of the migrations of the Akan nation through many centuries, the novel traces their evolution through slavery, exile, Arab and European conquests to emerge into the modern period and the possibility of reconstruction thanks to a philosophy influenced by Pan-Africanism. Though the narration includes individualized characters, the main subject of this novel is the nation itself which evolves from destruction to possible reconstruction. The narrative voice adopts that of traditional griots and often speaks in the first person plural, as though to reassert the values of community which far transcend individual desires and ambitions. The tone is deliberately elevated and sometimes repetitive. The orality of the tale does not always adapt well to written fiction. Still the particular poetic power of the novel emerges in part from the rooting of the people

---

[1] *The Theory of the Novel*, p. 56.

in the cosmic forces surrounding them: they are creatures of the desert, of the seasons, of the sun and moon:

> Springwater flowing to the desert, where you flow there is no regeneration. The desert takes. The desert knows no giving. To the giving water of your flowing it is not in the nature of the desert to return anything but destruction. Springwater flowing to the desert, your future is extinction.[1]

The elements become the source and the metaphors of life, of death and of possible regeneration. Here one may also note the way in which the desert is a metaphor for the sterility and death brought about by the Arab invasions.

The novelist fully assumes the role of educator traditionally associated with the function of the *griot*. His narrator apostrophizes the responsible readers who might feel concerned with the revolutionary mission of artists:

> You hearers, seers, imaginers, thinkers, rememberers, you prophets called to communicate truths of the living way to a people fascinated unto death, you called to link memory with forelistening, to join the unaccountable seasons of our flowing to unknown tomorrows even more numerous, communicators doomed to pass on truths of our origins to a people rushing deathward, grown contemptuous in our ignorance of our source, prejudiced against our survival, how shall your vocation's utterance be heard? (p. xi)

The conception of the artist evoked here is clearly reminiscent of the romantic function of the creator as a beacon for humanity. Armah claims that only such visionaries can divert people from the deadly path on which they are bound. What is suggested is nothing less than the creation of a utopia on earth. In the conclusion of the novel, communal values are privileged above all for 'there is no beauty but in relationships. Nothing cut off by itself is beautiful' (p. 206). Though the narrator constantly refers to the 'way', the implications of this remain very general and unclear. Too much didacticism interferes with the dynamics of what remains nevertheless a bold and worthy attempt at finding a genuinely epic voice.

Without going to such extremes of abstraction, numerous other post-colonial novelists have attempted to give epic dimension to their works. Would the image of Colombia be the same without García Márquez's creation of Macondo in *One Hundred Years of Solitude*? Would readers

---

[1] *Two Thousand Seasons*, Heinemann (London, 1979 [1973]), p. xi. All further references to this edition will be included in the text.

throughout the world know so much about the struggle between small agricultural workers and the owners of the *fazendas* in Brazil without the epic recreation in Jorge Amado's *Terras do sem fin* (1943). Similar clashes between small peasants and the local authorities in Peru might have passed unnoticed without Manuel Scorza's epic novel *Garabombo, el invisible* (1978).

These few examples belie Mikhail Bakhtin's excessive generalizations concerning the epic which, to him, is concerned with 'a world of 'beginnings' and 'peak times' in the national history, a world of fathers and founders of families, a world of 'firsts' and 'bests'... In its style, tone and manner of expression, epic discourse is infinitely far removed from discourse about a contemporary reality'.[1] The examples given above show that there is far more to the epic genre than the Greek and Roman texts implicitly evoked by Bakhtin. The epic has influenced the post-colonial novel, providing it with strategies to repossess an alternative discourse which positively re-evaluates reality.

4- The Allegory

In recent years, critics have tended to use the term 'allegory' often in connection with - or even as an alternative to - the epic. Literary texts in which the characters or situations are meant to represent more than their individual occurrence and to illustrate certain social, political or historical situations have been called allegorical. Strictly speaking, this term refers to a mode rather than a genre, since it may be found in any kind of literary text in which the agents, the action or the setting signify another order of persons, things, concept.

The hero of Witi Ihimaera's *Tangi* is not just a particular Maori but Tama,[2] the archetypal son, who, after the death of his father, has to take on the task of keeping the family going without the necessary support of shifting social structures. Unlike traditional elder sons, he has not stayed in the village to look after his mother, brothers and sisters. Instead he has sought his fortune in Wellington like so many Maori people of his generation and contributed to the disruption of age-old social patterns. His plight epitomizes that of many post-war 'sons' and becomes allegorical of a vast movement of change affecting his whole society.

In 'Monuments of Empire: Allegory/Counter-Discourse/Post-Colonial Writing',[3] Stephen Slemon considers that the new writers are engaged in

---

[1] Michael Holquist, ed., *The Dialogic Imagination: Four Essays by M.M. Bakhtin*, p. 13.

[2] 'Tama' means 'son', 'boy', 'child' in Maori.

[3] In *Kunapipi*, IX, 3, 1987, pp. 1-16.

providing new allegories which run counter to the appropriative forms always used by the colonizer. In his mind, 'a textual counter-discourse seeks to interrogate those notions of history which colonialism leaves in its wake by reiterating those notions on an allegorical level of significance' (p. 11). He quotes texts ranging from Armah's 'An African Fable' and *Why Are We So Blest*, Omotoso's *The Combat*, Naipaul's *Guerrillas*, Ngugi wa Thiong'o's *Devil on the Cross*, Okara's *The Voice*, to Hearne's *The Sure Salvation*, Lamming's *Natives of My Person*, Coetzee's *Waiting for the Barbarians*, Stow's *Tourmaline*, Rushdie's *Midnight's Children*, Hulme's *The bone people* and Harris's *Carnival*. Though in different degrees, these texts question hegemonic ideological and literary representations provided by the colonizer. But none of them can be fairly described as just an allegory. Allegorical intent is present besides many other features which Slemon ignores in his desire to find an all-encompassing term. Yet, undeniably, many post-colonial novels show their authors' fondness for history and politics, for myth-making and for projecting abstract entities onto individual characters.

5- A South African Allegory: Rabie's 'Drought'

Apartheid society in South Africa seems a fruitful ground, if not for the rights of individuals, at least for the production of literary allegories Jan Rabie's story 'Drought',[1] originally written in Afrikaans and translated by the author, opens on the evocation of an arid scene with 'whirling pillars of dust [that] walk the brown floor of the earth.... Tiny as two grains of sand, a white man and a black man build a wall. Four walls. Then a roof. A house' (p. 181). Obsessed with self-protection from the tide of black people around, the white man shuts himself inside his doorless and windowless house which the black man is building around him. At the end, realizing that the white man is trapped between the four walls, the black man tries to convince his 'baas' to come out, but to no avail.

The opening scene stresses the minuteness and seeming insignificance of human beings in this empty land dominated by a never-ending blue sky. The vastness and the drought epitomize the landscape and the climate - both physical and social - of South Africa with its strict separation between ethnic groups. Here each of the two major 'races' is represented allegorically by just one anonymous individual and the

---

[1] In Stephen Gray, ed., *The Penguin Book of Southern African Stories* (Harmondsworth, 1985), pp. 181-3.

drought can be seen as an indication of the sterile lack of communication between the black man and his white master.

What matters is the rarefied allegorical impact of the story, the richness of evocation and significance of each detail which becomes over-determined, and not individual psychological analysis . However the explicitness of the allegory does not detract from the poetic value of a text whose chief merits are its pregnant allusiveness and its extreme economy of means.

The power of evocation is reinforced by a tightly structured rhetorical organization. In terms of imagery, the hot pillars of dust frame the story at the beginning and at the end. Initially enigmatic, they are later related to the ritual dance of the black man who is thus reinstated as the rightful owner of the land.

The central theme of the house being built - also found in V.S. Naipaul's *A House for Mr Biswas* - is a common metaphor in the New Literatures which was interpreted by the authors of *The Empire Writes Back*[1] in terms of the constitution of post-colonial identity. In Rabie's story, the action of erecting the white man's house soon evokes building the 'house' or nation of South Africa, a struture in which the two 'races' should be able to cohabit. The white man insists on his own plan of action regardless of any criticism, even when his ignorance of the black man's sensible objections - obviously shared by the author - eventually leads him to a catastrophe.

This story lays bare a series of white ideological stereotypes: the image of the Black people supposedly cursed by God is based on a tendentious interpretation of the episode in *Genesis* when, after drinking too much of the wine he had produced, Noah fell asleep naked under his tent.

And Ham, the father of Canaan, saw the nakedness of his father, and told his two brethren without./ And Shem and Japheth took a garment, and laid it upon both their shoulders, and went backward, and covered the nakedness of their father; and their faces were backward, and they saw not their father's nakedness./ And Noah awoke from his wine, and knew what his younger son had done unto him./ And he said, Blessed be the Lord God of Shem; and Canaan shall be his servant./ God shall enlarge Japheth, and he shall dwell in the tents of Shem; and Canaan shall be his servant' (Genesis 10: 22-27).

Among racist people, these biblical lines confirmed their conviction that the black people - referred to as Egyptians in the holy text - were inferior. In South Africa, they justified the official Dutch Reformed

---

[1] See Ashcroft, Bill, Gareth Griffiths and Helen Tiffin, *The Empire Writes Back*, p. 28.

Church's initial acceptance of apartheid. Supported by these religious certainties, the white settlers in South Africa - and the Afrikaners in particular - considered that they had a divine mission to act as the black men's protectors since they knew what was best for their welfare.

The roles in the story are distributed in conformity with the white man's conception of the 'natural' order of things: the black man does the unqualified building work, whereas he supervises the undertaking. Rabie's preference for the oppressed black appears unambiguously at the end when the unrepentant white 'baas' shuts himself into his own doorless house and is condemned to silence.

The white master evokes the myth of his founding fathers, the colonists who came in tall ships and then started to move across the land to take it over from those considered as 'barbarians'. Once the white people had decided that they would prefer to lead a sedentary life, they imposed their own conception of peace on the 'uncivilized' blacks. This is a classical allusion to the 'white man's burden' which the Boers considered they had to bear. In their mythology, they remember the 'Great Trek' as a metaphorical flight into Egypt prior to their return to the 'promised land'.

Along their journey, the white people clashed with the semi-nomadic blacks living in the interior. In order to prevent night attacks, every evening the Boers interposed the fortress-like protection of their chariots arranged in a 'Laager'[1] around them. Throughout Rabie's story, the white man's unreasonable demands contrast with the black man's sensible arguments. The image of the master's cementing himself inside his own house without allowing for any doors or windows is a proof *ab absurdo* of the stupid 'Laager' mentality characteristic of some white South Africans.[2] Here Rabie suggests that, ultimately, too much protection will lead to the extinction of the 'white tribe', a feature which seems to alarm the black man. Perhaps this is a sign of Rabie's desire to see the development of genuine understanding between the races.

Allegories prosper when artists feel bound by a sacred duty to transmit a 'message' to perpetuate ancestral values or reform a society which is felt to have gone astray. With a crude writer, this leads to boring didacticism. Rabie's 'Drought' shows that sophisticated writers can use this much maligned genre in a fruitful way.

---

[1] The word 'laager' means a fortress in Afrikaans.
[2] The term has been used frequently to refer to the Afrikaners' sense of being surrounded on all sides by hostile populations from which they feel they have to protect themselves at all costs. The series of ghettos constituting South African society have only reinforced this tendency.

6- Nadine Gordimer's 'Is There Nowhere Else Where We Can Meet?'

Nadine Gordimer dramatizes the ideological contradictions of white South Africans in 'Is There Nowhere Else Where We Can Meet?',[1] the story of a fortuitous meeting between a white woman and a black man in the middle of the *veld*. Each stage of the woman's experience is evoked through a series of apparently disconnected impressions triggered off by the changes in her situation. At the beginning, the white woman appears in complete harmony with the cool and peaceful setting. The narrator is fascinated by the particular quality of the sky which has the liquid sheen of the sea, with gentle, silent waves lapping at the horizon. A purring dove adds to the impression of serenity. Paradoxically, even the cold has a soothing quality about it. Though this is a wintry landscape, the woman has pleasant memories of what this particular stretch of land looks like in summer when the bone-like shrub near her comes out in bloom. When a black man, who has just crossed her path, suddenly turns back and grabs at the parcel she is holding, the woman's head swings up and she notices a crane flying over majestically, gliding like the figurehead of a ship striding the waves. So the air provides a source of beauty which remains strangely unaffected by the woman's distress.

Initially the elements of the landscape are perceived in pictorial terms; they appear as lines (the scribble of twigs, the curve of the trees) structuring space and dots that bring a focus to the eye. The narrator remarks on the absence of definite colours. The view is merely an arrangement of different shades ranging from black to platinum through a gradation of greys.

Even her first acknowledgment of a human figure in the distance brings to the woman the same satisfaction as what she felt when she could add the dot-like figure of a man in a landscape painting. The appearance of the black man far away with his red cap similarly provides the first element of colour in what is otherwise a rather plain variation of greys and whites. The smouldering *veld* fire in the grass near the woman might have been disturbing and potentially dangerous. But it is now reduced to a gentle plume of smoke that presents no particular risk but is a beautifully poetic addition to the setting.

These elements of the landscape suddenly become hostile when the woman runs away in panic after the attack. The trees and plants which were so much part of a harmonious composition now turn into

---

[1] From *The Soft Voice of the Serpent* (1953). All further quotes related to this story will refer to pages in Nadine Gordimer's *Selected Stories*, Penguin (Harmondsworth, 1975).

hindrances, into so many hands clutching at her clothes to prevent her from escaping as fast as she would like: the mimosas and blackjacks cling to her. A fence with barbed wire holds her back and it is only when she reaches houses, the promise of protection and 'civilization', that she can calm down and start cleaning herself by getting rid of the blackjacks which are signs of the intruding presence of hostile nature, itself a reminder of the attacker.

At the beginning of the story, after the initial evocation of a visually pleasing landscape and a remark on the cold air which clung (pleasurably?) to the woman's eyes, the narrator mentions the protagonist's definitely enjoyable handling of pine needles which she collected on her way. Maybe we could interpret this action as the mere caressing of a familiar item taken as a 'transitional object'[1] to use a term coined by the English paediatrician Donald Woods Winnicott. One is also reminded of the *fort-da* game played by the child in Freud's *Beyond the Pleasure Principle*: Freud had observed a child playing at throwing away from him a spool with a string round it and then at recovering it. Each time the game was punctuated by exclamations (*fort* = far; *da* = here it is). Freud interpreted the game as the child's attempt to control the appearance and disappearance of a familiar object which, to the psychoanalyst, represented the mother figure.

One might view the handling of the pine cone by Gordimer's heroine as a simple masturbatory act with the obvious phallic connotations attached to the needles because of their shape and because of the way the woman holds them in her fingers. Yet here the protagonist's compulsive action suggests that reality is double-sided: by caressing the needles in one direction, they are smooth; in the other they snag at the skin. But these needles also leave a persistent scent on the fingers after handling them. Obtrusive olfactory memories also plague the woman after her encounter with the black man: the odour of his stale sweat is described as a burning sensation in her nostrils. When the attack occurs, the mugger's smell chokes her. This feeling echoes a common manifestation of racist attitudes in people who complain that other 'races' stink and that their cooking gives off an offensive stench. In a country like South Africa where blacks were considered as little more than animals,[2] this feeling in a white woman is not unexpected.

---

[1] An object which the child fondles and which, in her case could serve as an intermediary which helps him/her in her process of individuation, in his/her apprenticeship of autonomy in relation to his/her mother.

[2] This perception of the man as a variation on the animal is suggested on several occasions: 'as a cow sees you go' .... 'the sound of a hare running in fear' (p. 18).

The black man does not seem to have premeditated his attack. It is only after meeting the woman by accident that he suddenly comes back, as if seized by an overwhelming urge to get hold of the parcel she has under her arm, a desire which reduces him to the state of a ravenous beast. But, more unexpectedly, the woman too is reduced to animal reactions under the shock of the encounter: 'animal sounds came out of her throat. She gibbered [italics mine]' (p. 18). When she eventually escapes his clutch, she runs away like a frightened creature blindly blundering through the bush.

The smell of pine needles which remains on her fingers helps the woman to overcome the sensation of disgust that she experienced when the black man turned against her. It is pleasant because it is natural, 'clean, unhuman' (p. 18). The association of ideas suggests that, to her, anything human is necessarily tainted and dirty. In this story, the woman finds unpleasant anything linked with the odours of the body; not only is the smelly black man offensive to her; her own sweat is also perceived as a distasteful manifestation of fear, especially when it runs down beneath her armpits and buttocks. Even the pleasant smell of the pine needles is not altogether devoid of unpleasant connotations. Because these are slightly sticky with resin (another possible sexual allusion), the protagonist feels the need to wash her hands carefully afterwards in order to free herself from what appears as an obnoxious sensation.

The woman cannot control her feelings when the attack comes. The man evoked now in terms of fragments, tears, gaps and fissures does not appear in control of the situation either: he stands there panting, out of breath. She does not even think of how cold he could be on such a morning with his tattered clothes. He, who appeared as so much part of the landscape initially, is now an image of dislocation. The red of his woollen cap, a pleasant touch of colour on the landscape in the early stages, is now transferred to the haggard appearance of his eyes.

The woman's disconnected image of her attacker inspires abstract fear in her. His foot is cracked 'like broken wood' (p. 19). She notices a scratch in his flesh where the skin appears red under the general black colour. These fissures and fragments reflect her inability to interpret the scene in terms which might suggest a sense of wholeness, of harmony. The world and her own reactions remain a mystery to her. She fails to see the black man as a total individual. She perceives his limbs as parts of a machinery disconnected from the source of energy which activates them. One is reminded of Kafka's characters who never have access to the central authority or power of decision which rules over their lives. This disconnectedness may also be read as an allegory of the white people's inability to see blacks as other than the embodiment of their wildest destructive fantasies. Here these fantasies take several forms: initially the black man is just an element in the landscape, a distant point, just like any other tree or flower, a part of the background but not really a distinct individual. During the attack, the white woman is overwhelmed by what she sees as an oral threat.[1] Though this remains unexpressed, we may wonder whether the woman's reaction does not stem from a fear of being sexually assaulted by the black man. Such fantasies were common in white South African society as these represented a radical infringement of the law against sexual relations across the racial border. Moreover raping the enemy's women is a common way of humiliating them, of reducing them to a status less than human. The woman attempts to defend herself by throwing her parcel and handbag at the aggressor without realizing that these objects are precisely what the black man is after.

'Is There Nowhere Else Where We Can Meet?', an allegory of the radical misunderstanding between black and white South Africans, reveals common prejudices in the dominant society. Gordimer proceeds indirectly through tracing the woman's varying perception of the landscape and of the black man as the story reaches its climax. Though, initially, the woman is the only character explored in depth by the narrator, the feelings she experiences during the attack ruin her sense of communion with her environment and bring her paradoxically closer to the animal condition which she unconsciously associated with black people.

Because post-colonial writers often feel an urgent need to create counter-models to those vehicled by the colonizers, they instinctively use allegorical representations in a less self-conscious manner. Without being necessarily didactic in the reductive sense of the word, they fully assume their role as the arousers of people's consciences and see literature as an integral part of the process of nation building.

In order to achieve their aims, they frequently resort to new modes of enunciation, which correspond to different relationships between writer and potential reader and also to different attitudes towards what one conventionally considers as 'reality'. Though post-modernism has naturally affected most English-speaking regions of the world, post-

---

[1] She imagines herself falling into a gaping hole in the earth under her or being devoured by a beast.

colonial writers have also shown a renewed interest in the potential of the realistic mode.

II - REALITY, REALISM AND MIMESIS

In any discussion of a literary work, 'reality' has no objective existence. It cannot be proven through scientific methods. What can be considered as 'realistic' is what is believable. Far from being a mere replica in a mirror, fictional reality is only validated by the readers' acceptance of artistic illusion.

A- A Brief Historical Reminder of the Relationship between Art and Mimesis

Mimesis has been a key concept in the emergence of the novel. Historically speaking, nineteenth-century fiction with such artists as Balzac, Dickens or George Eliot provides widely accepted paradigms for the genre. The relation between art and imitation has always been a basic concern in any study of the creative process. Aristotle, one of the earliest scholars to have examined aesthetic questions, already stressed human beings' natural taste for imitation. In *On the Art of Poetry*, he declared that:

> the instinct for imitation is inherent in man from his earliest days; he differs from other animals in that he is the most imitative of creatures, and he learns his earliest lessons by imitation. Also inborn in all of us is the instinct to enjoy works of imitation.[1]

When he used the term 'imitation', Aristotle did not mean that people are duped into believing that what they see or hear in art is reality. They realize that it is not but they also know that the mental image it evokes possesses enough features which they recognize intinctively from their own experience for them to accept these representations as valid. The conventions governing the 'encoding' of realistic details are equally accepted and recognized as such if the work is to function properly in its relationship with the recipient.

When something has not been experienced previously, human beings 'reason out'[2] and build a credible mental picture of what they have not seen before. Readers of post-colonial fiction are often faced with unknown environments, which may cause some problems in their response to the world represented. Our pragmatic knowledge of literature teaches us that, whereas Kipling's India might have seemed perfectly acceptable to a British person in the Indian civil service, the same picture

---

[1] Aristotle, Horace, Longinus, *Classical Literary Criticism*, p. 35.

[2] see *Ibid.*, p. 35

becomes objectionable to most modern South Asian intellectuals. So this 'reasoning out' of reality closely depends on historical and geographical conditions.

In the post-colonial field, the 'experience gap' between the author and the recipient of the work is sometimes so wide that an effort of adaptation or imagination will be necessary for readers to accept the 'reality' of the imaginary world presented to them as other than exotic.

Aristotle's developments on the question of mimesis are closely linked with the didactic function of art. It is therefore not surprising that didacticism, a strong motivation in the creative drive of many artists in the New Literatures in English, should also go hand in hand with a special interest in the 'realistic' tradition. A *caveat* must be introduced when the term didacticism is used. Too often this means monolithic unproblematic discourse. But this need not be so, as many subtle uses of this type of discourse in post-colonial novels show.

The school of writing which has most vocally proclaimed its belief in the importance of representing reality in art was the movement called realism, whose theory was elaborated most systematically in nineteenth-century France. The notion of 'realism' implied faith in the materiality of the world perceived by the senses. The role of art was then taken to be to imitate reality, not to recreate it.[1] In the nineteenth century, 'realistic' writers were attempting to go beyond what they saw as the excesses of subjectivity or the uncontrolled outpouring of feelings associated with the romantics. Beyond this theoretical credo, they had social motivations: they were trying to extend the realm of literature beyond the narrow circles of the aristocracy and the bourgeoisie in order to account for the whole of society, including the lower classes.

In a similar reaction against what they felt was the confiscation of literary representation by an unacceptable group of outsiders, the first generation of post-colonial writers often reacted to the use of their home environment as the background for sentimental exotic stories in which the 'natives' were merely used as decoration for plots concerning mostly Europeans. With his novels *Things Fall Apart* and *Arrow of God*, Chinua Achebe radically questioned this tradition by placing peasant African society at the centre of action, thus seeking to redress a biassed picture of his own society.

The so-called school of realism in nineteenth-century France was extremely diverse and it overlapped into 'naturalism'. Like most similar terms, the appellation 'realism' was of more interest to critics who

---

[1] This is purely a theoretical statement though since every artist refashions reality.

classified the movement a posteriori than to the practising artists at the time. Still the birth of the movement corresponded to a new apprehension of reality which became possible because of the tremendous progress of science and industry. Intellectuals were fascinated by the possibility that human beings could harness the forces of nature for their own purposes and this optimistic mood led some writers to believe that they could give an accurate description of reality in their works. Novels tackled ambitious subjects encompassing a whole society with its many social groups and diverse characters, as opposed to what was considered to be the restricted view of romantic poets, with their concern for the individual mind.

These generous ideals sometimes went together with much naïveté and great writers were prompt to pinpoint the weaknesses in the explicit aims of the movement. Faced with the blind belief that art could 'mirror' reality, Zola, one of the revolutionary theoreticians of the new 'scientific' method in literature, admitted that 'realism signifies the frank and complete expression of individualities'.[1] The less sophisticated realists represented by Champfleury were able to oppose the complex and self-conscious writers, whom they disliked, and the 'sincéristes', who cultivated simplicity and sincerity, notions which the modern reader now finds suspicious.

Zola's theoretical position[2] opposed the didactic value of literature and the escapist tendency which he condemned. Among realists, social usefulness was preferred to individual or private soul-searching. In some regards, the enthusiasm of the nineteenth-century realists was comparable to the optimistic faith which one finds in some post-colonial writers; both felt that a major breakthrough had been made and that the artistic drive could be put to social use. This originated in their desire to legitimize their activity by seeking social recognition of their usefulness to the whole human community. They came to consider themselves as the educated guides who could show the way to liberation. In the New Literatures, this attitude to art was most frequent in countries such as Nigeria where the tradition of literature as a tool for education remained very much alive. Another illustration of this attitude can be found in the 1960 'ghetto poets' in South Africa (Serote, Sepamla, Mtshali...) and among novelists such as Alex La Guma who hoped to raise consciousness among the readers and contribute to the liberation of their fellow-countrymen.

Realists, whether in nineteenth-century Europe or in twentieth-century Africa, have depicted social classes which the dominant discourse had

---

[1] *Roman expérimental*, p. 307. Quoted by Damian Grant in *Realism*.
[2] In art too, theory often differs widely from practice.

neglected. Unavoidably a number of them found their inspiration in the new socialist or Marxist analyses of society. Marxists have paid particular attention to the conflicts between the different classes in a given society. They have often argued that the relationship between the bourgeoisie and the workers was not significantly different from that between imperialists and the subjects of their colonies. In both cases, they analyze the dominant class's attitude to the others as one ruled by the process of reification: the underdogs are considered as objects and means of producing more added value, and not as free subjects.

Marxists have illustrated themselves in art with their special fondness for 'socialist realism', a genre admired by a number of radical writers in the New Literatures. Socialist realism is an offshoot of realism and naturalism. Like nineteenth-century French writers such as Zola, Marxist creators have privileged the working classes and glorified their resistance to the exploiters. Such analyses, modified to fit the post-colonial situation, inspired the Kenyan novelist Ngugi wa Thiong'o in his depiction of political corruption in *Devil on the Cross* and *Matigari*. In that period of his writing career, Ngugi wa Thiong'o simplified his message and used the fable to denounce a system of exploitation whose victims, the landless peasants and the inhabitants of the urban ghettos, did not always realize the ruthlessness and cynical efficiency of their rulers. But such literary expression, with a willing abandonment of all the complexity of language and characterization which made earlier novels such as *A Grain of Wheat* and *Petals of Blood* masterpieces, appears to some as a form of artistic mutilation for the sake of (problematic) social efficiency.

Underpinning Marxist literary theory lies the belief that the creator must describe society 'really', with its superstructures; and this purpose is best achieved by outlining class conflicts. According to a number of Marxist critics, the really innovative writers are those who can dramatize, in an artistically satisfactory form, the basic conflicts and evolutions at work in their societies. This approach has led to the privileging of revolution as a decisive step towards the empowerment of the deprived working classes. Some critics have even come to the conclusion that such social changes can have consequences in literary practice too: for David Craig, the rise of a new genre is 'likely to occur along with the rise of a new class.... Such an upheaval is likely to take place at a time of social upheaval and rapid change'.[1] This analysis seems confirmed by the emergence of the novel in eighteenth-century Europe, a period which

---

[1] David Craig, ed. *Marxists on Literature*, p. 160.

corresponds to the rise of the bourgeoisie and the parallel decline of the aristocracy.

In the post-colonial context, the maturity of written literature also corresponds to the period just before or around the independence of each former colony. Initially the elites were essentially members of the local bourgeoisie who had had access to European-type education and were suddenly given an opportunity to take on social and political responsibilities. The evolution of this rising social class can, to a certain extent be compared to the emergence of a new social category in eighteenth-century Europe. Intellectuals such as Jomo Kenyatta and Julius Nyerere provide good examples of this phenomenon, even though many of them soon abandoned their revolutionary rhetoric once they obtained power. Others chose to remain in teaching or in writing fiction and contributed to revitalize the realistic genre.

According to Craig, altered social conditions often lead to the emergence of new genres or to the transformation of old ones. But, besides purely sociological or historical causes, one has to take into account fashionable artistic theories or discussions largely extraneous to the 'objective' evolution of societies. In an age of global communication, ideas travel as fast as technologies allow and artistic forms inevitably undergo influences from outside the narrow geographical confines in which the artists work. What is happening in the New Literatures in English partly confirms Craig's axioms. Yet his explanation is slightly too mechanistic to account for the various phenomena at work in art. These early formulations express a naïve conception of literature as the mere 'reflector' of 'reality'. They ignore the problematic nature of reality as well as the complex situations of enunciation which determine the writers' relationship with language. Post-colonial writers frequently view both Western representations and autochthonous values with a mixture of familiarity and distance, which renders their attitude to 'reality' often paradoxical and complex.

Though he remained basically within the Marxist framework, Georg Lukács made an essential distinction which swept away the cruder interpretations of realism as a pure 'mirroring' of reality. For him, a mere copier who accumulates superficial details leaves the reader with a chaotic mass. Similarly a writer who seeks to impose 'a system originating in his own mind'[1] to order the world founders in abstract considerations which fail to express reality. Instead Lukács favoured those creations which can unveil inner truths through an artistic

---

[1] *Ibid.*, p. 291.

presentation which centres round reality 'freely and naturally'.[1] This legitimate criticism of meretricious realistic scribblers perhaps raises more questions than it answers. The mystery of this miraculous synthesis achieved by some and missed by most is what distinguishes a major writer from a more ordinary one. Reducing success to a faithful rendering of the social forces at work merely presupposes a judgement of value which many would question. In his criticism of naïve realism, Lukács abandons 'scientific' criteria and resorts to some sort of organic link, which seems a very 'subjective' tool to use for a dedicated materialist.

Other Marxist-inspired theoreticians shed an interesting light on the concept of reality and that of realism: for Bertold Brecht, who rejected purely formal or literary criteria to define the term, realism cannot be taken as a literary model *per se*. Because reality changes, 'the means of representation must alter too'.[2] Yet, when pressed to give a precise definition, Brecht abandoned subtleties and reasoned in terms of preconceptions which resorted to faith rather than logic. To him, 'Realist means: laying bare society's causal network / showing up the dominant viewpoint as the viewpoint of the dominators / writing from the standpoint of the class which has prepared the broadest solutions for the most pressing problems afflicting human society / emphasizing the dynamics of development / concrete and so as to encourage abstraction'.[3] There may be some measure of truth in the arguments advanced. But this type of reasoning excludes from the 'realistic' genre anything that does not express the point of view of the proletariat. Many would argue that class analysis, though useful, does not suffice to describe the situation in countries widely different from those of Europe on which the Marxist theory was based.

Strict Marxist opposition between realism and formalism is equally simplistic. Strangely enough, for Lukács, Kafka 'belongs with the great realistic writers'[4] because the 'diabolical character of the world of modern capitalism, and man's impotence in the face of it, is the real subject-matter of Kafka's writing'. At that point, ideology takes over. The word 'realistic' is used in the sense of anything that Lukács, the critic, approves of. If Kafka's writing were reduced to its social message, it probably would not have passed on to posterity. His unique style of presenting reality, with the help of overpowering obsessions and fantasies is closer to the world of nightmares than to the most pessimistic

---

[1] *Ibid.*
[2] *Ibid.*, p. 425.
[3] *Ibid.*, p. 424.
[4] *Ibid.*, p. 380.

interpretation of 'reality'. Lukács' remark ignores all the unconscious desires at work in Kafka's fiction.

However Kafka's particular mixture of facts and fantasy may well have prefigured some of the work of the 'magic realists'. He too was a man of the margins, because of his family's cultural roots and because he belonged to the German-speaking minority in Czechoslovakia. He too had to recreate his own reality in nightmarish terms because he was not satisfied with the representations offered around him. But, with him, as with many post-colonial novelists such as V.S. Naipaul, the border between horror and comedy was never clearly-defined.

This rapid survey of traditional Marxist uses of the term 'realism' shows that the word has positive ideological connotations within the system but does not necessarily correspond to any clear definition. It becomes one element in a polarity whose negative opposite is 'formalism'. 'Formalism' is seen as subjective, divorced from reality, its own logic being based on abstract notions which have nothing to do with the 'real' processes of positive evolution in a society. So maybe, in an ironical way, Brecht's remark about 'realism' being no *a priori* formal model holds true. One cannot take the term 'realism' to represent a form outside its historical context of production. Or, to put it another way, like many other terms, it is determined by ideological representations rather than by essences. Does this mean one should abandon it altogether?

A number of French Marxist critics have gone beyond the rather sketchy theorizing of their predecessors. Because they have resisted the temptation to ostracize 'formalism' at first sight, they propose a subtler method of analysis. Pierre Macherey[1] rejects any form of empiricism and declares: 'the objects of any rational investigation have no prior existence but are thought into being'.[2] So literary criticism or the activity of reading produces its own object. Knowing does not mean coming closer to the 'true object' of knowledge. This is never offered as an unproblematic reality. 'The act of knowing is not like listening to a discourse already constituted, a mere fiction which we have to translate. It is rather the elaboration of a new discourse, the articulation of a silence'.[3] This emphasis on the irreducible gap between criticism and the work of art,

---

[1] Macherey, *A Theory of Literary Production*.
[2] Macherey, p. 5. The English translation does not quite do justice to the original in which Macherey writes that the object of research is *produced* by the activity of the one who searches: 'ce sur quoi porte la recherche rationnelle n'existe pas déjà mais est produit par elle' (p. 13).
[3] Macherey, p. 6. Again the translation slightly alters the meaning of the original French: 'inventer une nouvelle parole, donner la parole à ce qui par essence garde le silence' ['... give voice to what, in essence, remains silent'] (p. 14).

between the work of art and its reference, leads to the practical consequence that the realistic work can never claim to blend with the reality it evokes. 'The illusion that it produces is its own peculiar norm'.[1] Any analysis of realistic effects focuses on discourse and on its conditions of production.

Macherey agrees with Balzac that a book is entitled to create a world of its own. The novel thus builds its own norms, which does not mean that it can move in any direction whatsoever. The logic for the development of the work is inscribed within its letter. For Macherey, the characteristic of inferior literary production is that it inevitably seeks a pretext outside itself, in a tradition, in moral principles or in an ideology. Yet a work of art is autonomous but not independent with regard to what lies outside itself. A novel or poem does not exist in isolation as extreme formalists would have us believe. *Through language*, literature is related to history, to sociology, to ideologies, but always in a problematic manner. It must always be constructed by the reader. Unlike earlier Marxist critics, Macherey has integrated the discoveries of Saussure and of semiologists. The study of signs need not inevitably lead to 'escapist' enterprises. For Macherey, the writer's language builds meaning, sets out to produce illusion, a phenomenon whose primary characteristic is veracity. It produces the conditions which make it possible for other people to believe in it without having to validate their perception by means of external criteria. This 'reality effect' ('effet de réalité') is based on people's fascination for the images the artist creates. These remain virtually endless and therefore can be infinitely 'rehearsed', to use in this context the beautiful phrase coined by Wilson Harris, the Guyana-born author of *The Infinite Rehearsal*.[2] A work never emerges on its own; it is always characterized by its relationship with other works that came before or with other discursive forms. Art is neither absolutely free, nor completely predetermined. It constitutes its own norm and creates its own 'literary space' ('espace littéraire').

One of Macherey's positive contributions to Marxist criticism lies in his questioning of Lenin's oversimplifications on literature; for Macherey, the analysis of literature cannot be content with using scientific concepts pertaining to the study of history or ideology.

---

[1] Macherey, p. 44. 'L'illusion qu'il produit est à elle-même sa propre norme' (p. 56).
[2] Faber and Faber (London, 1987).

'It will require new concepts which can register the literariness of the text'.[1] '... a writer never reflects mechanically or rigorously the ideology which he 'represents, even if his sole intention is to represent it; perhaps because no ideology is sufficiently consistent to survive the test of figuration.... the writer always reveals or writes from a certain *position*... in relation to this ideological climate: he constructs a specific image of ideology which is not exactly identical with ideology as it is given'.[2]

For Macherey a great work of art is riddled with ideological contradictions. Often the main 'message' from which the writer starts is contradicted by incompatible ideological lines in the course of the narration. 'The structure of the work... is this internal displacement, this caesura, by which it corresponds to a reality which is also incomplete which it shows without reflecting'.[3] While examining Tolstoy's art, Macherey meditates on Lenin's idea of literature as a mirror: 'the relationship between the mirror and what it reflects (the historical reality) is *partial*: the mirror selects'.[4] One may at this point question the term 'historical reality', which, in classical Marxist theory, tends to be given as a relatively unproblematic object, which can usually be explained in the context of class struggle. Here, because of ideological preconceptions, Macherey may well be resorting to simple points of reference, thus jeopardizing the subtlety of his other analyses. Despite this, Macherey's formulation of a mirror which reflects fragments and reveals instead of mechanically duplicating is particularly enlightening. This mirror is also meaningful because of what it does *not* reflect.

> If the mirror constructs, it is an inversion of the movement of genesis: rather than spreading, it breaks. Images emerge from this laceration. Elucidated by these images, the world and its powers appear and disappear, disfigured at the very moment when they begin to take shape. Hence the childish fear of the mirror which is the fear of seeing *something else*, when it is always the same thing.

---

[1] Macherey, p. 119. 'Il lui faut de nouveaux concepts qui permettent de rendre compte de ce qu'il y a de littéraire dans le livre' (p. 141).
[2] Macherey, p. 195. 'Un écrivain ne reflète jamais mécaniquement, ni rigoureusement, l'idéologie qu'il 'représente', même s'il s'est fixé comme seul but de la représenter: peut-être parce qu'aucune idéologie n'est suffisamment consistante pour survivre à l'épreuve de la figuration.... Toujours il donne à voir (ou à lire) une certaine position... par rapport à ce climat idéologique: il en fabrique une image particulière qui ne se confond pas exactement avec l'idéologie telle qu'elle se donne' (p. 220).
[3] Macherey, p. 79. 'La structure de l'oeuvre, c'est ce décalage interne, cette césure, par le moyen duquel elle *correspond* à une réalité incomplète elle aussi, qu'elle donne à voir sans la refléter' (p. 97).
[4] Macherey, p. 120. 'le rapport du miroir à l'objet qu'il réfléchit (la réalité historique) est *partiel*: le miroir opère un choix' (p. 143).

> It in this sense literature can be called a mirror: in displacing objects it retains their reflection.[1]

For Macherey, the process of literary mirroring is intimately linked with the creation of illusion and the notion of a contract between the writers and the readers who accept to suspend their disbelief.

At the same time as the realists were stressing the mirroring of reality, other writers, though on the surface equally concerned with depicting tableaux of society, highlighted the element of illusion always present in artistic activity. Maupassant stressed the illusory nature of reality in his preface to *Pierre et Jean* (1888):

> What childishness ... to believe in reality since every one of us carries his own in his thoughts and in his body.... Every one of us simply forms an illusion of the world... Great artists are the ones who impose their own particular illusion on humanity.[2]

Without going as far as Maupassant who has a very subjectivist view of reality, one has to acknowledge the importance of the artist's capacity or inability to have the reader share his vision and impose it as a valid substitute for reality.

Ferdinand de Saussure's linguistic theory has shown the irreducible gap that always remains between the signifier and the signified. In the 1950s and 60s, the French structuralists followed up with the exploration of the semiotic reality of language. In *Littérature et réalité*, Roland Barthes declares:

> The truth (of referential illusion) is that, once eliminated from realistic enunciation as a denotative signified, the 'real' reappears as a connotative signified: for at the very moment when these details are supposed to denote the real directly they only signify it, without saying it explicitly.[3]

---

[1] Macherey, pp. 134-5. 'Si le miroir construit, c'est dans le mouvement inverse de celui d'une genèse: loin d'épanouir, il casse. C'est de cette déchirure que sortent les images. Par elles illustrées, le monde et ses pouvoirs apparaissent et disparaissent, défigurés au moment même où elles commencent à faire figure; d'où la peur enfantine devant les miroirs, d'y voir autre chose, quand c'est toujours la même.
C'est en cela que la littérature peut être appelée miroir: en déplaçant les choses, elle garde leur reflet'. (p. 157)

[2] 'Quel enfantillage, d'ailleurs, de croire à la réalité puisque nous portons chacun la nôtre dans notre pensée et dans nos organes.... Chacun de nous se fait donc simplement une illusion du monde.... Les grands artistes sont ceux qui imposent à l'humanité leur illusion particulière'.

[3] 'La vérité (de l'illusion référentielle) est celle-ci: supprimé de l'énonciation réaliste à titre de signifié de dénotation, le 'réel' y revient à titre de signifié de connotation; car

Many passages in Salman Rushdie's *Midnight's Children*, notably those when the narrator describes places in Bombay, illustrate this definition; they do not mean as much as connote the fictional existence of a place, which a local reader with a similar experience to Rushdie's may share and identify with. So accumulation does not aim at producing a 'realistic' effect in the primary sense of the word; it rather creates the conditions for the readers to use their imagination in order for them to take possession of the 'reality' described.

In his 'Introduction à l'analyse structurale des récits',[1] Roland Barthes plays down the importance of mimesis in narration. For him, 'the function of a narrative is not to 'represent' but, instead, to constitute a spectacle which still remains very enigmatic for us but in any case is not of a mimetic order. The 'reality' of a sequence lies not in the 'natural' succession of the actions composing it but in the logic there exposed... the origin of a sequence is not the observation of reality, but the need to vary and transcend the first 'form' given to man, namely repetition...'[2]

The phenomenon is further complicated by the particular conditions of enunciation which often preside over the reading of post-colonial fiction in which writer and reader do not necessarily belong to the same culture. This is even truer when the artist possesses a complex multicultural background.

Barthes' remark which aims at breaking the surface of referential illusion raises the problem of the readers' attitudes towards the world represented in the work of art. Do they expect it to stand for the 'real' world or are they acutely aware of the symbolic contract which binds them to the writer? The question cannot easily be answered because the common ground of expectations between the two parties remains extremely varied in the case of the New Literatures. Barthes' remark applies to a post-modern environment in which the reader's attention is drawn to the artificiality of the sign and to the implications of this perception based on an awareness of semiotic problems.

---

dans le moment où ces détails sont réputés dénoter directement le réel, ils ne font rien d'autre, sans le dire, que le signifier' (p. 89. translation mine).

[1] *Communications*, 8, 1966, pp. 1-27.

[2] Susan Sontag, *A Barthes Reader*, p. 294. 'la fonction du récit n'est pas de 'représenter', elle est de constituer un spectacle qui nous reste encore très énigmatique, mais qui ne saurait être d'ordre mimétique; la 'réalité d'une séquence n'est pas dans la suite 'naturelle' des actions qui la composent, mais dans la logique qui s'y expose... l'origine d'une séquence n'est pas l'observation de la réalité, mais la nécessité de varier et de dépasser la première forme qui se soit offerte à l'homme, à savoir la répétition' (*Communication*, 8, p. 26).

Semiosis and mimesis are, according to Michael Riffaterre,[1] the poles between which the 'referential illusion' operates. He prefers the term 'reference' to 'things' because the *référent* marks the absence which the presence of signs makes up for. Riffaterre believes that, beyond the world of words there undeniably exists a non-verbal reality but there is no natural adequacy between this reality and the words that refer to it. Words belong to a conventional system specific to one social group. They arbitrarily express concepts related to *référents* although most people act as though words gave birth to reality. Referential illusion leads people to mistake representation for reality.

Michael Riffaterre's analysis centres here on poetry for the analysis of which he feels the need to introduce the concept of *significance* which he differentiates from *signification*. To him, in everyday language, words appear to be linked vertically to the things they signify. In literature, a horizontal network woven as the text develops tends to cancel the individual meaning of each word. Thus the *significance* results from this conflict with apparent referentiality. It is *'produced and regulated by the characteristics of the text'*.[2] Riffaterre's emphasis is laid on the syntagmatic logic of the poem. His remarks hold true especially for pieces with a high semiotic value.

Between 'mimesis', in which the readers believe that the verbal construct does mirror reality, and 'semiosis', in which they are aware of the symbolic function of the literary object as a text which is also the inheritor of other texts, the difference is one of degree rather than of kind. There is always more or less of this 'je sais bien mais quand même' (of course I know. And yet...), the essential dimension studied by Octave Mannoni in *Clefs pour l'imaginaire*.[3] This corresponds to the reader's willingness to confer authority over the control of 'reality' to the writer. The reader knows that the book is not real. And yet, there always remains that moment of hesitation. It is precisely this ambiguity, this belief *and* disbelief which the reader contemplates in the same instant.

The degree of mimesis and semiosis is not always easy to determine when writer and reader belong to the same culture. Interpretation depends very much on the shared values and cultural references. One easily imagines the difficulties in the case of the New Literatures when, for instance, an African or a South Pacific writer is read by a European or a North American. Similar misunderstandings may occur when a

---

[1] In Barthes et al., *Littérature et réalité*.
[2] 'La significance, c'est à dire le conflit avec la référentialité apparente, est *produite et régie par les propriétés du texte*' (*Ibid.*, p. 94).
[3] Octave Mannoni, *Clefs pour l'imaginaire ou l'autre scène*.

Caribbean or a Maori reads a text by a European author. The situation may even be worse in the first case since the former colonial will have been acquainted with the culture of the colonizer whereas the reverse does not always apply. How can we judge the mimetic quality when we are almost ignorant of the reference? Can we easily appreciate the inside allusions when we know little of the culture concerned? In the case of a reader foreign to the culture evoked in the book, what would appear as the semiotic character of the text is sometimes masked by the pleasure that the reader takes in being transferred to another 'exotic' universe for which the author is a sure guide. The greatest risk lies in using the text as a purely escapist representation of an idyllic society whose quaintness ravishes the senses just as a traveller's tale distorts the picture of a society by only highlighting its curiousness, a reaction which Edward Said rightly stigmatizes in *Orientalism*.

It is more difficult, especially for a critic who is an outsider to the literatures concerned, to judge of the 'mimetic' or 'semiotic' effect of genres imported from the dominating culture. There was no novel as such in Africa before the Europeans introduced it there. But there were oral narrations and folk tales whose aim was to teach values as well as to entertain. How then are we to judge Nigerian novelists who have adapted fiction for the sake of traditional didactic purposes? The success of such creations among modern Africans may indicate that they correspond to a deep necessity in their cultures. Otherwise how could we account for the constant discussion of their merits (as opposed to what some call the 'escapist' literature of Tutuola or Soyinka). Similarly, when an author uses a recognizable grid (for example that of Fanonian Marxism in the case of the latest phase of Ngugi wa Thiong'o's novels), the suspension of disbelief is even easier among readers or spectators steeped in the same approach of society.

This success does not mean that such authors are realistic but that they merely fulfil a function: they justify the existence of intellectuals as socially useful character - a position which need not be the same in other, more individualistic societies. This constitutes a further proof of the primordial role of ideological determination in the appreciation of mimesis.

One may also examine the process insofar as it affects the receiver of the 'message' or the relationship between signifier or signified. This second viewpoint has been fruitfully explored by A.D. Nuttall in *A New Mimesis*. Despite his sometimes excessive caricature of formalist or 'opaque' criticism, Nuttall reassesses the merits of 'realism' in a manner which is relevant to much post-colonial writing. He refers to Auerbach's description of mimesis as a form incompatible with the presence of a marked style. For Auerbach, the very concept of reality underwent a drastic change (transcendent in the Middle Ages, naturalistic in more recent times). Nuttall argues that 'all representation of reality is conventionally ordered; it is never possible in a finite work to exhaust reality' (p. 182). Rather than oppose Auerbach's arbitrarily termed 'marked style' and the more transparent mimesis, Nuttal prefers to stress the fact that mimesis is 'mimesis of something, or it is not mimesis. It exists in tense relationship with that which is other than itself' (p. 182). Ironically enough, after his severe berating of critics inspired by Barthes, Nuttall resorts to the notion of 'relationship', one of the keystones of Barthes' theoretical reflexions. The weak point in his argument is that he does not say much about the 'other'. Perhaps he means it in the sense of that pragmatic perception which can be recognized as true by others. His insistence on the possibility for us to ask ourselves the questions 'Is this true? Is this likely?' suggests an interpretation of this kind. It does not solve the problem of truth or the inferences of the term 'likeliness'; yet it reasserts the possibilities of communal agreement on the relevance of such notions. He does not think that reality is unified or objective. His remarks do not constitute a return to nineteenth-century positivism. He acknowledges the variety of reality and insists on its shifting appearances. In the last resort, Nuttall describes as mimetic 'any deliberate relation to the real' (p. 190). And this he opposes to playing with empty categories. Some might object that the term is stretched so much that it may include almost anything. Yet its merit lies in the reassertion of the pleasure of identification and projection of the audience into the work of art which they consider as mimetic. This does not leave aside problems of formal organization. But Nuttall does not consider them as the essence of a work of art. Instead of simply talking of realism, Nuttall comes to use the interesting notion of 'problematic mimesis' (p. 190), which has to do with the fact that language is at the core of literary creation. For Nuttall, 'language grows when certain schemes prove operable in relation to the real' (p. 192), a typically pragmatic definition which might infuriate more theoretical thinkers. The meanings with which language plays 'must first have worked, or they would not be meanings' (pp. 192-193). Private composition is subservient to the unavoidable fact that one was born in a language which constitutes a reality outside oneself. One can use it, bend it, make it evoke new meanings; but they have to be shared by others. One lives in language, while sometimes being under the impression that one possesses it, a particularly frustrating feeling for post-colonial writers who are fighting consciously for the repossession of their territories in their own terms with sometimes more than one language at their disposal to express their reality.

Nuttall here makes a plea that 'no form of literature be regarded as wholly insulated from this varying world' (p. 193), a belief that very few post-colonial writers would query.

B- Art and a New 'Repossessed' Post-Colonial Reality

Post-colonial literature is often concerned with repossession of the writers' 'reality'. In this enterprise, language is the only weapon at their disposal, and in the case which concerns us, the language is that of the colonizer. Language, the writer's means of expression, is rooted in a particular culture and it varies with the specific historical moment at which it is used. Recent quarrels about nationalism or 'regionalism' have highlighted people's concern with the disturbances which may be inflicted on children who have to use a second language in their elementary education. What happens then, we may ask, when creators consciously choose to write in the former colonizer's idiom which is not always their mother tongue? Is it then possible for him or her to avoid the preconceptions vehicled by that language? Will the cultural representations contained in their works be perceived as other than exotic by metropolitan readers tempted by the lures of ethnocentrism? Abdul R. JanMohamed outlines the agenda required of such readers:

> Genuine and thorough comprehension of Otherness is possible only if the self can somehow negate or at least severely bracket the values, assumptions, and ideology of his culture.[1]

The 'older' generation of mature post-colonial writers have all had a 'Westernized' education which tended to alienate them from a sense of distinctiveness and originality. Many of them wrote with a Western publisher in mind and, whether they liked it or not, the strong possibility that their reading public would be in the West. At an initial stage, the West's artistic fashions inevitably influenced the development of post-colonial writing; The West provided models which, even after their canonical works had been rejected, could be taken as valid prototypes for the development of the New Literatures.

In the 1930s, a number of novelists grew increasingly concerned with the fate of the unemployed and the under-privileged in society. As a

---

[1] 'The Economy of Manichaean Allegory' in Ashcroft et al., eds., *The Post-Colonial Studies Reader*, p. 18.

movement, proletarianism was a reaction against literature produced by and for the upper classes; it questioned the monopoly over culture held by a small group of intellectuals. Their fight was one which some writers in the New Literatures could easily embrace because it represented a rebellion against arrogant British upper-class cultural canons. These 'proletarian' writers made disciples in several post-colonial countries where people were in search of an 'authentic' voice to express the grievances of the common people and provide a fresh interpretation of reality. Areas most affected by this phenomenon were those in which literature was beginning to develop in an autonomous way at that time (Australia, New Zealand, Canada, the 'White Commonwealth'). In the 'Third-World', India was probably the country where writing by indigenous people was most advanced. Mulk Raj Anand's brand of realism was inspired by Marxist ideas, which, to him, provided a grid of interpretation different from that implicit in traditional British representations of the colonial situation. John A. Lee's *Children of the Poor*, a novel depicting the lower classes in New Zealand, corresponded to a similar urge to get rid of a colonial system of references in order to create native heroes and values; Lee's autobiographical protagonist rebels against smug morality and asserts himself through transgression of middle-class principles. The European proletarian novel may have served as an initial model. But this does not mean that all the realistic works in the New Literatures accepted metropolitan models wholesale.

Still it would be wrong, because of these origins, to think that proletarian novels are all that the New Literatures can produce. It would be equally false to consider that this realistic discourse is a mirror image of that of the colonizing culture. At present, there is also a spate of so-called metafictional works in the 'Old Commonwealth'[1] or among writers such as Rushdie, who were born in a developing country but have spent much of their existence in the West. These may, on the surface, seem to imitate the metropolitan post-modernist works. But a closer examination shows that the borrowing of a Western mode is associated with the use of many other sources of inspiration which reflect the multiplicity and complexity of the writers.

Marginality and rebellion against authority often figure prominently in a novelist's early works. Yet, in the New Literatures in English, this marginality manifests itself differently. Rejection of the father figure is often transposed as an attempt to overthrow colonial values and replace them by new ones with which the colonial readers can identify. These

---

[1] See, for example, C.K. Stead or Ian Wedde in New Zealand.

provide them with a sense of identity which owes less to the metropolis. Consequently post-colonial works often violently question ideological representations or images of themselves which, they feel, have been confiscated by the colonial master. As Stephen Slemon says, the post-colonial writer has a 'dual agenda to continue the resistance to (neo)colonialism through a deconstructive reading of its rhetoric *and* to achieve and reinscribe those post-colonial social traditions that in literature issue forth on a thematic level and within a "realist problematic", as principles of cultural identity and survival'.[1]

Post-colonial intellectuals tried hard to react against the reality imposed by the colonial culture, that of Worsworth's 'daffodil', the only poem known by many Trinidadians a few decades ago, if we are to believe V.S. Naipaul. This flower which does not exist in the West Indies was then supposed to epitomize beauty in a literary form. Canons which had no relation to the colonial everyday experience contributed to 'de-realize' the colonial child's reality. When Naipaul refers to the campaign led against this poem in the West Indies,[2] he denounces this selective 'decolonizing' discourse which rejected Wordsworth but did not seem to object to the increasing americanization of Trinidadian society. Movements of liberation are always selective. Post-colonial artists sometimes overreact and create a reality of their own which is only the reverse side of what they are rejecting. Frantz Fanon's *Peau noire masques blancs* offers many examples of this negative reproduction of the model explicitly rejected. Wole Soyinka's criticism of the Negritudinists bears precisely on this point. The strategy of repossession adopted by these liberators sometimes replaces the monolithic colonial representations by an equally monolithic conception of their own roots which makes little of each culture's complex and hybrid history. For the sake of liberating themselves from one rigid vision of reality, they are sometimes tempted to substitute a ready-made and at times equally oppressive model endowed with supposedly 'authentic' values. Reactive cultural politics are in danger of creating other narrow forms of nationalism which have little to do with the richness and complexity of the nation. Some writers are obsessed by the idea of a miraculously pristine state before the 'fall' brought about by the colonizers. This type of dream cannot stand as other than an 'exotic' mode, a sterile utopia with only escapist values. A much more constructive attitude is to acknowledge that many 'colonial' elements have seeped into what they consider as their culture and try to account for the valuable syntheses

---

[1] 'Modernism's Last Post' in *Ariel* 20-4, 1989, p. 3.
[2] See *The Middle Passage*, p. 70.

which have been achieved. History never stops and when several cultures have come into contact, whether by choice or by accident, the 'stronger' (in technological and monetary terms) generally influences the 'weaker'. But the result need not be systematically felt as pure alienation. In turn, the colonized alter the world of the colonizer, at least culturally speaking. Any survey of the contemporary British novel has to take into account Salman Rushdie, Timothy Mo, Kazuo Ishiguro, Wilson Harris and V.S. Naipaul. My purpose here is not to downplay the deleterious effects that colonization has had on the colonized cultures. This is unquestionable and has been rightly highlighted. But the wave of justified reaction can sometimes lead to the ignorance of the obvious European component in that new and evolutionary sense of identity thanks to which some formerly colonized countries define themselves.

This questioning is made easier by the slightly marginal position of post-colonial writers - marginal in relation to these Western systems of thought. Marginality is not meant in a derogatory sense; on the contrary, the so-called 'margins' are a way for the artists to define themselves in relation and in opposition to the main centres of culture's pretension to sophistication and creative worth. People living in the West[1] tend to consider themselves as the centre of the 'civilized' world. Studying the New Literatures is therefore an excellent way of having a new and fresher viewpoint on some of the more questionable aspects of the West and on its cultural impact on the rest of the world. The Caribbean critic Michael Dash argues[2] that Third-World writers must go beyond the feeling of total loss and alienation which inevitably seizes them when they contemplate the destructive consequences of colonization. Using the example of Wilson Harris and Jacques Stephen Alexis who turned to the myths and folk legends 'in order to isolate traces of a complex culture of survival which was the response of the dominated to the oppressors', he advocates what he calls a 'counter-culture of the imagination'.

In order to set up such a counter-culture, post-colonial writers had to take possession of their own reality by 'naming' their environment in terms which clearly belong to them. For many realists, the question of localization and the creation of a believable environment are essential questions. The most realistic text is one in which time and space are recognizable. The realistic pact between writer and reader implies that,

---

[1] We use this term, as a means of simplification, to refer to the formal colonial powers or to the new world powers — such as the USA.
[2] 'Marvellous Realism: the Way out of Negritude'. Our references are to the republication of this text in Ashcroft, B., G. Griffiths and H. Tiffin, eds., *The Post-Colonial Studies Reader*, p. 200.

once localized, the text presents itself as a believable artifice. The writer in some ways guarantees the authenticity of the events narrated.

In the New Literatures, localizing a novel in the region concerned 'makes it exist' fictionally, gives it a status equal to Dickens' London or Balzac's Paris. V.S. Naipaul expresses this feeling using a rather provocative remark when he writes that 'landscapes do not start to be real until they have been interpreted by an artist'.[1] One should add 'until they have been interpreted by a local artist in ways which do not betray an insider's vision of the place'. In the early stages of post-colonial literatures, this task required a measure of courage on the part of the writer. The creative impulse originates in a moral impulse to correct a biassed picture.

Achebe's long digressions in the middle of *Arrow of God* which describe some key-moments in the existence of his Ibo community are not merely gratuitous. They aim at making this society exist, in all its manifestations, through the written word. The history of the Umuofia people is inscribed in their rituals and in the description of the utensils they use. Here these details are not only meant to be recognizable by a reading public which already knows them. Their presence in the text makes them exist in the minds of the public. Achebe uses this particular form of 'realism' not because he wants to cause a feeling of recognition giving birth to verisimilitude. He indulges in descriptions to wrench a whole culture out of oblivion. The reader soon discovers that the picture painted is credible and that the characters are believable, even if very different from contemporary people.

Post-colonial artists have consciously sought to redress pictures of their own environment and people, which they judged too colonial. In doing so, they have sometimes been tempted to brand any European writing on their countries as valueless in terms of evoking the reality of the place. In an analysis whose weakness lies in its anachronistic criticism, Achebe wrote against Conrad's 'biassed' vision of the Africans in *Heart of Darkness*. Yet, in doing so, Achebe forgot that the present consensus on the evils of colonization is relatively new. Conrad's perceptive view of the ambiguities of imperialism has to be envisaged in the ideological context of the time. And then the newness of his viewpoint becomes evident. The Polish-born novelist's ability to dynamize the relationship between past and present and his depiction of the powerful ambiguities inherent in any attempt to find the 'truth' about a situation have led radical post-colonialists such as Ngugi wa Thiong'o

---

[1] Robert D. Hamner, ed., *Critical Perspectives on V.S. Naipaul*, p. 18.

to acknowledge their debt to the visionary author of *Nostromo*.[1] Even
Ngugi wa Thiong'o, who sometimes tends to simplify his arguments for
the sake of political efficiency, insists that the reality produced in a work
of art is 'more than just a mechanistic reflection of social reality. As part
of man's artistic activities, it is in itself part of man's self-realization as a
result of his wrestling with nature.... it is ... a symbol of man's
creativity'.[2] The position of the Kenyan writer is fraught with the
contradictions inherent in a number of post-colonial writers. As a
practitioner of fiction, especially in the early stages of his career, he was
marvellously aware of the complexities of the situation in his native
country. Still the idealistic part of Ngugi wa Thiong'o led him to
sometimes abandon what he probably saw as the onanistic pleasure of
complex creation in favour of more direct social or cultural action. In
many of his essays, he demonstrated that literature cannot stand outside
the framework of social reality which he described as a class struggle
between the oppressors and the oppressed. Quoting Arnold Hauser,
Ngugi wa Thiong'o envisaged the relationship between writer and reader
as one close to that of *Agitprop*:

> All art aims to evoke; to awaken in the observer, listener or reader emotions and
> impulses to action or opposition. But the evocation of man's active will requires
> more than either mere expression of feelings, striking mimesis of reality, or pleasing
> construction of word, tone or line.[3]

Ngugi wa Thiong'o's evocation of mimesis here sounds unproblematic,
similar to the conception held by socialistic realists. His theoretical
discourse contrasts on this point with his own complex representation in
his early fiction. For the author of *Writers in Politics*, intellectuals have to

---

[1] On this subject, Jacqueline Bardolph's analysis in her *Ngugi wa Thiong'o: l'homme et
l'oeuvre*, possibly the best monograph to date on the Kenyan writer, is particularly
perceptive. Talking of intertextuality in relation to Ngugi wa Thiong'o's works, she
writes: 'Conrad, le Polonais exilé qui choisit de ne pas écrire en langue maternelle, fut
dès le début le modèle le plus fort et le plus intériorisé. Chez lui, Ngugi a appris a faire
jouer le passé et le présent à la fois dans une intrigue et à douter qu'il y ait jamais une
' vérité ' sur un fait, en présentant la même situation diffractée dans de multiples récits'
(p. 33).
(Conrad, the Polish exile, who chose not to write in his mother tongue, was, right from
the beginning, the strongest and the most interiorized model. With him Ngugi learnt to
juxtapose past and present in the same plot and to doubt that one may ever reach the
'truth' concerning a fact through the depiction of the same situation diffracted into
multiple narrations. [translation mine])
[2] *Writers in Politics*, p. 6.
[3] *Ibid*.

help in the becoming of a new society by suggesting directions towards which it has to move in order to improve its conditions. They cannot merely reflect reality; they have to act upon the reader or audience either by means of obviously didactic techniques or through influencing the imagination and feelings of their recipients. The latter strategy is usually more efficient and less tiresome than the former. The Kenyan novelist denounces the falsely neutral attitude of uninvolved literature:

> ... because of its social involvement, because of its thoroughly social character, literature is partisan: literature takes sides, and more so in a class society.... A writer is trying to persuade us, to make us view not only a certain kind of reality, but also from a certain angle of vision often, though perhaps unconsciously, on behalf of a certain class, race, or nation.[1]

Ngugi wa Thiong'o chooses his side, that of the voiceless peasant and worker's classes. To him, the political role of the writer is to confront the colonialist or neo-colonialist picture with another, which is more in conformity with the interests of the dispossessed. His action, which he bases on key concepts developed by Fanon and Marxists, aims at the control by the workers of the means of production. The land ranks uppermost among these, perhaps because of Kenya's particular history: most of the fertile areas were confiscated by white settlers, a situation which affected the author's family very much.

Ngugi wa Thiong'o's extreme dedication to his cause has led him to a position rarely adopted by other post-colonial writers: desirous to have leverage on the common uneducated people who could not have access to his publications in English, he decided to write in Gikuyu and have other people translate his works. This remarkably consistent stance is not devoid of ambiguities: with the obvious love that Ngugi wa Thiong'o has for the English language, is this not a form of artistic castration? In the context of Kenya where the movement of liberation was confiscated after independence by politicians using Gikuyu culture as the alternative to British culture, is there not a risk of reinforcing the monolithic neo-imperialism of one Kenyan culture over the other minorities who had little say in the process of decision-making? Was there any other solution to reach the people whom Ngugi wished to address? We are not trying to condemn a remarkably courageous intellectual forced into exile but only to show the ambiguities inherent in any radical stance in a place where seeking an alternative to the dominant culture is likely to lead to the under-evaluation of other strands of national culture.

---

[1] *Ibid.*

A danger in this repossession process would be that of believing that the reality reappropriated constitutes firm roots, an anchoring in a past tradition which has been recovered whole, unadulterated. Taking up this question, Homi K. Bhabha refers to Fanon who, according to him, 'recognizes the crucial importance, for subordinated peoples, of asserting their indigenous cultural traditions and retrieving their repressed histories. But he is far too aware of the dangers of the fixity and fetishism of identities within the calcification of colonial cultures to recommend that 'roots' be struck in the celebratory romance of the past...'[1] For Bhabha, the experience of 'unhomeliness' is characteristic of cross-cultural situations. But it is in no way reserved to them.

As we have seen with Ngugi wa Thiong'o, the process of 'repossession', with all its ambiguities, is closely linked with interrogations concerning language. Language is never neutral; it always vehicles preconceptions and cultural codes. The solution does not always consist in finding an alternative native tongue to replace that of the colonizer. In her essay 'Post-Colonial Literature and Counter-Discourse',[2] Helen Tiffin forcefully demonstrates the working of linguistic decolonization. For her, 'the processes of artistic and literary decolonization have involved a radical dis/mantling of European codes and a post-colonial subversion and appropriation of the dominant European discourse. This has frequently been accompanied by the demand for an entirely new or wholly recovered 'reality', free of all colonial taint' (p. 17). The last sentence, though underlining a major problem, leaves room for essentialist interpretations. The question is not to recover a pure unadulterated primeval entity which has possibly never existed. Culture and codes are always inscribed in history and languages have a potential for both reproducing and leaving possibilities of displacing stereotypical meanings. What is recovered is articulated through language and therefore refashioned, the difficulty being that the object thus transformed was itself a form of discourse. Though the signifier can be identified, the signified always remains trapped in a hall of mirrors. Still the effort made by the colonized people to reconstitute symbolic forms relevant to their own experience and which give positive value to their sense of identity cannot be ignored. Even if the language in which the colonized people express their sense of self is that of the colonizer, they can use it in such a way that it will subvert some of the constricting ideology vehicled by the language.

---

[1] Homi K. Bhabha, *The Location of Culture*, p. 9.
[2] *Kunapipi* IX, 3, 1987, pp. 17-34.

Because post-colonial writers express themselves in a language which may not be their own native one, or because it is merely one of several at their disposal, the possibilities of linguistic mirroring or interplay can be more fully exploited than in the case of monolinguistic writers.

On the other hand, when words are the colonized persons' main possibility of recreating worlds they can genuinely call their own, the fear of words betraying their conceptions are perhaps stronger. They may therefore choose to mask the problematic quality of language in order to create a stronger artistic reality which will be a form of repossession of the universe around. This temptation may be reinforced by the fact that the writers are expressing themselves in a language brought by the colonizer and therefore pregnant with Eurocentric conceptions. The writers may not wish to question the semiotic reality of language because it is the only tool at their disposal to try and master the world. This possibly accounts for the great number of 'realistic' narrations in many developing countries and for the relative lack of sophistication of some of their narratives.

In the case of English being used by writers from the former colonies, the problem is compounded by the complex class-system inherent in British and colonial society. 'Reality' in a work of art is perceived through language. When that language is felt to be tainted with colonial prejudices, the writer may wish to 'decolonize' it. English is kept as a medium for international communication but it is adapted to make it fit the particular reality referred to. In order to adjust it to the requirements of a local public, the artist may adopt a modified sort of English. Many possibilities are open, from the use of a 'nation language'[1] professed by the Caribbean poet E.K. Brathwaite and practised by Earl Lovelace to Albert Wendt's modified pidgin, Chinua Achebe's transliterations of Ibo phrases or Frank Sargeson's rendering of lower-class 'Kiwi' English.

One form of reaction to the imposition of the imperial language is to try to outdo the former colonizer at his own game. In *Razón de ser*, Alejo Carpentier talks of this inferiority complex which has led to excesses and prevented some American writers from developing their own idiom:

---

[1] 'Nation language is the language which is influenced very strongly by the African model, the African aspect of our World/Caribbean heritage. English it may be in terms of some of its lexical features. But in its contours, its rhythm and timbre, its sound explosions, it is not English, even though the words, as you hear them, might be English to a greater of lesser degree' (*History of the Voice*, p. 13).

> Within us, this preoccupation with linguistic purity is somehow a sediment of colonized consciousness. We would like to prove to the old colonizer that we can handle his idiom as well as he does.[1]

Carpentier adds that, from the 1930s on, creators lost that complex and began to treasure their 'americanismos'.

The West has not only influenced the way writers should write. It has often determined ways in which the New Literatures are; in Britain, after the initial refusal to acknowledge the validity of the New Literatures, these were often pigeonholed as ethnographic material. The teaching structure of the New Literatures in many British universities still bears witness to this non-literary status given by the establishment. When the New Literatures first attracted critical acclaim, it was often in the form of slightly patronizing statements in which the artist became a twentieth-century version of Rousseau's Noble Savage.

Unfortunately the West is not alone in its reductionist readings of the New Literatures. The Third World also imposes such narrow-minded interpretations of works of art written by people from the West. Post-colonial critics are sometimes too sensitive to any allusion to their present state of subservience and consequently tend to label any text written by a white artist, especially in the colonial period, as a racist or colonialist book. We have already mentioned the case of Conrad. Kipling was even more generally reduced to the chauvinistic imperialistic figure that he became at the end of his life. And yet such novels as *Kim* show far more complexity and understanding of India than some post-colonial readings would have us believe. In this novel, as Edward Said convincingly demonstrates in his preface to the book,[2] the author may be displaying an early form of hybridity which prefigures most other forms of the same phenomenon.

It would be equally unreasonable to impose Conrad's vision or Kipling's image of India on colonial or post-colonial pupils and expect them to accept it without criticism. Post-colonial critics have basically objected to the canonization of works proposed as 'the truth' on a particular question or situation. Their initial rejection of Conrad or Joyce Cary must be interpreted as a historical phenomenon. There are ways of teaching *Heart of Darkness* to African students which may help them to enrich their understanding of their environment. What was initially

---

[1] 'Esta preocupación de pureza lingüística era en nosotros, en cierto modo, un sedimento de conciencia colonizada. Queríamos demostrar al antiguo colonizador que sabíamos manejar su idioma tan bien como él.' (*Razon de ser*, p. 71. Translation mine).

[2] See his preface to the 1987 preface to the Penguin edition of *Kim*.

rejected was not so much the text in itself as the text as a pretext for the imposition of values which failed to prove constructive for the Africans' vision of themselves in their own environment.

It would be equally dangerous for the Africans to be intolerant of other visions of African texts under the pretext thet they were born in the place and know better. Nationalistic excesses led to the elimination of European authors from some African curricula. This attitude is just as narrow-minded as that which consists in systematically ignoring texts from the New Literatures in courses taught in British, French or American universities because they are considered as 'non-literary'.

Initially, many post-colonial writers only had a foreign audience (mostly liberal-minded intellectuals). A misunderstanding may arise from the lack of common ground which may lead some foreign readers to take the novelist's word at face value and to trust the exactness of the picture given with no concern for the specifically fictional quality of the writing. The referential value of a novel is complicated by the fact that most texts are variations on former texts. What is taken by the foreign reader as a completely faithful account of reality is a viewpoint heavily influenced by other linguistic or cultural models which have fashioned the writer's expression.

Among other influences, behind Ngugi wa Thiong'o or Achebe lurks the figure of Conrad. Behind Soyinka stand the Greek classics as well as Yoruba traditional tales. Camus, V.S. Naipaul, the negritude poets and R.L. Stevenson are perceptible presences behind Albert Wendt's novels. No text is born out of nothing. In the case of the New Literatures in English, the diversity and apparently contradictory character of some of these sources account for a greater complexity of viewpoint and for equally problematic responses on the part of the readers.

This situation accounts for the new narrative strategies which correspond to the diverse perspectives simultaneously or alternately held by the writers. In her article 'The Mouth with Which to Tell of their Suffering',[1] Angela Smith convincingly studies Achebe's particular use of the narrator in *Things Fall Apart*. According to her, the reader is tossed back and forth between the point of view of the anthropologist and that of the traditional oral storyteller.[2] Angela Smith sees that as a schizophrenic pattern, which can be questioned. There is certainly a lot of nostalgia for the lost old ways in Achebe's fiction. But he is a modern African, who cannot eternally be described as 'divided'. The way in which the characters of *Anthills of the Savannah*, his latest novel, constantly play on

---

[1] In *Commonwealth* 11-1 (1988), pp. 77-90.
[2] *Ibid.*, p. 88.

their multiple cultural references shows that, far from being a handicap, this situation is felt to be an asset, as opposed to Americans such as Lou, the journalist, who only has a stereotyped view of Africa. Achebe's characters are capable of self-irony, a faculty which non-Africans in the novel seem to lack totally.

Writers such as Achebe may well be taking their revenge on the unfortunate tendency on the part of outside observers to fossilize Africa at a certain point in its evolution, forgetting that cultures never remain static. Any examination is necessarily rooted in a certain historical period. In 'L'Ethnographe devant le colonialisme',[1] Michel Leiris shows the link between such a tendency and colonialist ideas:

... as soon as a culture appears in a constant process of flux, constantly overreaching itself as the human group which supports it renews itself, the desire to preserve the cultural particularities of a colonized culture ceases to have significance. Or rather, such a desire means that it is the very existence of a culture that one seeks to oppose.[2]

In their problematic vision of society, Achebe and other similar writers are precisely proposing an antidote to that colonialist view of reality in their non-monolithic visions of their society. They force the readers to accept different and more complex points of view, showing them societies in the process of assimilating different elements and building different syntheses.

The readers' appreciation of the degree of realistic illusion on which the generic classification of a work of fiction depends is closely determined by their expectations and experience of being confronted with similar forms. And this recognition stems from the common ground of reference between the producer of the work of art and its recipient. In his study of autobiography entitled *Le Pacte autobiographique*, Philippe Lejeune developed the notion of a pact between reader and writer. This is only to be taken in a loose metaphoric sense since no agreement of this sort was ever signed. But the merit of the term is to point towards a common area of expectations. This preoccupation with the pact between writer and reader is more important when the writer sets out to show how

---

[1] In *Cinq Etudes d'Ethnologie*.
[2] '... dès l'instant que toute culture apparaît comme en perpétuel devenir et faisant l'objet de dépassements constants à mesure que le groupe humain qui en est le support se renouvelle, la volonté de conserver les particularismes culturels d'une société colonisée n'a plus aucune espèce de signification. Ou plutôt une telle volonté signifie, pratiquement, que c'est à la vie même d'une culture qu'on cherche à s'opposer.' ([my own translation] p. 92).

a different culture, which has been threatened with extinction, reacts or behaves. As we have shown, the New Literatures do not ususally produce much purely narcissistic fiction. Conversely the didactic dimension occupies a major place in this field. A number of post-colonial novelists have felt the need to alternate action and commentaries in which a narrator, who stands outside the story, fills in information about the context or the background, which some readers might miss because of their ignorance of the world evoked. The narrator thus becomes a specialist adding to the reader's experience. This attitude is particularly frequent when the reader and writer belong to different cultures. Sam Selvon's early Trinidadian novels provide examples of this type of narration which presupposes a certain relationship between writer and reader. Another more subtle alternative leading to the filling in of information is to present events in such a way that the reader will guess the organization of the social structure or culture described. It is what the Maori writer Patricia Grace does in many of her stories collected in *Electric City*.

In more established literatures where writer and reader share cultural or moral values, this informative content is not so necessary and the mixture of identification and distance created by traditional realistic discourse is relatively easy to produce. Writers can resort to numerous unwritten markers which make it unnecessary to embark on long explanations. Because of this shared code of understanding, literary discourse can leave more to the unsaid than in the New Literatures in which the reader's expectations are extremely varied. So even verisimilitude, the effect produced when, in realistic fiction, the 'pact' between reader and writer, is correctly respected, becomes problematic. Because the rules governing social relations sometimes have to be explained, the narrator's presence becomes more obtrusive, which sometimes limits his/her possibilities of playing with irony. It may also increase the reader's pleasure if, as in the case of Rushdie, the artist has an encyclopaedic culture and, catlike, enjoys playing with the reader. Some would remark that Rushdie panders more to the taste of western readers than to those of his native countrymen, as the recent controversy seems to indicate. But there we may have reached the limits of communication of the novelistic experience, when fictional material is confused with reality and when a plot ventures into sensitive areas of belief or non-belief in a world where a number of people are ready to adopt any ideology provided it offers absolute certainties. Because one of the main themes developed in *The Satanic Verses* is precisely the question of belief and doubts, it is anathema to the puritans of all denominations.

Different audiences may appreciate different levels of reality. In the case of theatre particularly, African writers seem to have produced multi-layered works which can appeal to people with various degrees of literacy. *A Dance of the Forests* by Wole Soyinka often baffles readers of the script. And yet, when the play was first performed on the occasion of the celebrations marking Nigerian independence, the author remembers common workers coming to watch it night after night and apparently enjoying it on their own terms. But then perhaps *A Dance of the Forests* includes the same ingredients which brought together the little people and noblemen to watch Shakespeare's comedies or tragedies. On a different scale, the Elizabethan period was one in which several cultures were suddenly being forced together under the benevolent authority of the Queen. We may be going through a similar period of transformation, only this time more radical since it involves the possibility of exchange and communication around the globe. Concepts such as reality and artistic illusion thus become even more problematized and appear in singularly hybridized forms.

Because of the particular resonances it has with a local readership, the language used will ring familiar (or strange) to a local audience. On the contrary it may look like local colour to an ill-informed outsider, who may be encouraged to look further into the particular anchoring of a type of idiom. Therefore what appears 'realistic' to some may sound 'exotic' to others. If the bewilderment of the latter leads to an attempt to understand the strange cultural environment of the text, the artist will have fulfilled much of his aim. If, on the contrary, the reader cannot see further than exoticism, then much of the potential richness of the book will be lost.

The ambiguities of 'realism' appear particularly vividly in the case of the New Literatures. The Haitian writer and activist Jacques Stephen Alexis describes his people's particular apprehension of their own world in terms which question some of the common presuppositions concerning reality. In 'Of the Marvellous Realism of the Haitians' he argues[1] that his people's particular use of the 'marvellous' must be taken seriously. He opposes the positivist stance imposed by the major technological powers on Third-World countries with a particular disregard of their own

---

[1] In 'Of the Marvellous Realism of the Haitians' (originally published in *Présence Africaine* 8-10, 1956). Our references are to the republication of this text in Ashcroft, B., G. Griffiths and H. Tiffin, eds., *The Post-Colonial Studies Reader*.

relationship with their environment. Alexis stresses the fact that Haitians 'express their own consciousness of reality by the use of the Marvellous' (p. 195). To him, resorting to the Marvellous does not just mean using a second-rate form of perception. It is 'the imagery in which a people wraps its experience, reflects its conception of the world and of life, its faith, its hope, its confidence in man, in a great justice'. The interesting feature about Alexis' argument is that his rhetoric is tinted with some Negritudinist concepts and yet deliberately sets out to prove that the Marvellous is not part of an escapist enterprise:

> Haitian artists made use of the Marvellous in a dynamic sense before they realized they were creating a Marvellous Realism.... Creating realism meant that the Haitian artists were setting about speaking the same language as their people. The Marvellous Realism of the Haitians is thus an integral part of Social Realism.... The treasury of tales and legends... all the forms of Haitian popular art are there to help the nation in solving its problems and accomplishing the tasks which lie before it. (p. 197)

For Alexis, the Haitians' use of the Marvellous is attributed to their being close to nature, with the people having 'for centuries been compelled to sharpen their eyes, their hearing, their sense of touch' (p. 194). Such remarks do echo some of the ideas defended by Senghor. Alexis also paradoxically tries hard to show that this admiration for popular art is not incompatible with his dedication to socialism. Beyond these justifications, the fact remains that Alexis is suggesting that one people's reality must be seen in its own terms, that reality cannot be circumscribed merely through science and that imaginary representations and beliefs in the marvellous may form a valid part of the people's construction of their own reality.

In the New Literatures in English, perhaps more than in any other literary field, questions of cultural relativity are of utmost importance. So any usage of the term 'real' or 'reality' becomes problematic, which does not mean that it cannot be used. Provided the writer can create a universe which one can easily recognize as valid 'reality', the mimetic pact between author and reader may operate. It requires an effort, mostly on the part of the reader foreign to the culture described. Often the reader will be less equipped than a native person to judge of the local reference of the work. Some, who wish to recognize every detail of their environment will consider the work 'unrealistic'. On the contrary others - in many cases more sophisticated readers - will be able to accept the selection and condensation of information as well as the 'milieu' described as probable. When we talk of the 'reader', we do not mean here the 'implied reader' or the narratee, whose place is organized in the narration. We mean the public which the book actually reaches, sometimes despite the author's desire.

When the process of mimesis functions within a fairly closed social system, a slight effort of distancing enables the reader to distinguish between what is documentary and what is not. When Third-World writers refer to their familiar environment in their works and the reader is a European or a North American, the tendency of the latter to take the work as documentary will be even stronger. This has led some critics of the New Literatures in English to denounce them as too elementary because their 'referential' content is too strong. This comes from the confusion between mimesis and exact reproduction. Just like any other creators, post-colonial writers adapt, fashion and reconstruct their perception of 'reality' in their own terms. But, because they deal with realities unfamiliar to the European critics, they run a greater risk of being misunderstood.[1] In their inital attitudes to post-colonial works, Europeans or North Americans may be heavily influenced by the more consecrated literary visions of the Third World or of the colonies dating back to the period of imperial rule. Unconsciously, the viewpoints of E.M. Forster, Joseph Conrad, Robert Louis Stevenson, James Anthony Froude, Evelyn Waugh or Joyce Cary may carry more weight in their opinion than the visions of contemporary artists writing from within the culture described.

The pleasure the reader derives out of mimesis in the New Literatures may take several forms. The most naïve approach is the ethnocentric one. Starting from the presumption that one's own cultural references and norms are universal, the work of art is examined by comparison with these norms. A perfectly normal feature of everyday life - such as sugar cane in a West Indian novel representing peasant life - may be taken as terribly 'exotic' by a foreign reader. By this term 'exotic', the reader will refer to an escapist world in which the said plant will connote holidays where sun, sea and sex are supposedly offered unlimited. The 'beauty' of the scene will depend on the evocation in the readers' minds of a more perfect world where the limitations and taboos of their own do not apply. The work may also reflect colonialist clichés and play on them to attract a certain type of audience. We will ignore these types of works - which might have a sociological interest - to concentrate on those which are more satisfying to our mind because of their rich and problematic and nature.

---

[1] Some will argue that this is no great damage since the European critic may not be the writer's main implied audience.

In *A New Mimesis*, A.D. Nuttall rehabilitates the representation of reality in literature. He opposes two radically different conceptions of art:

> There are two languages of criticism, the first 'opaque', external, formalist, operating outside the mechanisms of art and taking those mechanisms as its object, the second 'transparent', internal, realist, operating within the 'world' presented in the work. (p. 80)

In the New Literatures, at least in the early stages, this debate between 'opaque' critics and 'transparent' critics strikes a distant note and appears as a discussion with more relevance in the Latin Quarter. Writers in the New Literatures are so concerned with placing their country or area on the literary map of the world that their first preoccupation is to give shape to their national or regional experience by describing it in their own terms. Because of this fundamental reason and also because they are usually nourished in the Dickens, Jane Austen nineteenth-century classics, they naturally turn to the realistic tradition. Some of them have sought inspiration in the local and traditional when it existed and have produced strange combinations of the old and of the new literary conventions.

Usually the writers, following in this the tendency of most novelists whose first work is generally autobiographical, recreate their youth and possibly the story of their nation, going back to the time of their grandparents. Their personal need is compounded with a social responsibility they feel invested with as the inheritors of a long line of culture.

In the New Literatures in English, there is practically no partisan of the 'opaque' school'. Even when the writers' aims are to explore the possibilities of language, they do not wish to abstract themselves from the reality around. The obstacle to be overcome is not to do with the 'tyranny of mimesis' but usually with the alien forms superimposed on their representation of reality. The act of repossession requires some measure of belief in the power of mimesis. If the local readership is to be convinced, they have to be offered representations to which they can adhere mentally and emotionally. Any great distance taken in relation to this will involve the risk of the book being ill-received or rejected. One cannot easily become a hard-core formalist when the status of one's artistic reality is shaky.

Writers in the New Literatures in English are usually immersed in their nation's fight for self-identity. This leads them not to question the value of mimetic literature. This does not mean that they do not adapt it to their particular requirements. On the contrary, because of their particular background, they will be inclined to seek artistic syntheses between older, traditional forms inherited from their original cultures and genres or approaches borrowed from the West. This new blending of course influences the evolution of the concept of mimesis, which is very dependent on the readers' artistic expectations. Features adapted from the old oral epics may well be considered mimetic in the original culture whereas they will appear as pure fabrications or figments of the imagination to a foreign reader. The same of course applies to conceptions of the 'fairy' story.

In the constitution of a stable sense of reality, the post-colonials often resort to the idea of roots, a notion which raises as many questions as it answers. The degree of 'rootedness' of a social group is supposed to determine its sense of identity. The absence of roots is reputed to lead to alienation. If one follows this argument, the West Indies and, to a lesser degree, Fiji, may provide the most extreme examples of alienation: there the colonizer brutally subdued - and in some cases wholly eradicated - the native population to replace it by a more 'docile' slave contingent brought over from another continent. Though less cruel than the actual slave trade, the indenture scheme whereby Indians were brought over from Asia to the Caribbean or to Fijian plantations in the nineteenth century was often just a milder form of slavery.[1] Culturally speaking, this has caused a sense of isolation and uprootedness in the people concerned. Fijian Indians have clung to fragments of their Indianness, which, because it was no longer a truly dynamic constituent of their everyday lives, soon risked becoming fossilized. A similar process took place in the West Indies. Naipaul's *A House for Mr Biswas* - though in no way an exact description of the plight of every Indian in the West Indies - is particularly forceful in its description of that experience. Similarly the descendants of former African slaves sought to cling to fragments of their past which had to be preserved as precious relics. Their sense of alienation was extreme, not only because of the 'Middle Passage' they had endured, but also because, in one single plantation, many different cultures and African languages were represented, thus diminishing the possibility of finding a common ground. The unification arose out of their similar experience of bondage and ill-treatments and their own history was built around the emerge of resistance and rebellion. The non-conformist churches played a significant part in bringing the people

---

[1] Following in the steps of the slave system, just after its abolition, the indenture scheme relied on a similar social structure.

together, in retrieving some models of traditional worship and in building a sense of religious and cultural identity. The two aspects are still intimately intertwined, as we see with the modern forms of the Rastafari movement. In the twentieth century, before they became aware of their Caribbean roots, the white or 'brown' elites of the region had to fight against the sense of being second-rate colonial imitations of Englishness 'with no past of their own'. The more enlightened among them found it increasingly difficult to cope with the idea that their ancestors had been conquerors, exploiters and slave-drivers and that they themselves, in some ways, were the inheritors of that situation, with all the personal advantages that they still enjoyed. A similar - though probably less intense - guilt feeling has beset many Pakeha liberals in New Zealand during the past fifty years or so.

The least extreme sense of alienation is probably to be found on the Indian subcontinent where, during the colonial period, the cultural influence of the British mostly affected the upper classes and the people who acceded to the civil service. It may be one of the reasons why literature in English has continued to play a relatively minor role (in terms of the number of books published) by comparison with works written in the original Indian languages. This does not mean that no cultural synthesis has been achieved - quite the contrary when we read the works of R.K. Narayan, Raja Rao, G.V. Desani, Anita Desai, Salman Rushdie, Amitav Ghosh or Vikram Chandra - but that the original cultures have not had the same difficulty in continuing to play a major role with the people.

'Roots' and the Western realistic tradition have not always been considered incompatible. On the contrary synthetic forms appeared, initially in areas of the world which were once colonized by Spain. Any examination of genres, conceptions of composite reality and hybridity will be greatly enriched by a study of different forms such as magic realism or its related sub-genres in South and Central America. But first we must enquire into the advisability of still using terms such as 'fantasy' or 'the fantastic' in a post-colonial context.

III - FROM FANTASY TO MAGIC REALISM

A- The Fantastic and 'Magic Realism'

Much use has been made of the term 'magic realism' to refer to texts which introduce an important 'imaginary' dimension into 'realistic' evocations of the world. The Cuban Alejo Carpentier has also coined the phrase *lo real maravilloso* (marvellous reality) which he applies to a vision characteristic of Central and South America.

One cannot study such terms as 'magic realism' or the *real maravilloso* without referring to the so-called 'Boom', a literary phenomenon which brought to the forefront Latin American writers in the fifties and sixties. 'Magic realism' and its avatars cannot be understood without a reference to realism. But any discussion of this subject will inevitably lead to the mention of the 'fantastic', which differs from the realistic tradition and yet is historically connected with it.

Towards the end of the so-called period of the Enlightenment, a new type of literature emerged, which challenged 'reasonable' representations. In the heart of the nineteenth century, a time when positivism prevailed, when belief in 'reason' was uppermost, many celebrated 'realistic' novelists also indulged in what was then called 'fantasy'.

B- Definitions of the Fantastic

In his *Introduction à la littérature fantastique*, Tzvetan Todorov reflects on Roger Caillois' remark that the fantastic marks a break with the common order of things, an emergence of the inadmissible into the unalterable everyday legality. Wondering who should decide what is admissible or not, Todorov privileges the point of view of the reader. To him the reader's hesitation is the first condition of the fantastic. For Todorov, 'the fantastic requires the fulfilment of three conditions. First the text must oblige the reader to consider the world of the characters as a world of living persons and to hesitate between a natural and a supernatural explanation of the events described. Second this hesitation may also be experienced by a character... the hesitation is represented, it becomes as one of the themes of the work.... Third, the reader must adopt a certain attitude with regard to the text: he will reject allegorical as well as 'poetic' interpretations'.[1]

---

[1] Todorov, *The Fantastic: a Structural Approach to a Literary Genre*, p. 25. 'Il faut que le texte oblige le lecteur à considérer le monde des personnages comme un monde de personnes vivantes et à hésiter entre une explication naturelle et une explication surnaturelle des événements évoqués. Ensuite cette hésitation peut être ressentie

This essential role given to the reader implies that there is a common ground of culture, or at least a majority of shared values, between reader and writer or between the reader and the character who thematizes his/her place in the text. In post-colonial literatures, this identification is more difficult to establish because of the cultural differences which may exist between author and reader.

Todorov always relates the function of the fantastic to the breaking of personal taboos. For him, the fantastic enables the writer to approach forbidden themes such as homosexuality, incest, vampirism, necrophilia... The questioning of reality implicit in this particular point of view presupposes that literature is mainly concerned with individual rebellion against representations which are judged inacceptable. Todorov asserts that, through the hesitation which it causes, fantastic literature leads the reader to question the existence of an irreducible opposition between 'real' and 'unreal'

1- A Problematic Term in the New Literatures

Such a questioning can only take place in a context where a certain consensus exists about the nature of reality. The adepts of the fantastic have tried to show that, in the last few centuries, our civilization has privileged logic too much, thus ignoring a whole section of human experience broadly classified as 'imaginary' or pertaining to the unconscious, and therefore dangerous because unreliable and potentially deceptive.

The terms of this argument become problematic when applied to the New Literatures. Primarily images of reality have been offered by the colonizer and it is against these images that the new intellectuals are rebelling. Rather than reject reality in favour of the powers of the imagination, many post-colonial writers offer alternative interpretations of reality. They are often torn between two contradictory desires: one is to go back to the native sources; the other is to use the tradition offered by European realism to reinterpret their reality in their own terms. The 'colonialist' *logos* is often useful, provided it can be made to accommodate different forms of experience.

Often too, writers in the New Literatures feel that their responsibility as artists is not merely one to personal integrity. Many also feel invested

---

également par un personnage; ainsi le rôle du lecteur est pour ainsi dire confié à un personnage et dans le même temps que l'hésitation se trouve représentée, elle devient un des thèmes de l'oeuvre.... Enfin ... le lecteur ... refusera aussi bien l'interprétation allégorique que l'interprétation 'poétique " (*Introduction à la littérature fantastique*, pp. 37-8).

with a social and cultural mission. Because of these characteristics, writers will tend more often to present an alternative reality where the hidden side will be the old culture or the suppressed categories of thinking. This does not mean that personal themes are not treated. Only, in many cases, they will not be as important as communal issues.

Where, in European literature, the fantastic serves to protest against the tyranny of 'fact', in post-colonial literature it frequently serves to incorporate the old values and beliefs into the modern man's perception. It has a social function, whereas in European literature, it more often expresses individualistic rebellion. In *Fantasy, The Literature of Subversion*, Rosemary Jackson, taking after Bakhtin, sees the *menippea*, with its carnivalesque roots, as one of the ancestors of modern fantasy. Its social function is admittedly lost in modern forms. For African authors, a return to the world of ancient deities and heroes does not constitute a reversal of codes; it is an attempt to reclaim alternative rules which may replace or complement those in use at the present time. Such practice may contain regressive and conservative implications; but it may also provide an alternative form of organization available as a substitute for the alienating dominance of Western ways.

Yet such an approach is never innocent and always contains ambiguities; how can modern city-dwelling Africans of the 1960s steeped in missionary education seriously believe in the validity of the old beliefs? How can they integrate them into their own system of thought, which is so influenced by concepts inculcated by Western education? How do their readers react to what may be, for them, an exotic set of rules? In such a context, Caillois' concept of the 'real world' will necessarily be a very fuzzy notion. It will refer essentially to the world perceived as 'real' by the writer concerned, a notion which becomes even more problematic than when it is applied to Western writers.

Even in European literatures, the fantastic serves to question the tyranny of the *logos*. Rosemary Jackson insists that the fantastic comes as a necessary corrective to narrow conceptions of the real. She quotes Irène Bessière's *Le Récit fantastique: la poétique de l'incertain* and argues that 'it reveals reason and reality to be arbitrary, shifting constructs, and thereby scrutinizes the category of the 'real'. Contradictions surface and are held antinomically in the fantastic text, as reason is made to confront all that it traditionally refuses to encounter.... What emerges as the basic trope of fantasy is the oxymoron...' (p. 21). In literature produced in developing countries, 'all that it traditionally refuses to encounter' is often the native tradition, 'reason' being represented by Western categories of thinking. With the transposition just mentioned, Irène

Bessière's notion seems particularly apt in that the fictional world of post-colonial writers usually forces together two systems which were originally antonymous. But even the figure of the oxymoron may only correspond to the perception of a Western critic for whom one cannot simultaneously hold a western-type 'rational' discourse and another one belonging to another order of reality. What may appear as a figure close to the oxymoron to an outsider may well be perfectly natural to the insider - though, in the case of writers who have acquired a western education, nothing can be so unilaterally simple.

2- A Historical Progression from the Supernatural to the Fantastic?

Historically speaking, in Europe, the fantastic emerges roughly at the same time as romanticism. Roger Caillois compares the Middle Ages and the romantic period and declares that the former was so steeped in the supernatural that it could not possibly give rise to such a genre as the fantastic.[1] Probably there was too much continuity between people's beliefs and their certainties about another invisible world ruled by the gods and daemons. Caillois could thus draw a basic distinction between fairy tales and the fantastic:

> ... in the fantastic, the supernatural appears as a break with the principle of universal coherence... The fantastic comes after the fairy tale and practically replaces it.... The fairy tale is set in a world where enchantment is taken for granted.... The fantastic presupposes the solidity of the real world but only to ruin it more radically.[2]

Caillois' distinction between different clearly separate ages applies to Western Europe. In the New Literatures in English, this concept of a succession of eras (from the belief in 'fairies' to a rational age) is much more problematic because, in some cases, the two exist side by side and simultaneously. In much West African literature in English, there is no clear separation between the old beliefs in the supernatural and the new 'scientific' age. Far from being a sign of obvious 'progress', the advent of science and rationalism was often perceived as a perverse effect of Westernization which writers, conscious of their unique heritage, partly

---

[1] 'Le Moyen Age, qui baigne dans le merveilleux, ne sait pas donner à ses diableries ou à ses enchantements la tension nécessaire, le haut degré d'angoisse indispensable au frisson futur' (*Anthologie du fantastique*, p. 14).

[2] '... dans le fantastique, le surnaturel apparaît comme une rupture de la cohérence universelle.... Le fantastique est postérieur à la féérie et, pour ainsi dire, la remplace.... Le conte de fées se passe dans un monde où l'enchantement va de soi.... Le fantastique suppose la solidité du monde réel, mais pour mieux le ravager' (Caillois, pp. 9-10). Translation mine).

rejected and partly endorsed. The return to modern interpretations of the old beliefs may cohabit, within the same person, with a perfectly 'Western' mode of thinking and with Cartesian principles of reasoning. The former is merely a way of holding on to what is the uniqueness of the African experience of the world threatened with extinction by the invasion of 'progress'. The metaphysical interpretation of the universe characteristic of the old African civilizations may appear as a valid enough structure to account for every phenomenon which rational reasoning remains powerless to explore. Nationalistic motifs and a desire to preserve their originality often leads the Africans to adopt the two different (and, to a European, incompatible) systems of reasoning without feeling apparent strain. Wole Soyinka's mythopoetic world in *A Dance of the Forests* shows such syncretism at work with Ogun, the old god of iron and of metal workers, becoming the deity which presides over road transport and lorry drivers. Technology and the traditional pantheon are made to cohabit. Similarly, in Soyinka's autobiographical volume *Aké*, the Christian religion appears in no way incompatible with the spirits of the ancestors or with traditional evil deities.

3- An Illustration of the Problem: Achebe's 'The Sacrificial Egg'

When Rosemary Jackson talks of the fantastic as 'the underside' of realism 'opposing the novel's closed, monological forms with open dialogical structures, as if the novel had given rise to its own opposite, its unrecognizable reflection' (p. 25), the example of Achebe's story 'The Sacrificial Egg'[1] immediately comes to mind. Julius Obi, the protagonist, is a clerk in the offices of the Niger Company. From the window of the building where he spends his days, he can see the great market on the bank of the river. But, when the story starts, Obi contemplates an empty market-place because smallpox has hit the town and people fear they might be infected if they go out of doors. Obi re-lives his last meeting with his beloved and their final parting. After leaving Janet, he wandered along the bank of the river and suddenly realized that the time had come for the night spirit to run its race through the town. In his haste to reach his house, Julius squashed a sacrificial egg at the crossroads and wondered whether this would bring ill-luck on him. The reader learns in a final paragraph that the smallpox has carried away Janet and her mother.

---

[1] Original version first published in *Atlantic Monthly*, April 1959. Achebe has since produced a revised and extended version which is part of his collection *Girls at War and Other Stories*, Heinemann [London, 1972]. Our page references are to this first version republished in Anna Rutherford, ed., *Commonwealth Short Stories*.

Julius studied at missionary school and is very much a man of the
modern world whose rationality leads him to condemn what the narrator
calls 'superstitious stuff' (p. 239). This epithet refers to the stories
reported by Janet's mother, a 'devout Christian' and yet one who believes
that 'some of the beautiful young women you see squeezing through the
crowds are not real people but mammy wota from the river' (p. 239).
These *mammy wota* are supernatural beings who emerge from the water
and enchant men only to cause their final loss. So Janet's mother sees no
contradiction between believing in Jesus Christ as the son of the only
God and being afraid of these *mammy wota*. Her world is one in which
the supernatural, a blending of the new religion and some of the old
beliefs, accounts for the unexplained or the unexpected in the universe.
But where does Julius stand, he who thinks of himself as above such
irrational and archaic beliefs? And how can we define the narrator's
position in relation to the episodes described?

The story starts in the realistic mode with the description of the
setting, both geographical and historical (the town of Umuru has become
a centre for exporting palm-oil to the rest of the world). The details given
can lead the reader to see Umuru as the archetypal West African colonial
town whose activity hinges on the export of a crop very much desired by
the metropolitan masters. So far the reader might think that the story will
be yet another allegory of the imperial domination of Britain over Africa.

The narrator then proceeds to give the foreign reader inside
information about the economic and traditional functions of the Ibo
market which traditionally rotated from town to town and recurred on the
same day every week, the Ibo week being divided into four days. The
narrator here fills a gap for the external reader who ignores the Ibo world
organization or for the modern Ibo who has forgotten the old pattern.
Achebe is faithful to his self-imposed mission which is to 'teach' at the
same time as he creates a believable fictional reality.

The nature of the narrative voice becomes more complex when the
reader learns that the market had become daily because of the increased
trade in the town but 'it was still busiest on its original Nkwo day,
because *the deity that presided over it cast her spell* only on that day. *It
was said* that she appeared in the form of an old woman in the centre of
the market just before cockcrow and waved her magic fan in the four
directions of the earth (Italics mine)' (p. 238). An analysis of the two
syntagms italicized shows a different type of adherence on the part of the
narrator in relation to the facts described. In the first instance, belief in
the reality of magic powers is simply suggested unproblematically, as
though the readers could easily understand that they have to interpret this

in a context where the supernatural forms part of the general world-view of the author. The second syntagm underlined introduces a measure of distance between the speaker and the supposed appearance of the market deity. Instead of merely presenting the belief as self-evident, it relates this belief to a general consensus among local people. A further example of this slightly distanced mode of enunciation is to be found later on when a 'they say' precedes the mention of the *mammy wota* and links this belief to popular creed.

One soon realizes that the narrator's voice is intimately intertwined with that of Julius Obi. After the initial description, the protagonist appears, looking out of the window of his office and wondering why there are so few people about: 'Who would have believed that the market could be so empty? But such was the power of Kitikpa, or smallpox' (p. 239). Who is speaking there? The narrator? Obi? The disease is first mentioned under its Ibo name and the narrator soon explains that 'no other disease is feared by the Ibo people as much as they fear Kitikpa. It is personified as an evil deity' (p. 239). The anthropological explanation suggests that the narrator distances himself from a belief held by the Ibo as a whole.

But the 'modern' Julius with his blind faith in rationality is soon overshadowed by another when he runs away in panic on hearing the wooden gong of the night spirit after taking leave of Janet for the last time. His hurried flight shows that this Christian man has kept his fear of the dread spirits who are abroad and can harm the careless ones who stay out when they should be home.

Dashing away in the dark, Julius steps on something that breaks under his foot and proves to be sacrificial egg. 'There were young palms fronds around it. Someone oppressed by misfortune had brought the offering to the crossroads in the dusk. And he had stepped on it, and taken the sufferer's ill luck to himself. 'Nonsense', he said and hurried away, but Julius *knew* that distance did not apply to these beings (italics mine)' (p. 240). Again the phrase italicized shows that the belief in the possibility of being saddled with someone's misfortune through breaking the sacrificial egg that the person has deposited appears as a self-evident reality. Is it the external narrator speaking or is it a passage in free indirect style rendering the protagonist's thoughts. One has difficulty unravelling the two voices here. The protest uttered by Julius Obi sounds weak with regard to the evil forces he has apparently unleashed against himself. His act of transgression in relation to ancestral religion looms much larger than his feeble Western 'rational' remarks. A further proof of the convergent position of the narrator's and the hero's voices is provided when, referring to Julius's attempt to run away before the night spirit, the narrator remarks: 'but Julius *knew* that distance did not apply to these beings (italics mine)' (p. 240).

The enigmatic conclusion allows for various interpretations: referring to the events described above, the narrator merely adds: 'It was only a week ago, but already it seemed to be separated from the present by a vast emptiness. This emptiness deepened with the passage of time. On this side stood Julius, and on the other Ma and Janet, who were carried away by the smallpox (p. 240)'. One may consider that the final discovery confirms the supernatural cause behind the two women's death. But the lack of commentary on the part of the narrator also leaves room for more 'rational' interpretations suggesting that the sad end was merely coincidental with the breaking of the egg. I would personally be tempted to see Achebe's position as a condemnation of the simplistic 'modern' rejection of any old beliefs apparently incompatible with the reasoning of an educated person. Achebe might very well be suggesting here that the world makes sense to the modern African only if he does not reject the essentially dual system at his disposal. Instead of a mutually exclusive polarity between 'ancient or modern', perhaps a combination of the two, depending on which proves most efficient to structure one's vision of the world, remains preferable. Neither a complete syncretic fusion nor a strict separation between the two cultural traditions at Obi's disposal might best define Achebe's attitude insofar as we can define it in this story. The revised version of the story in *Girls at War* gives even more importance to the traditional viewpoint. I personally find this less satisfactory in that the 'ancestor-worshipper' takes over from Achebe, the complex multicultural artist. The increased didacticism of the second version also leads to a more heavy-handed narratorial attitude which privileges ideology rather than pluralism. For the sake of clarity, Achebe abandons the more sophisticated viewpoint perceptible in the initial version of the story.

In this context, ready-made definitions of terms such as the 'supernatural' or the 'fantastic' become less precise because consensus on what reality is and what belongs to the supernatural becomes more difficult to reach. Similarly, in civilizations where the religious domain can include elements belonging to Christianity and others pertaining to various forms of traditional faiths, the dividing line between reality and the supernatural is far from clear. It can be argued that writers expressing themselves in English, because they have often been educated in a Western-type establishment, may exaggerate the importance of traditional elements. Multiculturalism may at times become a way for writers to seek some kind on revenge on the Western reader by claiming an exclusive field of knowledge which might give them superiority and make up for the old hierarchy which ensured that the indigenous person always felt inferior to the colonialist. The old game of one-upmanship is then transferred onto a terrain where the Third-World writer is ensured an advantage.

4- Fictional Reality/Fantasy/Magic Realism: the Case of Witi Ihimaera

Witi Ihimaera's early works, *Pounamu Pounamu* (1972) and *Tangi* (1973) were the first fiction in English published by a Maori. They are usually described as 'village novels', somewhat in the same mode as Achebe's fiction. Basically set within the realistic conventions, they express the reality of the native population of New Zealand at a time when, during or just after the Second World War, people were forced to abandon their traditional rural lives to seek a living in the cities. Several of Ihimaera's texts, particularly his story 'The Greenstone Patu' published in *The New Net Goes Fishing* (1977) and his novel *The Matriarch* (1986), feature episodes which apparently infringe the prevailing code of realistic illusion. Patricia Grace's *Potiki* (1986), *the bone people* (1984) by Keri Hulme and 'I Will be Our Saviour from the Bad Smell'[1] by Albert Wendt could also be examined from a similar angle.

In 'the Greenstone Patu',[2] Witi Ihimaera tells of how a young Maori, based on the same model as the hero of his novel *Tangi*,[3] at work in Wellington one day receives a telephone call from his aunt Hiraina who asks him to fetch her immediately from the airport. When he arrives after making up an excuse for his boss, Auntie Hiraina informs him that she has come to claim the family's lost 'patu pounamu'[4] which she has managed to trace in a house in Porirua. When the protagonist and his aunt arrive at the said house, the woman who, over the phone and after threats of legal action, had initially agreed, though with reluctance, to give them the *patu*, declares that she has changed her mind and orders them out of the house. Then the *patu* appears mysteriously, glowing in the room;

---

[1] In *The Birth and Death of the Miracle Man*.
[2] In *The New Net Goes Fishing*, pp. 107-118.
[3] Like Tama in *Tangi*, the protagonist of the story works in Wellington though his family (the Mahana family, like in *Tangi*) lives in a country village called Waituhi. His boss is also called Mr Ralston.
[4] Ceremonial club made of greenstone (jade).

Auntie Hiraina seizes hold of it and they leave. The *patu* will now go back to the village of Waituhi where it rightfully belongs. All seems in order in the best of Maori villages. But is it really?

The Matriach appeared at the same time as a series of novels[1] written by various New Zealand authors on subjects related to the confrontation between Maori and Pakeha. These works were published in 1986, a period when the Maori's claims for land confiscated by the Pakeha following the Land Wars in the 1860s and 70s made headlines in the news. Many early reviews focussed on the topical relevance of *The Matriarch* and highlighted the author's relatively new stand clearly in favour of the Maori cause whereas some of his earlier novels had been interpreted as a sign of his assimilation in the official policy of multiculturalism.

The protagonist's special interest in the oral history taught by his grandmother Artemis is an essential feature of this multi-faceted and ambitious novel which spans nearly two centuries of history in Aotearoa. Artemis' stories to her favourite grandson tell of a fight for the chiefly title in the family. This strand of the plot, set at the present time, alternates with the narration of events closely modelled on a Maori vision of the Land Wars: the historical Maori rebel Te Kooti plays a major part there. As is often the case in Witi Ihimaera's works, the re-telling of history opens out on an evocation of foundation myths.

Beyond the immediate historical relevance or the explicit political stance - which are at times over-obtrusive and didactic - the novel possesses a complex structure whose sophisticated organization witnesses to Ihimaera's artistry. One of the novelist's main strengths is his ability to weave together several narrative strands in a carefully orchestrated manner.

The Matriarch unfolds in a non-linear fashion with its many anachronies and sudden changes from one sub-plot to another. Running through all these different narratives one finds the question of the *whakapapa*,[2] the origins of the protagonist, with an emphasis laid on the unbroken line of descent right up to the primal conquerors of Aotearoa,[3] who are said to have come from Hawaiki, the mythic land of Polynesian origins, on their famous canoes and settled the different parts of the new land.

---

[1] These included Maurice Shadbolt's *Season of the Jew* and Ian Wedde's *Symmes Hole* both also published in 1986 and concerned, though from different standpoints, with the re-evaluation of the Maori past in the light of recent historiography.
[2] A Maori word meaning 'genealogy'.
[3] The Maori name for New Zealand.

In the early stages of 'The Greenstone Patu', the hero's grandfather has had a premonitory dream. According to traditional Freudian interpretations, dreams often correspond to the realisation of forbidden desires. But here no such explanation can be invoked. From this point on, the old man urges the protagonist's father to promise to look for this lost *patu*. Several elements in the grandfather's dream turn the *patu* into more than a dead object in a museum or in a glass cabinet: first it is described swimming through water towards Nanny Tama. Then it calls its name to him. One night, after Auntie Hiraina has taken on the quest for the lost heirloom, as she is praying, another strange occurrence takes place:

> There had been a rushing sound of a river. She had seen the patu pounamu twisting and turning a glowing path through sunlit water. She heard it calling out its name. (p. 111)

Suddenly it is as though, knowing that the grandfather is no longer alive, she, the next authority in the line of inheritance, receives a message from this precious lost object.

The third moment when reality gives way to strange happenings is when Auntie Hiraina and the protagonist are trying to convince the reluctant woman in Wellington to let them have their *patu* back. First the woman lies and says that it is not in the house, shouting to the visitors to get out.

> Then it happened.
> The sun glowed upon a wedge-shaped object swimming towards us. Swiftly it approached, twisting and gliding through water shafted with sunlight. As it came, it cried out its name. Its calls grew louder, ringing in our ears.
> Suddenly they were accompanied by sharp cracking sounds snapping loudly through the room. The sounds came from a cabinet pannelled with glass like silver mirrors. As we watched, the panels began to buckle and snap and splinter into sharp broken shards. Imprisoned behind the glass was the patu pounamu.
> The woman screamed.
> Auntie Hiraina, with a cry of desperate longing, clenched her fist and punched through the breaking glass.
> - Aue, she cried.
> The patu pounamu was like a living thing, pulsating and bucking in her hand. The sheen of its polished surface glowed with a terrible fire. (p. 116)

This 'magic' scene is set in a city house whose owner is probably married to a Pakeha man.[1] The woman's idea of rightful ownership is closer to the

---

[1] While they wait for the man's wife to come back, he passes remarks which clearly distance him from their world: 'I thought you Maoris were supposed to have love for

Pakeha than to the Maori conception; she claims that the *patu* was left to her by her father and cannot understand that it may have belonged to the protagonist's family in the past. She has placed the object in her china cabinet where it features among other exhibits which are supposed to enhance her middle-class status.

Basically 'The Greenstone Patu' is narrated in a realistic mode, set in an easily recognizable city at a period corresponding to the 1970s and with characters who behave unsurprisingly. Yet several happenings come to disturb this apparently stable order and lead the story to shift into what some might call magic or fantasy. The exact status of this transgression of realistic conventions remains unclear.

One of the strong scenes in *The Matriarch* is one in which Artemis is confronted with Timoti, a Maori male chauvinist, on a *Marae*[1] where a special meeting of all the elders and the Prime Minister has been organized. Timoti is enraged by what he considers as the cheek of this woman who is spoiling the proceedings. During the *hongi* - the ceremonial touching of the noses which is a form of greeting with the Maori - he threatens to suck the breath of life out of her. The *hongi* itself is a ritual symbolic of the exchange of breaths between the host and the visitors. This episode in the novel represents a battle of wills between two mighty characters who both call traditional myths to their rescue, though choosing different episodes of the same story: Timoti recalls the story of when Tane, one of the primeval parents' sons, weary of being without a wife, fashioned a woman, Hine ahuone, from the red earth and breathed life into her. As he reminds the matriarch, '[Tane] gave [Hine ahuone] the breath of life, from his nostrils into hers, in the first hongi' (p. 251). To Timoti, this is a reminder of man's precedence over woman and he threatens to reverse the process with Artemis since she is rebellious towards male authority. But Artemis can fight the elder with his own weapons as she too is well versed in oratory and Maori tradition and she retorts:

> Be warned, lest the evil in your words and intentions be returned to you. For although Tane breathed life into Hine ahuone, and mated with her, it was their daughter, Hine Titama, who became Hine nui te Po.... And I, a woman, can claim my right to take your breath, my brother. For, just as Hine nui te Po became the great goddess of death, so too are all men returned to her embrace. (p. 251)

each other.... You seem to have very long memories. All I can say is that the sooner you forget about the past the better' (p. 115).
[1]   Area on which a Maori meeting house is erected. People gather on the Marae for ceremonial occasions.

What happens next suddenly changes the nature of reality: the old woman seems to turn into a kind of spider or to cause millions of spiders weaving their webs under the ceiling of the room to suddenly descend on Timoti and suck him dead. Even as these events are taking place, the matriarch is possessed of a force within her yet not entirely natural:

> And the voice she spoke with was not her own. And her body was not her own, also, seeming to have been possessed by some annihilating presence. And no matter how hard Timoti struggled, the matriarch only enfolded him more tightly in the web of her dark gown, and her face was like that of a black spider with its mouth parts tightening on the face of the old man. (p. 258)

Once the old man has fallen, two versions of the episode emerge: the first one, that of the journalist who reports the events, tells of intimations of strange happenings. Another voice describes the spider feeding on the old man and crunching his bones in its mouth. In no way can we, as readers, decide what is supposed to be the first level of reality.

The only indication given in the text is that the journalist's reporting is given in parenthesis while the vision of the spider appears as the plain, primary level of narration. Does this mean that the one holds supremacy over the other? It is difficult to tell. It could also mean that there are two ways of viewing this event, one, the Maori, which is closer to the 'supernatural' vision, the other, that of the Pakeha journalist, who is steeped in rationality and yet troubled by the impression that something unnatural is happening there.

Things seem to get out of control as the destructive powers unleashed by the matriarch threaten to turn against the rest of her family. And the matriarch advises the child to beware of such dangerous territories:

> 'Remember the spider', she said. 'It can so easily be done, when one walks too close to the border between the darkness and the light, to go too far onto the dark side. It is a lesson to me. It is a warning to you.' (p. 267)

Tamatea's link with Waituhi represents more than just the attachment anybody may feel with 'home'. The *wharenui*[1] provides his anchoring and his communication with what makes sense in his world, what links him to the forces of the universe. Tamatea remembers what can only be described as a vision during which he transcended the limitations of his present human form. He was in the meeting house with his grandmother, and suddenly it happened:

---

[1] Literally 'large house', another name for a meeting house.

> She felt the elements coming alive, the long silent dynamo of creation beginning to hum. The earth breathing. The sky taking the form of a giant tatooed god. The forces of life, animate and inanimate, stirring in the wind and flooding through a widening cleft of light.
> All of a suden, the veil between day and night lifted, and the matriarch and the child were in some otherworld where gods and men commune. Where timelessness begins and there is no separation of past and present. (pp. 108-109)

The grandmother and the child are put into contact with the basic forces of the universe to which they have no access otherwise. The metaphor of the dynamo, with its strangely modern connotations, shows how much, for the narrator, the old world can only be perceived through the words of the modern one.

Another example of a similar clash between ancient and modern is to be found when, after invoking the appearance of the spider against the hostile elder, the matriarch attempts to 'find the calm and quiet stream which flows in the time's tide' (p. 278). The boy suddenly becomes aware of currents which nobody else can see:

> slowly he began to divine various streams, like rivers of psychedelia, swirling between earth and sky. Some of the streams were filled with creatures of light, and others were filled with creatures of darkness. They swam, divided, united, and swam again in a dazzling son et lumière....
> Then the child saw a stream which was the colour of greenstone, folding itself within the blinding river. 'There it is,' he said to the matriarch. And she followed his gaze and saw the calm river swirling towards them. And she and the child stepped into it, and away from the conflicting elements of the tide of time, and were made luminous with beauty. (p. 278)

Calmness is regained when they reach this river of peace which flows through the conflicting currents. Interestingly enough, this river is the colour of greenstone, an element which always has positive connotations in the world of Ihimaera (see the greenstone *patu*), since it is linked with the *mana* (a word meaning 'prestige', 'charisma') of positive tradition.

The vision brings them back to a world where the invisible forces carrying life through the animate and inanimate elements of the universe are suddenly visible:

> The child saw into the essence of things. He saw the gleaming sap ascending the trees, and the sap and the dark red blood coursing through his transparent body were one and the same. He saw into the geological structures of the earth, and the diamond sparkling structure of the mountains were one and the same as the gleaming cellular structure of his body. He saw the movement of light and wind and cloud, and they were one and the same as his own life force. (p. 109)

Like in Australian aboriginal bark paintings, the viewer can see the inner structure of things. This mode of vision, which is basically holistic with its emphasis on the unicity of all life forces, is also interpreted through the findings of modern crystallography and of cellular biology, a strange mixture.

The episode is also an occasion for Tamatea to go through an experience of death and rebirth: passing through the different stages of creation in a reverse manner, he reaches the origins, according to the Maori tradition, *Te Kore*, the void. Then he comes back to life, following the stages narrated in the accepted Maori tradition:

> ... and he felt, more than he knew, that he was ascending from the void. From out of Te Kore he came, and began the journey back through the twelve changings of the Night. The chanting grew stronger and louder as he voyaged in that timeless time. He saw creation. He felt the first ray of light. He was part of the cauldron of energy which laid the foundations of the universe.... He saw the gods. He saw the creation of woman. He saw legendary canoes glittering in emerald seas and escorted by fabulous creatures of awesome power. He saw a huge fish being pulled out of the sea by a magic hook, transforming itself into a cloud-steaming land. (pp. 109-110)

Tamatea's despair and experience of nothingness is given meaning through the mythic story associated with the beginnings of life. This allusive summary of Maori creation mentions how Tane created Hine-ahu-one, the first woman, by fashioning a human shape with earth found on the shore of the ocean and how the hero Maui fished Aotearoa out of the sea, how the first tribes are supposed to have come from Hawaiki, the mythic land to the north, to lay the foundations of contemporary Maori society. Tamatea's narration is a shortened summary of the myth generally considered by the Maori as the story of the origins of life.

The search for the lost *patu* in 'The Greenstone Patu' may seem futile to a Pakeha unaware of the importance of such sacred objects symbolic of the Maori's link with their roots. The quest is motivated by Tama's desire to claim for himself and his own family this portion of *mana* which was unduly confiscated by somebody else. This claim rests on the belief that one is not a separate individual; one exists only as the descendant of a long line of ancestors who somehow still live within oneself. In the traditional Polynesian view, this collective identity transcending European conceptions of time is of utmost importance and Tama may well be motivated by his adherence to such principles. In this case, the *patu* may have supernatural properties.

To a Maori such as the protagonist or his aunt, the *patu* is essentially a living link with the past. It is a piece of the old *mana*, of the life force belonging to the group which was handed down through the generations. It represents this undying energy which can survive all kinds of disasters. The *patu* seems to need the contemporary people as much as they need him. His cries out to them witness to this urge to be reunited with the narrator and Auntie Hiraina.

The main value extolled in this story is undoubtedly the importance of keeping alive the link between the generations. When referring to her dead father, Auntie Hiraina insists on the work he did to trace everybody's ancestry: 'He didn't really need to collect the whakapapa of the whole village, you know. But he did it because he wanted us all to be a village family again' (p. 118). The task of the conscious Maori is then to remind the people of the sacred bond between them, a bond which constitued their strength in the old days. To Aunti Hiraina, this *patu* is made for the Maori 'to fight back with... to remind us who we are' (p. 114). It is a symbol of the people's resilience, of their desire not to be swamped in the dominating Pakeha culture. But, so far, this desire for resistance is not articulated in any concrete programme. The young narrator in particular seems to entertain only a distant and nostalgic relation with the rural world of his youth from which he seems largely estranged, and perhaps for good.

In *The Matriarch*, the personal quickly fuses with the allegorical in that Tamatea becomes a representative of the fate of the whole tribe if not of the whole Maori population of the country. The boy's concern is with the maintenance of an unbroken link with the past. Yet how can this link be unbroken when so much has changed in the situation of the Maori, including their assimilation into their culture of many features belonging to the Pakeha? They have been converted to Christianity and this has brought in new values which have merged with their own traditions. The very idea of a direct unbroken chain of beings suffered many exceptions in that period of colonization. Tamatea's ancestors are Pakeha as well as Maori and only his own personal choice - or that of his grandmother - can lead him to privilege one strand rather than another.

Tamatea is himself married to a Pakeha and he leads the life of an urban, largely assimilated Maori in a predominantly Pakeha environment. His grandmother Artemis has spent part of her life in Venice where she acquired a taste for Italian opera and for European culture.

Curiously enough, the problems of urban Maori occupy a relatively minor part in this novel, with the exception of the figure of Raina,[1] the

---

[1] See the chapter starting p. 357.

protagonist's cousin, who sinks into drug-addiction and loose living after breaking off relations with her parents. But, even then, Raina appears more as an exception than as a symptom of a wider social problem: the narrator explains that she was always given everything she wanted by her parents, which encouraged her to behave as a spoilt baby.

So, on the one hand Maori authenticity is extolled as a value to be cherished, while, on the other, the main characters are part of a complex society which is the result of a *métissage*, with the native population being placed very much in the situation of the dominated.

The manner in which Auntie Hiraina in 'The Greenstone Patu' managed to trace the *patu* resembles a detective inquiry with much luck added to it. Each time she thinks she is on the right track, a link in the chain is left missing because the person to be contacted has died or moved without leaving any address. Only pure chance allows her to find the location of the woman in Porirua whose father gave her the *patu* on his death-bed. And this person exemplifies what happens to the Maori who have been contaminated by Pakeha ways to such a degree that they have forgotten the sacred values of the old tradition.

Does the text allow us to talk of chance or should we believe that, in the world described, a *patu* is sacred and powerful enough to actually 'talk' to people? If such is the case, then the world of the narrator still leaves room for the supernatural. If not, then we may use the word 'fantastic' to characterize the sudden shift from rational to non-rational explanations for the phenomenon.[1] Perhaps an intermediary stage might be the belief in the reality of magic happenings in the midst of a world basically ruled by rational causality. Most characters do not seem to

---

[1] In a note to his essay 'Witi Ihimaera and Patricia Grace' (in Cherry Hankin, ed., *Critical Essays on the New Zealand Short Story* [Auckland: Heinemann, 1982] p. 175), Bill Pearson perceptively raises the same kind of question: 'Since I wrote this essay I have learned that there is a belief, widely held by older people though not freely revealed, that a greenstone weapon, once it has been prayed over with karakia and curses, can take on occult powers and might move of its own volition and swim through water to return to its owners. Clearly I have missed something in my response to 'The Greenstone Patu' and to the rainbow in 'Return from Oz'. *The question is raised, however, of the extent to which a western literary tradition, which requires of the reader no more than a willing suspension of disbelief in its tales of the supernatural, can accommodate the more deeply held occult beliefs of another culture.* Witi Ihimaera's disregard for the scepticism of the unconvinced reader reflects an understandable reluctance to expose the beliefs to profane minds. For some Maori readers, I am told, he is not reticent enough. A further question is raised: whether Mr Ihimaera, if he wishes these stories to have their full effect, is wise to address himself only to readers who share the beliefs'. (italics mine)

doubt the reality of the supernatural. Yet the narrator seems strangely distanced from traditional existence. Though he says he would love to be back to the village where his family still lives, the possibility of his actually returning for good is doubtful. It is as though there were a split in himself between wishes and memories linked with childhood and the reality of his everyday existence which seems to be firmly based in the city with its ruling Pakeha values.

The description made of the fantastic happenings, especially the moment when the *patu* is finally returned to its original owners, contains some elements of popular cinema magic which may echo *The Wizard of Oz* just as much as they reflect traditional Maori conceptions. The glow that suddenly surrounds the apparition of an object illuminated by shafts of light belongs to the convention of fairy stories.

After the mysterious happenings in the house at Porirua, the tone of the narration reverts abruptly to a very rational description of the conversation between Auntie Hiraina and the owners of the house who suddenly comply with their visitors' desire:

> We had talked and after a while the woman had formally asked us to accept the greenstone patu of our family.
> - It belongs to your people, she had said. You must take it back to your people.
> (p. 117)

It is as though the power of the *patu* had changed the situation and led the woman to adopt what, according to Maori custom, was a perfectly normal attitude. Traditional order is restored. Victory is with the people who respect the old law - or at least what is presented as such here. Is the situation as simple as this explicit conclusion might lead the reader to believe?

Is the *patu*'s power and its 'fantastic' coming to life any more than the result of a perception filtered through the imagination of American movie directors? A difference exists between Aunt Hiraina's undoubted faith in the unity of Maori culture and belief and the protagonist's rather distanced attitude. Can his dream of Maori society appear as more than a profession of faith based on nostalgic fragments of memory? Can these wishes turn into more than passing fantasies about a life that has already largely disappeared?

At the end of the story, he watches his aunt's plane soaring 'through the sunlit sky. It seemed like a greenstone patu swimming its way back to a forgotten world beyond these hills' (p. 118). The assimilation of air and water as well as the constant presence of the liquid element through which the *patu* travels towards its people may lead some to interpret the

scene as an evocation of the archetypal 'return to the womb', with all the
regressive connotations that this may entail.

The flickering status of the *patu*'s 'reality' illustrates this hesitation
between a dreamed world of organic unity between men, nature and the
supernatural and the urban atmosphere of individualism, rationality,
materialism and loneliness. Is it not already too late? In the gaps between
imaginary representations and the reality of the protagonist's life lie the
contradictions which the young man faces uncomfortably.

In *The Matriarch*, the old woman's retelling of the story of Maori
origins for her *mokopuna*[1] corresponds to the received version. It must be
said that there are many other stories which vary with this one, depending
on which tribal group you collect them from. But this is the one which
seems to have become standard, possibly because it was taught in New
Zealand schools and not necessarily because it was more acceptable to
the Maori. The idea of a unique legend served to classify in the same
category all these 'natives' who appeared threatening only until one had
dominated them not only physically but also through the digestion and
unification of their myths in a form acceptable to the Pakeha. The 'native
tradition' was collected and reformulated by the early Pakeha
anthropologists and became the official version of a tradition which they
helped to save but in a form which suited them.

An important Maori belief is reasserted by the matriarch, who tries to
comfort her favourite *mokopuna*: 'We had eternity in us,' she said. 'And
you began your life back then, e mokopuna, many thousands of years
before you were born in Waituhi.' (p. 108)

This refers to an important belief among the Maori that individuals do
not exist by themselves. Each person is the repository of life forces
inherited from all the forebears. So Tamatea is the continuation of a long
line of ancestors whose *mana* and high feats he carries within him. He is
not alone to face the difficulties of life since the ancestors, though
invisible, are still there, around him, as a support. But this also implies
that he has a responsibility, a duty towards them.

In the last part of *The Matriach*, reports of unnatural happenings are
mentioned. Chapter Fifteen alludes to the sighting made in 1891 by the
captain of a ship called the *SS Rotomahana* of a sea monster which the
Maori believe was one of the supernatural creatures which accompanied
the Takitimu, one of the legendary canoes, on its journey to Aotearoa.
The crew appear to have been struck by the appearance of this creature

---

[1] Maori for 'grandchildren'.

which 'dared the crew to believe in its existence and to open their minds to the possibilities of the unknown' (p. 340).

The vocabulary used by the narrator to tell this episode interestingly suggests alternatives to the reality commonly held to be objective by the Pakeha. Talking of the last decade of the nineteenth century, he says it was a world in which the Maori still believed in the 'communion between gods and man, the *fabulous* (italics mine) with the real' (p. 340). Further on, he adds that the 'sea serpent was a reminder of the past, ripping through the fabric of the real world, and bringing with it the remnants of *fantastic* (italics mine) dreams' (pp. 340-341). It is to be noticed that the narrator does not talk here of the supernatural but of the fantastic and the fabulous, two terms more frequent among people who believe in the prominent existence of objective reality.

So the reader is faced with two different and apparently incompatible systems of reference: one which sees the primal forces of the Maori world as efficient, perceptible by dedicated Maori, and the other which uses the terms of Western rationality, a rationality still interspersed with what almost appears as superstition. The first logic is holistic, the second binary and oppositional. And yet the two cohabit within the same work, thus reflecting the predicament in which some modern Maori find themselves.

Further on, the narrator describes at length the interior decoration of Rongopai. In this episode, the continuity of tradition suggested by the preceding quotation is questioned, or perhaps presented from a different angle, which sheds light on the particular contradictory situation of Witi Ihimaera himself:

> Taken as a whole, the paintings were schizophrenic, a virtual kaleidoscope of colour and form, which began from a traditional premise and then were embellished with the appogiaturi of the oppressed. (p. 190)
> ... the meeting house was like a strange Rorschach Test, unveiling the subconscious of the Maori, the persona, in highly romantic and yet realistic terms. (p. 191)

Instead of the traditional carved panels evoking ancestral forms, the panels at Rongopai are painted, a new technique brought by the Pakeha, and they represent persons who were alive at the time when the house was built, another infringement of tradition. That is why the narrator talks of a galaxy that has left its orbit and collided with others, gravely damaging itself and the others in the process. The language used to describe this new form of art, which alludes to modern psychological tests and to Jungian psychoanalysis, echoes this mixture of tradition and the contemporary world.

The protagonist's ancestry includes one person of mixed Maori and Pakeha blood, Wi Pere, a real historical figure who became one of the earliest members of parliament at the end of the nineteenth century, after the Maori had been defeated in their rebellion against the seizure of their land by the British Crown. He defended the Maori in parliament though he is rumoured to have become more self-interested at a later stage in his life.

Besides containing a portrait of Wi Pere, Rongopai was also dedicated to the glory of Te Kooti, the Maori leader of the Hau Hau rebellion against the Pakeha, who exiled him to the Chatham islands. But Te Kooti succeeded in escaping back to the Urewera area from which he organized resistance. His action also exerted itself in the religious field when he founded the Ringatu religion, a faith based on Christianity which reinterpreted the conquest and exile of the Maori from their own land in the light of the children of Israel's own deportation under the Pharaoh. Te Kooti came to be seen as the prophet leading the Maori out of the desert back into their sacred homeland. In a syncretic vision reminiscent of the vocabulary used by Rastas in the Caribbean, the narrative voice even refers to the Pakeha as 'Pharaoh'.

Te Kooti - a hero of Ihimaera's own region - partakes of the old Maori fighting spirit and pride and of a desire to compromise with the Pakeha. Ihimaera depicts him as one who sought to reason the British out of the disastrous land policy which led to the confiscation of so much Maori land. He is presented as a leader who was left with no other alternative but to take up arms after having tried to use all other peaceful means at his disposal to convince the invaders that they had inflicted a grievous wrong on the Maori people. Much rhetoric and didacticism are used by the narrator to counteract the common prejudice concerning this figure often officially presented as a bloodthirsty savage and a killer of innocent victims.

In *The Matriach*, traditional patterns form a backbone to a general design where individual creativity has projected itself in a particularly free way. The narrator evokes this new mood as the creation of people whose 'world [is] out of kilter, spinning off its axis and out of its own orbit around the sun that Maui had tamed, ripping other galaxies apart and, in the process, severely damaging its own' (p. 191). The metaphors used in this quote condense elements belonging to widely different domains. They refer to the strange helplessness of creators who, dissatisfied with purely traditional forms to express their radically new world, painted novel shapes onto the walls of the meeting house as though to explore the meaning of these conflicting forces which they could not articulate within themselves.

Ihimaera moves from the personal subconscious to the cosmic in an evocation which alludes to the demi-god Maui's feat when he is supposed to have regulated the course of the sun across the sky. Here the implication is that the planets have come out of their normal alignment and threaten to go wild in their orbits. Perhaps a new Maui, a saviour, is needed to tame the mechanisms of the new world. But such a figure has not come yet. So all the Maori can do is to look deep into their past and into their dreams and build an image of themselves which will provide an anchoring for a (still hypothetical) move forward.

For the narrator, the time of communion with the great life-forces is long gone. He talks in terms of a major break which is supposed to have happened with the advent of 'the juggernaut of progress rumbling across land, seas and skies, with an inevitability which threatened the realm of dragon, or sea serpent, mermaid or siren... The cities spread across the lands where once had been enchanted forests and fabulous kingdoms' (p. 437). Clearly here the disaster happened with the great conquests, when Western people began to travel and settle new territories. It also happened with the spread of cities in areas which had been mainly rural or covered with forests. Here the reference to the New Zealand situation is more precise in that the narrator deplores the end of rural life and the drift of populations to the cities (an allusion to the situation of the Maori in the post-war period). The narrator even puts a date to this degeneracy in New Zealand. He traces it to the second decade of this century:

> The next year was 1914. It was the year of the beginning of the Great war. The long-held communion between man and the gods was coming to an end. From that year we can date the beginnings of the world of man. From 1914 we can trace the start of the silence
> which descended when
>
> the
>
> communion
>
> stopped. (p. 439)

Even the layout of the words on the page outlines the sense of a world ending and of another, more flawed, emerging. The tone is one of nostalgia for a past harmony which is idealized as opposed to a drab present where man is no longer in communion with the gods or with the basic forces of the universe.

The only places where the protagonist can escape (Rongopai or Venice) are distinct from modern life, preserved relics from a past which he imagines as better. They act as echo chambers to his deeper longings, as stimulators of dream journeys into a mythic time where time did not exist to separate men from their origins. An element which has disturbed many commentators concerning this novel is the way in which the author weaves in a visit to Venice. Some objected to this episode, arguing that this was non-Maori and therefore out of place. Ihimaera has retorted that he lives in the modern world in which Maori can have international experiences which are in no way incompatible with remaining a Maori. The narrator's description of Venice where he has just arrived with his wife on a visit to Europe sheds a new light on his own descriptions of Waituhi:

> Venice, it seemed to me was the product of two worlds in collision, the supernatural with the real, the fantastic with the natural, the bestial with the sublime - and it had me in its thrall. I felt I had entered a timeless chamber, rather like Rongopai, whose very buildings, stones and statuary communed with men. (p. 431)

Venice and Rongopai are places of the imagination, where the creative mind can roam free and escape the limitations of everyday life:

> Venice is a mistress of deception, for she asks us to substitute our objectivity with melancholia and, once in the grasp of that most romantic of senses, only then can the possession begin. (p. 432)

The same terms could almost be used to describe the protagonist's relation to his own Maori culture. A new world dimension, which is wholly contemporary and not traditional at all appears when the narrator draws a parallel between the fabulous beasts carved on the monuments of Venice and those of his home culture:

> These were the monsters of the Venetian myth, tapping a source as deep as the Maori and displaying the reality in the light of the world. Perhaps that, also, is why I felt so much akin to Venice, for here were the manaia, the marakihau and taniwha of a culture far to the south. (p. 433)

Such a level of comparison would probably have been unthinkable in a traditional world where mythic representations were more than myth. But the narrator clearly lives in a world where comparative religion has become a scientific pursuit and relativity enables the scientist to point out parallels between different religious systems without establishing a significant hierarchy between them. The protagonist is more of a relativist of the holistic kind than a believer in traditional Maori lore.

In their handling of mimesis, Achebe and Ihimaera waver between the Western logos and an uneasy acceptance of ancient spirituality. In such a context, categories such as the 'fantastic' become almost inapplicable because what might be called 'reality' presents many metamorphic faces. Possibly because of this difficulty, critics have sometimes resorted to the term 'magic realism', a 'genre' which needs to be examined in the context of its genesis and history before it can be adopted for the purpose of classification.

C - Magic Realism: the Building of a Literary Genre

1- Fantasy? Magic Realism?

From the 1960s on in formerly colonized countries several 'schools' of literature emerged which attempted to combine the old realistic tradition with elements variously referred to as the supernatural or magic. One centered around the use Wole Soyinka made of myth in such works as *A Dance of the Forests*. Soyinka himself claimed he sought his inspiration in the oral Yoruba tradition transcribed in modern times by such artists as Chief Fagunwa or Amos Tutuola. The most brilliant example of this type of writing in recent years has been Ben Okri whose *The Famished Road* (1991) explicitly inserted itself into the tradition established by Soyinka and Tutuola. Another branch of this literary revolution grew from the so-called 'Boom' which emerged in South America and was imitated in such diverse countries as Western Canada and India. What do all these writers have in common apart from the qualification 'magic realist' often used to characterize their particular approach of reality?

The debate is complicated by the fact that, in the 1960s this term became fashionable in literary criticism to designate different types of fiction which actually had little in common: 'magic realism', or 'marvellous realism', a variation of the former, was applied indifferently to the writings of J.L. Borges and García Márquez. To make matters even more confusing, the Cuban Alejo Carpentier introduced the term *lo real maravilloso* to refer to his literary experience of Latin America as opposed to the European tradition. Faced with such a diversity of implicit definitions, it appears essential to explore and delimit the field of each category as much as possible.

According to Jean Weisgerber,[1] the term 'magic realism' was first used outside literature: in 1923, G.F. Hartlaub projected to organize an exhibition on the theme of the *Neue Sachlichkeit* (new reality, objectivity), a project which came to fruition in 1925 in the Kunsthalle in Mannheim, Germany. According to Hartlaub, this current, which is posterior to expressionism, is divided into two branches: the first is verist in inspiration.[2] This current strongly reacted against the campaign led by the Expressionists against naturalism. The return to everyday experience meant that the eye of the onlooker focussed differently on its objects which were often seen in closeups, overexposed, in isolation. Familiar items became strange. The discovery of otherness in the heart of what was commonly taken for granted was at the source of the individual artistic emotion in this case. The second branch of the movement was more in line with classicism and advocated a search for the intemporal value in objects. In his study *Nach Expressionismus. Magischer Realismus. Probleme der neuesten Europäischen Malerei*, Franz Roh called the whole current 'magic realism'. In the 1960s, German art criticism preferred to keep the term *Neue Sachlichkeit* for the first kind and used 'magic realism' for the second.

For Roh, 'magic realism' was preferable to 'idealer Realismus', 'Verismus' or 'Neuklassizismus', each referring to only part of the movement. Roh insisted on the cold 'cerebrality' and on the static character of the works discussed. Though carefully represented, the objects appeared as 'strange schemes'. Their 'inner face' was unveiled. Their spiritual texture was shown. This world of painted objects became a recreation of reality. The psyche reconstituted reality which could not be wholly accounted for through empirical means. The magic of being was linked with the spiritual. According to Roh, this had to do with an authentic form of rationalism which venerates as a miracle the 'rational' organization of the world. Roh's references to literature were slight. He merely evoked two main tendencies in literature, one linked with Rimbaud, the other with Zola.

Roh's text found an echo in South America in 1927 with the publication in the *Revista de Occidente*[3] of extracts from his book. By the time the term was used in Buenos Aires, it had acquired new connotations and was applied to the writings of Cocteau, Chesterton and Kafka.

---

[1] 'La Locution et le concept' in Weigerber, ed., *Le Réalisme magique*, pp. 11-32.
[2] Verism refers to the artistic use of contemporary everyday material, as opposed to the use of the heroic, the mythical and legendary, or the historical.
[3] V, 48, June 1927, pp. 274-301.

Angel Flores' paper 'Magical Realism in Spanish American Fiction'[1] was read in New York in December 1954. For Flores, the term concerned the writings of Gallegos, Borges, Bioy Casares and Asturias. For him, magic realism possessed the following characteristics: there must be symbolism in action - a fairly unspecific characteristic, especially considering the numerous and contradictory acceptations of the term 'symbolism'. The episodes must be represented according to the neo-objectivist theories of Hartlaub and F. Roh. The discordant element must be a sign which suggests otherness (the absurd, mysticism, anxiety). There must be extraordinary facts, a tense and unreal atmosphere and an ambiguous ending. The plot must reflect an arbitrary conception of the passing of time and a vision of a new reality created in a more complete form. This definition is very wide in its application and suggests a reference to phenomena more currently described as the 'fantastic'. The presence of mysticism also adds a new dimension.

'El realismo mágico en la literatura hispanoamericana'[2] by Luis Leal argued that magic realism was not a way of avoiding everyday reality. It did not derive, unlike what Flores said, from the world of Kafka. The main point was not the creation of imaginary beings or worlds but the discovery of the mysterious relationship between man and his environment.

2- Alejo Carpentier and his Concept of the *Real Maravilloso*

In his book *Razon de ser*, Alejo Carpentier criticizes Roh's use of the term 'magic realism' using arguments which throw an interesting light on many post-colonial works. According to him, the German art critic was really referring to expressionist painting which had nothing to do with a concrete political intention.[3] For him, Roh chose art without a social purpose. Carpentier criticizes surrealism because, according to him, this school showed a fascination for the marvellous, but essentially as a premeditated prefabrication.[4] He stigmatizes the surrealist search for artificial effects which were the result of calculation. He refers to Salvador Dali's 'relojes blandos' (soft watches) to illustrate his point. Carpentier clearly situates his criticism in the context of a moralistic Marxist conception of art which was to be judged mostly through its social use. From this ideological standpoint, he moves on to assert that a

---

[1] Published in *Hispania*, XXXVIII, 2, May 1955, pp. 187-192.
[2] *Cuadernos Americanos*, N° 4 (July-August 1967), pp. 230-235.
[3] 'En realidad, lo que Franz Roh llama realismo mágico, es sencillamente una pintura expresionista ajenas a una intención política concreta' (p. 57).
[4] 'era lo marravilloso fabricado premeditadamente' (p. 59).

very different and potentially more fecund form could be found in its native state in South America. This he calls *lo real maravilloso*. Reversing the traditional hierarchy which situated metropolitan writing before whatever could emerge from the colonies, he argues that the books of chivalry which were written in Europe were actually inspired by the conquistadors' realization that this 'marvellous reality' was an essential feature of America.[1] In a salutory revisioning of priorities, truly interesting reality here is said to belong to America whereas Europe is reduced to the status of a place remarkable for its dull ordinariness. In *Razon de ser*, Carpentier quotes Bernal Díaz contemplating the city of Mexico and exclaiming that it is just like in the writings of Amadís. Thus Carpentier implicitly adheres to the feeling of wonder experienced by the conquistadors. This type of perception seems marked by ethnocentrism: In typical colonial fashion, Europe is reality, whereas America is the materialization of dreams. One is not very far from conceptions of the Noble Savage, with the New Continent being endowed with all the qualities which Europe does not possess. Europe is the reference, unlike America which becomes the object of man's desires. This contradiction possibly reflects Carpentier's very special position: the son of parents of European origin, he was always very strongly attached to his homeland of Cuba despite his long residence in France as cultural attaché at the Paris embassy. This cultural filiation was externally noticeable in his strong French accent when he spoke Spanish.

Carpentier opposes the static character of Europe and the dynamic quality of the New Continent. He describes the New World as baroque in its architecture but also in the complexity of its vegetation, in the polychromy around, in the telluric pulsion to which the people are submitted.[2] One almost finds the same images as Victor Hugo used in his preface to *Cromwell* (1827) which he wrote as a manifesto against classicism, opposing the 'jardin à la française' of classical literature and the luxuriant forests of the New World which represented his own conception of drama. Carpentier has a fondness for artistic

---

[1] 'Aquí lo insólito es cotidiano, siempre fue cotidiano. Los libros de caballería se escribieron en Europa, pero se vivieron en América, porque si bien se escribieron las aventuras de Amadís de Gaula en Europa, es Bernal Díaz del Castillo quien nos presenta con su *Historia de la conquista de la Nueva España* el primer libro de caballería auténtico.... los conquistadores vieron muy claramente el aspecto real maravilloso en las cosas de América' (p. 60).

[2] 'Nuestro mundo es barroco por la arquitectura — eso no hay ni que demostrarlo — , por el enrevesamiento y la complejidad de su naturaleza y su vegetación, por la policromía de cuanto nos circunda, por la pulsión telúrica de los fenómenos a que estamos todavía sometidos' (p. 61).

revolutionaries who rebelled against Aristotelian rules and classical French theatre with its *règle des trois unités*.[1] He sees them as men of action: far from being intellectuals in their ivory towers, young Wagner was expelled from Münich because of anarchism and Lord Byron died in Missolonghi for the liberation of Greece. Carpentier's romantic heroes are described in terms which privilege action, pulsion, movement and violence.[2] One is almost reminded of the ideals of the Futurist artists. In his revolutionary rhetoric, Carpentier opposes academism, which, to him, is a feature of well-established societies, and the baroque which corresponds to periods of transformation and innovation.[3]

This telluric frenzy does not lead to gratuitous violence. In his basically humanistic view, Carpentier stresses the blending of cultures. The Latin American Creole, a category to which he belongs, possesses an identity based on symbiosis and represents the transformation of all the components of the country into one metamorphic whole. Carpentier admires the changes and the general dynamism which, to him, have characterized Latin American art ever since great mythological texts such as the *Popol Vuh* or the *Chilam Balam*.[4] The baroque provides an alternative system of values which integrates only one part of European culture (that which is judged most lively and creative) and relates to other world civilizations. The abhorred 'classicism' is replaced by a long tradition which, for Carpentier, includes Hindu and Iranian literature, *Los sueños* by Quevedo, *Los autos sacramentales* by Calderón, Góngora's poetry, Gracián's prose, the Ariosto's *Orlando Furioso*, Shakespeare and Rabelais (who is admired for his concatenation of multiple verbs to describe a situation). It is probably not fortuitous if Rushdie and García Márquez, who, to my mind, offer the best examples of magic realism in post-colonial literatures, are both great admirers of Rabelais. Rabelais as well as a few other European writers seem to escape the general climate of smug self-satisfaction which, for Carpentier, characterizes the Old Continent.

This search for a South American alternative to the European heritage leads him to call the great Aztec and Maya cultures definitely baroque.

---

[1] According to these rules, a play should have unity of action, of time and of place.

[2] 'el hombre del romanticismo fue acción y fue pulsión y fue movimiento y fue voluntad y fue manifiesto y fue violencia' (p. 49).

[3] 'El academismo es característico de las épocas asentadas, plenas de sí mismas, seguras de sí mismas. El barroco, en cambio, se manifiesta donde hay transformación, mutación, innovación' (p. 51).

[4] 'América, continente de simbiosis, de mutaciones, de vibraciones, de mestizajes, fue barroca desde siempre: las cosmogonías americanas, ahí está el *Popol Vuh*, ahi están los libros de *Chilam Balam*...' (p. 51).

Illustrating his point with a description of the Mexican temple at Mitla, he describes their art in terms of 'proliferating cells'.[1] One may notice that this admiration, which also inspired the writings of the Guatemaltecan novelist Miguel Ángel Asturias, was not solely the result of Latin American pride; it was also largely fed by the courses being taught in Paris concerning pre-Columbian mythologies. Perhaps the teaching of French anthropologists was a determinant factor for the arousal of Carpentier's interest in South and Central American mythologies. One reaches here the limits of the re-evaluation of a culture carried out largely through the lenses of scientists with inevitably metropolitan biases. Seen from a pessimistic viewpoint, this only confirms Carpentier's colonial alienation. But then at least field workers from Europe drew other people's interest to cultures which might have otherwise remained unknown. There lies one of the unsolvable ambiguities of ethnology which may be a source of discovery of other civilisations but has also often provided a scientific excuse for colonial domination.

Carpentier's vision of America is largely influenced by the socialist ideals of Cuba: When he talks of the baroque as being characterized by transformation, mutation and innovation, he immediately evokes Mayakovsky and a society about to give birth to a new and better one, an obvious evocation of a revolution such as that then in process in Cuba.[2] Carpentier stresses that his *real maravilloso* is different from 'magic realism' because the latter is identified with the artificial quality of the surrealist search. On the contrary, his own conception is rooted in America, latent in the native landscape, which is full of movement, transformation and violence, and therefore symbolizes for him the great international revolution which a small country like Cuba can export to the rest of the world.

This vision is a strange combination of revolutionary ideals and European ethnocentrism; for Carpentier, the American artist is organically immersed in the dynamics of his continent, whereas the European creator, often entrammelled in his 'classicism', can only look for an escapist kind of art, which is not really concerned with the reality of the world around. With Carpentier, through some particular merit inherent in the American landscape, the individual subjectivity of the writer is more directly in line with the essential forces of his

---

[1] 'células proliferantes' (p. 54).
[2] 'el barroquismo siempre está proyectado hacia adelante y suele presentarse precisamente en expansión en el momento culminante de una civilización o cuando va a nacer un orden nuevo en la sociedad' (p. 51).

environment, which herald a new order. In a reversal of the traditional situation, the former colonies will then export rejuvenation and progress to the old, fossilized continent of the colonizer.

His preoccupation with the epic is characteristic of his general outlook. For him literature in the New World is concerned with great feats and heroic characters, who may be humble or apparently weak, but whose influence on the world around is spectacular in producing a change for the better in the whole structure of society. We find here Carpentier's concern with moments of history when, after an uprising, a strike or a revolution, some form of dictatorship is overthrown.

Paradoxically enough, Carpentier's style is one in which descriptions proliferate even more than action. There are long passages in which action is temporarily suspended by a narrator whose power of revelation is manifested by an accumulation of details expressing his wonder at the dimension of the world described.

Carpentier's view combines elements of revolutionary fervour inspired by Fidel Castro's particular version of Marxism and ethnological visions of an alternative origin susceptible of replacing the outmoded European representations, a possibility opened up by ethnological research into Central and South American mythologies. Thus Carpentier's position can be explained by the Cuba of his times and by the influence of the Parisian intelligentsia where he found so much of his inspiration. The particular vision of his American roots is provided by the external and at times somewhat patronizing enquiry of French anthropologists. Here Carpentier embodies a contradiction typical of many other post-colonial writers. Perhaps a comparison with the Guatemaltecan novelist Miguel Ángel Asturias will serve to clarify his stance.

According to Claude Couffon in *Asturias*, the author sees his realism as magic because it is close to the idea of dreams as conceived by the surrealists, but also as conceived by the Mayas in their sacred texts. Asturias's reading of these texts led him to believe that, besides palpable reality, there was another one, created by the imagination, and which was just as 'real' as the other. Here we find a strange parallel between the collective world of the supernatural conceived by the Mayas and that of an individual dreaming. A bridge is built between the individual's subjective creation and a community's founding myths. The evocation of the surrealist method is not really appropriate in that the supernatural is born out of the myths belonging to another society and not merely out of the discovery that, besides one's 'reality', lies another. Asturias's method is that of an individual claiming the myths of a society to which he is originally foreign, but which he eventually calls his own. In 'Transposición del surrealismo francés al *real maravilloso* latino americano: el caso de Miguel Angel Asturias con *Hombres de Maíz*',[1] Eliane Karp examines the parallels between the use made by Carpentier and Asturias of the *real maravilloso* and surrealist theories and native myths. She traces the origins of this term back to André Breton's *Entretiens*,[2] when Breton drew a parallel between the anticolonialist fight and the aims of his own movement:

> Surrealism is intimately linked with coloured people, first of all because it has always been on their side against any kind of imperialism and white robbers, and also because the most profound affinities exist between so-called 'primitive' thinking and surrealistic thinking in that they both aim at getting rid of the hegemony of consciousness, of everyday preoccupations, in order to reach for the conquest of enlightening emotions.[3]

Both Asturias and Carpentier were, at various moments, in contact with the surrealists. But this biographical reason cannot altogether account for Breton's deep influence on them. Breton and the surrealists (if, for the sake of clarity, one may consider the 'movement' as unified, which it was not) were exploring new territories opened by the discoveries of Freud concerning the unconscious. The surrealists were rebelling against what they saw as 'bourgeois' modes of thinking, which had to do with logic and rationality.

Asturias and Carpentier were rebelling against a vision of Latin America entirely conditioned by the European point of view. They were seeking for an alternative language which might better correspond to their own perceptions. The native element in their societies provided an alternative to this Eurocentric vision. Using the arguments of the surrealists, the European interpretation was logical and imprisoning whereas the native tradition was illogical, based on emotions, sensitivity, associations of ideas. Surrealism over-idealized the potentialities of what they considered as the more authentic perceptions of 'primitive' societies which had not become entrammelled in the degenerate rituals of modern Europe. One perceives similar systems of opposition in the concepts

---

[1] *Lexis* VI-1 (1982), pp. 99-116.
[2] Gallimard, 1969.
[3] 'Le surréalisme a partie liée avec les peuples de couleur, d'une part parce qu'il a toujours été à leurs côtés contre toutes les formes d'impérialisme et de brigandage blancs, d'autre part parce que les plus profondes affinités existent entre la pensée dite 'primitive' et la pensée surréaliste, qu'elles visent l'une et l'autre à supprimer l'hégémonie du conscient, du quotidien, pour se porter à la conquête de l'émotion révélatrice.' (pp. 237-8) Translation mine.

evolved by the *Négritude*, especially in its most caricatural opposition between the black people's supposed innate sensitivity, their taste for rhythm, music and dancing on the one hand, and the European fondness for the *logos*.

At this point it may be interesting to examine the judgements of value implicit in the terms used by both Asturias and Carpentier: Europe is considered dull and static. The surrealists also object to bourgeois conformity and lack of imagination. On the contrary, Latin America appears baroque, active, imaginative. In the New Continent, the contradictions of old Europe can be resolved; a novel society can come into existence.

Despite these similarities in their approach, Asturias did not accept all the premises of surrealism; Eliane Karp quotes his remark in 'Magía y Política':[1]

> It must be also said that surrealism was also too intellectual and that ourselves, with our primitive mentalities related to the indigenous world, have access to this subterranean, sub-magic world more directly, not as an intellectual construct but as something natural. The indigenous people and ourselves generally have two realities: one palpable, the other dreamlike.[2]

This type of remark opposes the surrealists' 'artificial' approach and his own 'natural' one. It sounds as if, through some magic union with the world he was born in, the Latin American writer were gifted with a particular feeling for the mysterious realities of his country. In a curious re-working of the opposition evoked by Edward Said between 'us' and 'them', these Latin American writers take on the 'native person's burden' without questioning the implications of their essentialist stance which simply reverts the order of priorities without truly questioning the terms of the argument.

Eliane Karp talks of the comparison made by Asturias between himself as an artist and the Maya priests. She also ventures an interesting interpretation of his attitude in terms of the Jungian concept of the collective unconscious. Asturias appears as the recipient of a collective native memory handed down from generation to generation.

---

[1] *Indice* 226, Madrid, Dec. 1977.
[2] 'Hay que aclarar también que el surrealismo fue acaso demasiado intelectual, y que nosotros, los de mentalidad primitiva relacionados con el mundo indígena, tenemos este aspecto de un mundo subterráneo, submágico, más directamente, no como producto intelectual, sino como un producto muy natural. Los indígenas y nosotros tenemos generalmente dos realidades; una realidad palpable y una realidad soñada' (p. 39).

In his very perceptive thesis on the contemporary use of Maori myths,[1] Georges-Goulven Le Cam shows the shallow seams of such a theory of 'cultural remanence'. According to him, though parts of the same myths are to be found both in pre-European Maori wooden lintels and on pictures painted by modern artists, the function of these myths is different: in the old days, they served to reassert the existence of a strict hierarchical order on which the society was based. Such notions as *tapu* and *noa*[2] marked the territory of exclusion and interdiction, of sacredness and of deeply coded rituals. On the contrary, in modern visual and literary representations, what is kept of myths is essentially those elements that reaffirm man's link with the elements and the environment, all preoccupations which have recently acquired political and ideological relevance. So the question is not that of the unmodified transmission of cultural representations but rather the particular use that can be made in the contemporary world of representations whose 'age-old' existence provides them with unparalleled legitimacy irrespective of the modifications that they may have undergone in the process.

Both Karp and Le Cam's arguments stress the modern artist's desire to show a continuity between native past and the present time, whereas a closer examination shows, on the contrary, that a radical break took place with the massive imposition of European culture and viewpoint. Karp sees this 'double exile'[3] as one of the foundations of the *real maravilloso*. For her, an artist such as Asturias was estranged both from the colonial mentality of the conquistadors and from the possibility of returning to a system of thinking which existed before the conquest of America by Europe. Asturias was led to reformulate the present and to find a 'third formula' with syncretic potentialities. Neither wholly 'native', nor really an outsider, he claimed some intuitive links with the Indian tradition. While rejecting surrealism's 'artificial' game, he adopted some features of its discourse and used them to reformulate Maya myths. Karp insists on the transformations undergone by Francisco Ximénez's written transcriptions of the *Popol Vuh*, a collection of the oral Maya-Quiche

---

[1] See Georges-Goulven Le Cam, *Mythe et stratégie identitaire chez les Maoris de Nouvelle-Zélande.*

[2] For the Maori *tapu* means 'sacred', 'forbidden', 'set apart from common life', whereas *noa* means 'more spontaneous', free from *tapu*.

[3] Gareth Griffiths develops this notion very convincingly in *A Double Exile: African and West Indian Writing between Two Cultures.* Griffiths sees this as a major characteristic of a number of writers from the New Literatures who are 'exiled culturally from the sources and traditions of that language and linguistically from the landscapes and peoples they write about' (p. 9). This notion of exile, which I would interpret as a trope, has since been variously evoked under the names 'difference' or 'otherness'.

traditions, which Asturias used as a source for many of the myths included in his *Hombres de Maiz*. The mere fact of writing down and restructuring what was meant to be transmitted orally, in completely different conditions, altered the meaning of the tradition concerned. The result is a new mode of perception which Karp calls 'mestizo', neither native nor European, the result of a new hybrid sense of identity.

3- The Case of Juan Rulfo

Writing at the same time as Asturias and Carpentier, the Mexican Juan Rulfo also used a mixture of realism and of elements which many readers would consider as fantasy. Can he be considered as a magic realist for all that? Some commentators do apply the term in relation to his novel *Pedro Páramo*[1] (1955) whose plot unfolds on a realistic backcloth: Obeying the entreaties of his mother just before she died, Juan Preciado goes back to the village of Pedro Páramo, the father he never knew, to claim his due. The very arid environment ('Páramo' means 'desert land') of the Jalisco province where the author grew up may have served as a model for this harsh landscape where individual life is cheap and society still based on a master/slave relationship. The plot can even be situated more precisely in the 1920s when the 'Cristeros' rebelled against a secular government which wanted to do away with the influence of the Roman Catholic church. Real-life figures such as Pancho Villa are also referred to in the plot, thus making it possible to find a precise referential background to the story. The social practices described are typical of Mexico at that time: Pedro Páramo, the narrator's dead father, has accumulated land by stealing it from other people and considers all the women in the vicinity as potential targets for his lust which does not tolerate any opposition. Though awed by this formidable figure, some of the women whom he conquers are almost glad and honoured to have been chosen by such an exceptional person. Gerardo, the corrupt lawyer, brings his legal support to Pedro Páramo's tyrannical rule. This epitomizes the collusion between rich landowners and the legal profession. Father Rentería, the local priest, though full of moral misgivings, does not always resist Pedro Páramo's financial gifts to the church and often makes compromises. Towards the end of the novel, he deserts his parish to join the 'Cristero' guerrillas in the mountains.

On this strictly 'realistic' backdrop is grafted a story which has the poetic undertones of a journey into the underworld. Once Juan Preciado,

---

[1] English translation (with the same title) by Margaret Sayers Peden, Northwestern UP and Serpent's Tail (London, 1993).

at the end of his difficult journey, emerges into the streets of Comala, his native village, he discovers a ghost settlement where the distinction between life and death, past and present, reality and illusion is no longer clear. Abruptly the narration shifts from his point of view to many others, so that readers often wonder who is speaking to them and from what realm of existence or non-existence.

The first surprises concern the people who talk to Juan Preciado, generally old ladies, who are soon after said to have been dead for some time. In this novel, the deceased can communicate with the living. Gradually the readers discover that the first old lady who puts up Juan Preciado on his arrival at Comala has in fact been dead for some time. So has Abundio, the mule driver who came part of the way with Juan Preciado. But, even more surprising, Juan Preciado too dies of fright after so many encounters with ghosts. This complicates the relationship between text and reader since the narration is initially supposed to be a retrospective story told by Juan Preciado.

Using Faulknerian methods, the narrative voice changes suddenly and moves on to yet another present - or past - inhabitant of the ghost village. The readers often have to wait several pages before discovering who is actually speaking. In this novel divided up into sixty-two successive and apparently disconnected 'micro tales', the only link between the various sequences is the continuous presence of some characters or the reference to the same events. The narrative units which often do not occupy more than a page or two produce a strange impression of fragmentation. The writer seems to make it a point never to reveal who is speaking at the beginning of each unit. The same voice weaves out of one story and into the next one without any real break. And yet one soon realizes that the point of view has been radically altered. So the surface smoothness and false continuity give way to a deeper feeling of multiplicity and division. This makes it possible to read the novel in separate ways: one may choose to let oneself be carried away by these different voices without trying to distinguish between them, enjoying the strange dreamlike atmosphere as one appreciates the words of a poem. One may also reflect retrospectively on the origin of the different voices and recreate the main elements of a fractured vision.

If one chooses the second solution, one becomes aware of the fact that the novel is divided up between two major points of view, Juan Preciado's and Pedro Páramo's. Juan Preciado's dominates at the beginning. Pedro Páramo's is interspersed, first unobtrusively, then gradually in a more insistent way until it eventually takes over the second half of the novel. The shift parallels Juan Preciado's quest which aims at resurrecting his father's presence in his mind.

This strange and disturbing method brings alive a polyphonic world: Long-dead voices re-emerge. Memory produces a mosaic of fragmented testimonies which fall into place and make up a beautiful, though irremediably fragmented pattern of meanings.

Rulfo's story is allegorical of the unchallenged tyranny of local rulers over a population of poor and helpless peasants. It presents a modern version of the plantation system in the Americas, but without the trappings of social realism. The setting resembles the real world but the villagers disappear and reappear without any apparent logic. The living seem able to communicate with the dead, as though the novel could transcend the barriers between the two categories. One might argue that this corresponds to the old animism, a feature of Mexican civilisation in which the dead are very much part of the world of the living. It is difficult to decide whether this reflects Rulfo's possible belief in two different conceptions of reality simultaneously. What counts in this example is possibly not the author's own position but rather the influence he has had on a whole generation of South and Central American novelists from Carlos Fuentes to Mario Vargas Llosa. According to Susan Sontag,[1] 'García Márquez has said that, after he discovered *Pedro Páramo* (with Kafka's *Metamorphosis*, the most influential reading of his early writing years), he could recite long passages and eventually knew the whole book by heart, so much did he admire it and want to be saturated by it'. Possibly the voices from the dead that speak through this strange novel opened new possibilities for the use of popular beliefs in the treatment of a sociological reality deeply anchored in the history of the continent. Unlike the surrealists whose forays into the unconscious tapped essentially individualistic imaginary representations, this experiment was a way to use the imagination as an exploration in depth of a collective reality.

After evoking these early practitioners of a new mode often hastily labelled as 'magic realism', it might be useful to examine whether these different prototypes have features in common and where the differences between them lie. This will no doubt help us to check whether the term has value for the purpose of literary classification or whether it fulfils other functions. Our examples will be derived from novels, such as García Márquez's *One Hundred Years of Solitude*, which, according to

---

[1] In her foreword to the English translation of the novel, p. vii.

many commentators, have constituted prototypes in this 'genre'. Our discussion will also bear on Salman Rushdie's *Midnight's Children* and *Shame*, which share many characteristics with the Colombian novelist's best-known work. This 'school' has also had an influence on a series of Canadian writers such as Robert Kroetsch and Jack Hodgins.

D- Some Characteristics of Magic Realism in the Works of Rushdie and García Márquez

1- History, Fantasy and Allegory

Magic realism has affinities with the old carnivalesque tradition and the *menippea*. As such it shares many characteristics with the works of Rabelais. It is reputed to involve a return to native lore and folk magic, a question which must be relativized. Much of this literature - at least in its Latin American form - originates in a 'Criollo' environment, that is in the upper layers of society whose natural leanings brought the people closer to European culture than to popular beliefs. García Márquez was the first to admit that, initially in his native Colombia, he knew relatively little about the Amerindian component of the population. Perhaps the African tradition penetrated Criollo society more deeply through the special contact that the 'young masters' had with their servants and nurses. An examination of Jean Rhys's fiction - *Wide Sargasso Sea* in particular - shows the importance of magic and 'obeah' for people of her class.

The image García Márquez gives of his native environment contrasts with other conceptions commonly held by European or mainstream North American writers. If we believe what he says when he answers questions, in his native country, there is no dividing line between what appears real and what more positivist thinkers would call the supernatural. Is this phenomenon exactly similar to what Jacques Stephen Alexis calls 'marvellous realism'? Should we then jump to the conclusion that this represents García Márquez's own personal conception and say that what the 'West' calls his magic realism is just a 'realistic' representation of his compatriots' mental vision of their surroundings? In an increasingly urban society where the Western *logos*, the cult of progress and efficiency have permeated most layers of society, it seems difficult to admit such a presupposition unreservedly. We may even wonder whether García Márquez's remarks do not reflect the author's own natural adoption of the myth of the Noble Savage, a representation with clearly paternalistic implications.

Carpentier's *real maravilloso* and Asturias's interest in the myths of Guatemala which supposedly provide a privileged access to the creative processes of the 'collective unconscious' witness to a similar desire on the part of intellectuals to tap native sources in their homelands and to offer an alternative to the still largely dominant culture of the former metropolis. Such a store of popular lore is probably more abundantly available in Latin America than in the United States where the foreign settlers had a more destructive effect on the original populations of the continent. In this context, 'magic realism' represents a form of cultural assertion and a reaction to what was perceived as the dominant discourse. Yet, paradoxically, because of the nature of the readership for novels, the works classified in this category found an outlet mainly in the old metropolises. One may wonder whether the writers' awareness of this factor tainted their conception of the fictional reality they represented.

Commentators have used the term 'magic realism' to refer to so many different works of art - mostly written in Latin America - that the term has largely lost its value for making distinctions between genres. In order to bring some clarification, we will start with the examination of García Márquez's *One Hundred Years of Solitude* and Salman Rushdie's *Shame*,[1] which are often considered as prototypes of the 'genre'. *Cristóbal Nonato* by Carlos Fuentes and Manuel Scorza's *Garabombo, el Invisible* could probably fall into this category too. In order to decide whether the term has more than temporary relevance, we need to examine the circumstances in which it was most often used in reviews and critical essays.

It came into common usage in the late 1960s, a time when intellectuals and literary critics were often involved in Third-Worldism, civil rights and anti-imperialistic protests. Perhaps the success of the term reflects the demand of this captive audience as much as the necessities of the environment in which the writers were working. What many 'magic realistic' works have in common is this mixture of 'fantasy' and a clear concern with reference, historical allegory and social protest. Such novels often evoke the process of liberation of oppressed communities. The scope of these books largely transcends the individual fate of a few characters in order to constitute an imaginary re-telling of a whole nation through several decades. This proposed definition excludes more 'intimist' works such as those of Borges, whose writing bears similarities with the fantastic.

---

[1] In *The Writer Written*, I examine these issues in relation to *Midnight's Children*.

After *Midnight's Children*, whose plot revolves around the fictional recreation of the independence of India and its relation to a set of imaginary characters, Salman Rushdie published *Shame*, a novel which very closely follows the recent evolution of Pakistan. Most reviewers have underlined the similarity between the Iskander Harappa-Raza Hyder rivalry in the plot and the competition between Zulfikar Ali Bhutto and Zia ul-Haq in the sub-continent. The title of the fictional work suggests a grid of interpretation to account for major episodes in the history of contemporary Pakistan: shame, both in sexual and political matters, seems to frame the characters' actions. This notion refers to a code of honour primarily enforced within the family structure. Yet, despite the importance of such psychological motivation, the novel cannot be reduced to this single element. Salman Rushdie has proved with *Grimus* and with *Midnight's Children* that he is a master of storytelling. The author has absorbed the best of Eastern and world traditions and knows his *Rubaiyat* and his *Bird-Parliament* as well as his Sterne, his Günter Grass and his García Márquez. So *Shame* is not only a representation of a topical reality. It also reaffirms the author's paradoxical attitude towards major problems in fiction such as realism and verisimilitude, the relationship between writer, narrator, characters and reader, and works towards an original conception of art.

The novel combines two radically different conventions; it starts as an imaginary tale of the 'once upon a time' type. Yet twenty-five pages later the beginning of Chapter Two seems a direct extract from a personal diary written by the author:

A few weeks after Russian troops entered Afghanistan, I returned home to visit my parents and sisters and to show off my firstborn son. (p. 26)

Though the fictional plot clearly emerges as the major strand of the novel, the reader is never allowed to forget what appears as direct author's intervention hinting at a parallel between his own experience and what happens to the characters. Salman Rushdie's acknowledgements to different journalists at the end underline the referential value of the plot. Yet one would be misreading the book if one ignored the narrator's warnings about taking the story too literally:

The country in this story is not Pakistan, or not quite. There are two countries, real and fictional, occupying the same space, or almost the same space. My story, my fictional country exist, like myself, at a slight angle from reality. (p. 29)

The message is clear: *Shame* contains many elements belonging to the contemporary world. Yet artistic distance must always be kept so that reality may be restructured and made meaningful by the imagination. Rushdie does not deny his concern for discussing contemporary problems in a novel. He merely reaffirms his right to focus them in his own way. This method which brings together realistic and imaginary elements has bewildered some readers. But maybe this forms part of the writer's artistic strategy. Its merit and originality lie in the alternation of familiarity and strangeness which forces one to stay alert and to constantly question one's vision of reality. Rushdie suggests that what we commonly call reality or objectivity may have only relative value. When, in the novel, Bilquís becomes Raza Hyder's wife and is introduced into the family's gynaeceum, she has to tell the other women her own secrets in order to learn theirs in turn and be initiated through this 'rite of blood' (p. 77). The narrator insists on the shifting terrain of reality in which memory is anchored:

> Her story altered, at first, in the retellings, but finally it settled down, and after that nobody, neither teller nor listener, would tolerate any deviation from the hallowed sacred text. (p. 76)

This aside may well suggest that History undergoes a similar process of sifting, reorganization and finally of mythologizing in the sense that a community of people come to accept as their own true heritage representations which may have been rearranged many times and which consequently bear little relationship with actual facts. These characteristics cannot be interpreted as a direct commentary on the author's purpose in the novel; Rushdie introduces far too many levels of irony and self-irony for any single assertion to be seized upon as a final key to the understanding of the whole. Yet his art is also concerned with mythologizing, even if his mock-heroic tone often defuses the serious conclusions one may possibly draw from his fictional enterprise.

In *Shame* referential reality is used but the plot and characters frequently transcend verisimilitude. Some episodes such as the description of Old Mr Shakil, Omar Khayyam's grandfather, who hates to hear the noise of the town which he calls a 'hell hole', appear as parodies of epic feats or conventions. In his misanthropic delirium, he utters 'oaths and curses of a ferocity that made the air boil violently around his bed' (p. 11). His daughters, the hero's three 'mothers' - no one can tell who his actual mother is since all displayed signs of pregnancy simultaneously and the child was delivered without any outside witness - all have milk at the same time and feed the child in turn on their three pairs of breasts. Omar Khayyam himself sleeps very little and regularly suffers from giddy spells and dreams of 'falling off the world's end' (p. 127). Unlike the protagonist, the author is not unaware of the moments when dreams intrude upon 'reality' in his fiction. But he seems to favour characters who, because of their sleeplessness, frequent these peripheral areas where 'things skip between the unguarded bollards, avoiding the customs post' (p. 127). The frontier metaphor is here provided by the father of Farah Zoroaster, Omar Khayyam's first lady-love, who is sent as a customs officer on the frontier with Iran. Rushdie encourages the reader to interpret the border image as a metafictional remark concerning the true nature of creation which also implies familiarity with 'borderline' experiences. Omar Khayyam actually begins to stand on his own feet as an individual once he has passed the limits of Nishapur, the claustrophobic environment of his mothers' house where he was locked up throughout his childhood. He only becomes a man after going beyond the 'Impassable Mountains' which circumscribed his perception in his early days.

The narrator pretends to respect the conventions of mimesis and apologizes for the dubious reality of certain episodes by adding that he himself only heard of them through rumours, gossip or family legends. But he plays the detective game of sifting the truth from the lies. When they become pregnant, the 'Three Mothers' decide to sever all contact with the outside world and limit their dealings with the town to communication by means of a dumb-waiter whose builder dies a few weeks after the completion of his work, as if to carry into his grave the terrible secrets of that mysterious house. The man's death stirs a lot of controversy which the narrator feigns to echo faithfully:

> ... it got about that those Shameless women had had him poisoned to ensure his silence on the subject of his last and most mysterious commission. It is only fair to state, however, that the medical evidence in the case runs strongly against this version of events. Yakoob Balloch, who had been suffering for some time from sporadic pains in the region of the appendix, almost certainly died of natural causes... (pp. 17-18)

Such passages play on the confusion produced in the reader's mind between the fictional value of some events and the narrator's attempt to present them as real and rationally verifiable. The narrator's attitude dramatizes the two poles between which Rushdie's novel oscillates, that of popular myths and that of Western-type rationality. The adept juggling with different levels of 'reality' is meant to confuse and entertain the readers who hesitate between fully accepting the conventions of fiction - and consequently forgetting that this is fiction - and realizing that they remain in a world of make-believe. Much of the pleasure produced by Salman Rushdie's work is derived from this play on verisimilitude. Sometimes the narrator himself, far from pretending to clear the confusion, adds to it by reporting an event whose veracity he later questions: after drawing a fantastic picture of Omar Khayyam wandering like a time-traveller through a labyrinthine house, he shortly after brings the reader back to everyday reality by adding that, even then, nobody believed in these stories.[1]

Salman Rushdie encourages the reader to look out for possible historical echoes in his characters' names: Mrs Aurengzeb, the Joint Chief of Staff's widow and mistress to Iskander Harappa bears the famous name of the last great Moghul at the end of the seventeenth century. Similarly Iskander Harappa evokes Iskander Mirza, the President of Pakistan in the 1950s. Babar Shakil, Omar Khayyam's younger brother, is a very pale imitation of fifteenth-century Babar, a descendant of Tamburlaine, who seized Delhi and Agra. The modern version is only a fairly ridiculous freedom fighter who spends his time between hit-and-run attacks on government troops and fornicating with goats. The echoes of all the glorious names give a mock-heroic quality to the characters, hinting at a greatness which they do not possess.

For Michel Dupuis and Albert Mingelgrün,[2] magic realism has a fondness for generalizations and the allegory. Though this is not an exclusive property of magic realistic texts, the creation of a whole universe with multiple characters is certainly a common feature to most magic realistic texts. A similar concern is to be found in other novels such as Jorge Amado's *Tocaia Grande*, a story set in a new frontier settlement in Brazil. The same could also be said of major realistic novels such as those of Balzac. Yet the fondness of post-colonial writers for this type of environment is marked with a definite desire to bring to existence places and communities which traditional literatures had ignored or misrepresented. Bombay takes on a different relevance to non-Bombayites (and to Bombayites too, probably) after the reading of *Midnight's Children*. When he wrote his novel, Rushdie reacted to colonial interpretations of India by such 'experts' as Rudyard Kipling,

---

[1] See p. 31.
[2] 'Pour une poétique du réalisme magique' in Jean Weisgerber, ed., *Le Réalisme magique*, pp. 219-232.

E.M. Forster or Paul Scott, the author of the *Raj Quartet* (1966-1975). Following a now classical post-colonial process of reappropriation of his reality, he struck back at the centre which had confiscated India and bottled it into chutney jars which had been watered down and adapted to metropolitan tastes, if one may borrow one of the ruling metaphors in *Midnight's Children.*

In order to repossess their alienated reality, magic realistic writers frequently go back to the origins of their cultures; echoing the post-colonial desire to start with a clean slate, they set their novels in communities which are just coming into existence and whose foundation becomes a replaying of genesis. With his creation of Macondo in *One Hundred Years of Solitude*, García Márquez indulges in a particularly idiosyncratic exploration of his imaginary roots, with fiction almost joining up with the myth of origins. The beginning of his novel goes back to the time when the village was still isolated from the rest of humanity and only wandering magicians such as Melquíades could tell the spell-bound peasants about the great discoveries made outside their restricted world.

Similarly the 'Revelation Colony of Truth' in Vancouver Island described by Jack Hodgins in *The Invention of the World* is a pioneering settlement founded by Donald Brendan Keneally who took along with him across an ocean and a whole continent the people of his original Irish village. In the author's adept hands, the 'colony' becomes an archetype of all such new outposts founded by European emigrants in search of a better life.

Robert Kroetsch similarly outlines the origins of a small prairie town in the West of Canada in *What the Crow Said*, though in an even more playful mode than the other texts mentioned. While aiming to put the prairies on the literary map, he does not take his task too seriously and refuses to dwell on the issue of local or regional identity, a question which was much debated in Canada at the time. Though frequently larger than life, his founding fathers and mothers are more anti-heroic than truly admirable.

Following in *Shame* other 'magic realists'' tendency to merge individual and collective genesis, Rushdie sets a stage on which ghosts move, neither pure fiction nor simple mirrors of reality. Omar begins his life and ends it in Nishapur; he leaves his home-town only to end up finally in that house of the three mothers, that territory of childhood where everything started. The subplot alludes to parallels with the situation of the author, a self-avowed emigrant playfully concerned with the gravitational pull of his roots:

> I am comparing gravity with belonging. Both phenomena observably exist: my feet stay on the ground, and I have never been angrier than I was on the day my father told me he had sold my childhood home in Bombay. But neither is understood. We know the force of gravity but not its origins, and to explain why we become attached to our birthplaces we pretend that we are trees and speak of roots. Look under your feet. You will not find gnarled growths sprouting through the soles. Roots, I sometimes think, are a conservative myth designed to keep us in our places (pp. 85-86).

Maybe *Midnight's Children* and *Shame*, two novels linked with Rushdie's childhood and family homes, are attempts to reassess the respective powers of freedom from and attachment to the world of the origins. In *Grimus* and in *Shame* the author comes back to the old Norse legend of the Ash Yggdrasill planted with one root in the pool of knowledge while the second is being consumed by fire and the third devoured by a beast. This tree of knowledge with its precarious roots may compare with the writer in his relationship to the native soil.

The flight of the migrant may be an equivalent of Omar Khayyam's escape from the claustrophobic world of the mothers. But he eventually returns home. Similarly the migrant runs the risk of being 'stripped of history' (p. 63). The voice here echoes that of the author who arrived in to Britain in relatively comfortable circumstances: the son of an upper-middle class Bombay family, he went through the elite educational institutions of Rugby school and Cambridge University. Yet his experience as the child of two cultures has left its trace on his fiction. In *Shame*, the narrator declares[1] that he will stop writing about the East where he was born. But he still feels closely attached to his origins: 'It is a part of the world to which, whether I like it or not, I am still joined, if only by elastic bands' (p. 28). His physical distance in relation to the Indian subcontinent does not imply that he has given it up for good: 'No matter how determinedly one flees a country, one is obliged to take along some hand-luggage' (p. 39). And he adds that what is striking about the emigrant is the emptiness of his luggage.

---

[1] Unlike the author who has continued to write about the East in *The Satanic Verses* (1988), *Haroun and the Sea of Stories* (1990), *East and West* (1994) and *The Moor's Last Sigh* (1995).

I'm speaking of invisible suitcases, not the physical, perhaps cardboard, variety
containing a few meaning-drained mementoes: we have come unstuck from more
than land. We have floated upwards from history, from memory, from Time. (p. 87)

Remarking jocularly about the position of the emigrant, he declares:

I am an emigrant from one country (India) and a newcomer in two (England, where I
live, and Pakistan, to which my family moved against my will). And I have a theory
that the resentments we *mohajirs* engender have something to do with our conquest
of the force of gravity. We have performed the act of which all men anciently dream,
the thing for which they envy the birds; that is to say, we have flown. (p. 85)

This metaphor of gravity is used again at the beginning of *The Satanic
Verses* when two Indians are plummeting down towards England after the
explosion in mid air of their Boeing 747.

The narrator of *Shame* prefers to use his special position in order to
account better and more freely for the complexity of reality: like all
migrants, he 'build[s] imaginary countries and [tries] to impose them on
the ones that exist' (p. 87).

The power of the imagination enables the writer to escape from the
prison of conventions. The hero of *Shame* ends up in the house where he
started from, pulled by a compulsion to seek refuge in the only 'safe'
place that he can think of. Yet, even at the end of this regressive journey,
he is not absolutely sheltered from all dangers; his 'mothers' want to
make him pay for the death of his brother and his savage wife will seek
him out. Similarly the writer does not emerge altogether unscathed from
his novel. The world of the origins - the 'mother''s land or the field of the
imagination - may appear as a very attractive territory. Yet one can never
wholly reclaim it and, supposing one could, it would not be as beautiful
as one's idea of it. *Shame* demonstrates to the reader Salman Rushdie's
virtuosity in his handling of characters, situations and plot. Yet what
happens to Omar Khayyam might be an indication of the hidden pitfalls
which an artist has to face, even when he seems to have mastered all the
elements of his art.

Omar Khayyam has emerged from Nishapur with its hidden Shame -
the two illegitimate sons - into an existence based on freedom but also
Shamelessness and constant compromise. He has broken many of the
taboos of his society. He has almost 'created' Sufiya who later became
his wife, by bringing her back to life thanks to his medical expertise. But
this Pygmalion trick ends tragically: Sufiya turns into a ferocious beast
who decapitates all the men who approach her. She eventually tracks him
down to his refuge at Nishapur. The object which the creator thinks he
has fashioned completely turns back against its 'owner'. All creations

124 *Mimesis, Genres and Post-Colonial Discourse*

finally acquire their autonomy. This might well be an indirect reflection on the writer's illusion of mastery over his material. Finitude and death catch up with the marvellously gifted children in *Midnight's Children*. They also overcome Omar Khayyam and the narrator who is left with his 'figure of dreams, a phantom with one arm lifted in a gesture of farewell' (p. 286). The journey towards freedom has become a voyage into the heart of darkness.

2- Reality and Meaning

The process of birth is intimately linked with that of naming, of acquiring a social existence, of being introduced to the world of language. The parents' desire to 'appropriate' their child leads them to choose its name(s). This attempt to 'possess' one's creation parallels the writer's desire to master his/her material. Post-colonial writers seem acutely aware of the ambiguities of artistic mastery. Their fiction often thematizes the limits of such a process. It frequently explores a time when places and people had no name, had not yet emerged into the social sphere. In *One Hundred Years of Solitude*, García Márquez refers to a society which is so new that language has not fully accounted for all the universe: 'The world was so recent that many things lacked names' (p. 9). Its inhabitants' taking possession of their environment through naming may well appear as a representation of the South American writer's desire to make his Colombian reality exist by describing it and ordering it in his novel. Because the names given by the colonizers are often inadequate, the artist has to take up 'Adam's task of giving things their name', to use Alejo Carpentier's famous formula quoted by the St Lucian poet Derek Walcott in an epigraph.[1]

In his novel, García Márquez suggests that names can also be lost when people have been made amnesic. All begin to lose their sleep after the mysterious Rebecca is sent to José Arcadio Buendía by some distant relation whose existence everybody has forgotten. And the consequence of this disease is that people gradually lose the memory of the use of things. José Arcadio Buendía begins to write the names on different objects around him. When the complaint worsens, he even has to put a note on his cow saying 'This is the cow. She must be milked every morning so that she will produce milk...' (p. 46). So, as reality evades the characters, they try ever harder to keep their hold on things by endowing words with a special status. This comic exaggeration can also be taken as

---

[1] Epigraph to Section Two, 'Homage to Gregorias' of *Another Life* (1973), republished in Derek Walcott, *Collected Poems 1948-1984*, p. 189.

a metaphor of the role of the post-colonial writer who has to invent new ways of using language in order to offset the dangers of losing the memory of his roots and of being wholly absorbed in the 'de-realizing' colonial language. Beyond the comic mention of a sign which had to be put up at the entrance to Macondo saying that 'God exists', the author probably suggests that American reality is still partly unnamed or at least partly forgotten by those who inhabit the continent. Perhaps writing is a way for the novelist to imprison reality on parchment. The book thus becomes a memory bank similar to the machine dreamt of by José Arcadio Buendía and thanks to which he imagines he can revise every morning the total sum of all the knowledge he has accumulated throughout his life.

This encyclopaedic aspiration in the novel is also present in *Midnight's Children* when the narrator complains in the first page that there are so many stories to tell that he is afraid of not having enough time. There too the novel as a memory bank is thematized at the end with the metaphor of the chutneyfication of reality. Like Saleem in his savouring factory, the writer 'bottles' reality and preserves it, trying to keep its flavour intact.

When the insomnia epidemic starts in *One Hundred Years of Solitude*, people live in a state where there is no longer any separation between dreams and reality. Not only do they know their own dreams; they can also perceive those of their neighbours. This 'universal' power of communication might also well be a thematization of the narrator's own 'omniscience'.

This mode in which everything becomes transparent appears as an ideal state where frontiers between people fade away. Characters tend to merge with others, thus satisfying a fusional tendency also illustrated by Rebecca's very regressive attitude when she eats earth and scratches chalk off the walls to swallow it.

After a strike which was violently repressed by the owners of the banana plantation, the inhabitants of Macondo officially accept the official version of the events, which says that there were no deaths and no troops firing at the demonstrators. The strikers are supposed to have gladly accepted the proposals of the company. For most, a simple decree was enough to erase from their memories what actually happened. José Arcadio Segundo manages to jump off the train carrying away the bodies of the casualties due to be dumped into the sea. After walking back to Macondo, he hangs on to his memory that more than three thousand people were killed and barbarously disposed of. He makes every possible effort to transmit the information and keep it alive in successive generations. Two conceptions of memory are opposed here: on the one hand, an officially approved version is imposed on people. On the other, a heroic individual doggedly preserves the truth which may not please everybody but is necessary for a proper sense of identity and history to remain among the people. This too is a commentary on the Third-World artist's duty towards historical veracity when the memory of events is so frequently warped to serve base political or economic interests. And heroes too can be contaminated by this thirst for power: after acquiring a prominent position in society, José Arcadio also warps reality and starts confiscating other people's properties, which shows that Márquez's taste for 'magic' does not lead him to the creation of a perfect fictional utopia.

Rushdie too is a preserver of historical memory in *Midnight's Children*. Like Márquez and his involvement on the side of Colombian workers and peasants, Rushdie seeks to preserve the memory of the essential events which led to the independence of India, but also to the very repressive period when Indira Gandhi curtailed individual rights by declaring a state of emergency. The miracles that take place in *Midnight's Children* do not concern memory so much as other senses: after eavesdropping on his mother in her washing chest, young Saleem surprises her in the nude, a sight which affects him so much that he suddenly becomes aware of changes in his perception; he begins to be receptive to the voices of all the other Indian children born like himself at the precise moment when his nation became independent. Perhaps the most embarrassing phenomenon is his ability to read in his father's thoughts, even and especially when he mentally undresses his secretaries.

All these modifications of the normal rules of perception or memory playfully thematize the writer's overwhelming desire to shape his fictional world even in the most unusual fashion. As is the case with Rushdie's children, there are very few physical obstacles to the writer's ambition to reorganize the world of representation.

Tampering with memory also means that one changes one's own vision of reality. Márquez illustrates the consequences of such an attitude when, in his novel, the soldiers come into the Buendías' house to arrest José Arcadio Segundo and do not even see him, though he is sitting there on the camp bed in the same room. Because they have been so conditioned by their fabricated vision of reality, they fail to see the truth, even when it is there in front of their eyes.

A similar technique of using 'fantasy' to represent a state of mind can be found in Manuel Scorza's *Garabombo el Invisible* (1978): this book by the Peruvian novelist is based on the fight of Andean peasants against the encroachment of large Criollo landowners. When, in the first chapter,

Garabombo, the leader of the peasant uprising, faces the guns of the army, he becomes transparent to them and manages to go through their positions without being noticed. Of course this technique was not invented by Latin American writers; it is already present in Ralph Ellison's *Invisible Man* (1952), a novel which similarly deals with the biassed and partial view of reality that white people in the United States have, so much so that they fail to notice the protagonist, a poor black man:

> I am an invisible man. No, I am not a spook like those who haunted Edgar Allan Poe; nor am I one of your Hollywood-movie ectoplasms. I am a man of substance, of flesh and bone, fibre and liquids - and I might even be said to possess a mind. I am invisible simply because people refuse to see me.[1]

In the case of Ellison's hero, this is not always unpleasant, except that it sometimes leads him to doubt his own existence. Such does not seem to be the case with Márquez's or Scorza's characters. Invisibility only protects them from their enemies and becomes a form of superiority. In all these examples, the characters, who belong to an oppressed group, see the whole of reality, whereas their opponents have a warped view.

Rushdie resorts to a rather extreme form of this invisibility by using a magician who, in *Midnight's Children*, does a disappearing trick with the hero Saleem in order to transport him from Bangla Desh to Delhi in her wicker basket after the Indian army has helped the Bengali to secede from Pakistan.

Saleem too chooses to select in reality those representations which are acceptable. When remembering the horrors during the siege of Dacca, he ironically remarks:

> We saw the intelligentsia of the city being massacred by the hundred, but it was not true because it could not have been true, the Tiger was a decent chap... (p. 375)

Here the narrator playfully illustrates the manipulation of reality which can be made by unscrupulous people. But it also echoes the particular feeling of unreality which the colonized subject feels when the only rendering of his experience is filtered through the colonial viewpoint. In the case of Rushdie, this doubt concerning the nature of reality provides an occasion for a joyful manipulation of different fictional levels. Other writers express less jubilant attitudes towards what may appear as the colonial or ex-colonial's deep alienation.

---

[1] Penguin (Harmondsworth, 1982 [1952]), p. 7.

Márquez's *One Hundred Years of Solitude* illustrates this precarious hold that post-colonial people sometimes have on reality. The narrator ironically remarks on the reasons for human beings' taste for fiction: Aureliano, who has discovered the secret chamber where Melquíades, the old gipsy wise man, hid all his secrets, cannot resist being 'holed up in written reality' (p. 314). A parody of the passionate reader of fiction, he lives in a make-believe world where everything takes on dubious existence. When he leaves his room in the evening, it is to retreat to the 'burdelito imaginario' (the 'imaginary brothel', which the English translator renders rather tendentiously as the 'brothel of lies'). There nothing has real substance: the garden is planted with paper flowers, the framed pictures on the walls belong to journals which were never printed and even the little whores have no solid existence.

The more the narration advances, the more the characters mistake their desires for reality. But some have been encouraged to do so before. Fernanda del Carpio, who marries Aureliano Segundo, was brought up to believe in her own greatness, a feeling which the author ridicules with his insistence on Fernanda's taking her solid gold chamber pot everywhere with her. She entertains the absurd dream of becoming queen of Madagascar.

Such delusions of grandeur which appear as symptoms of compensation for the precarious hold post-colonial people have on reality also go together with a passionate search for order, meaning and significance around them. Rushdie's narrator in *Midnight's Children* declares straight away: 'above all things, I fear absurdity' (p. 9). He has a mania for interpreting events, for making the slightest incident meaningful. Saleem even reverses the normal relationship betwen character and historical reference: he explains major events in India's evolution in terms of his own interventions and not the other way round.

Similarly, at the end of *One Hundred Years of Solitude*, Aureliano declares that, if Sir Francis Drake attacked Riohacha, it was in order to allow him to meet Amaranta Ursula, whom he first thought to be his sister but who was actually his aunt, with whom he fell desperately in love. So, without going to the same extent as Rushdie, García Márquez also stresses the characters' desire to leave their mark on history. This may well illustrate the post-colonial people's desperate need to repossess history on their own terms. But, with sophisticated novelists such as Rushdie or García Márquez, this is never done naïvely. History is not considered as a hoard which merely needs to be uncovered in order to be restored to its proper place. Writers from the New Literatures feel doubly alienated from their past, first because of the imposition of a colonialist received version of it and also because they believe in the impassable gulf between language and what people call reality. The post-colonial experience makes the writers doubly aware of the precariousness of their - or anybody else's - knowledge or apprehension of experience and history. Rushdie and García Márquez share these doubts with the post-modernists. They know that fiction does not merely 'mirror' reality but also allegorizes its own functioning.

Magic realism could probably not have existed without the surrealist movement or without the influence of Rabelais, Sterne and Diderot. Yet these same writers have been claimed as a major influence by novelists who, starting from the premises of the *nouveau roman*, set about producing works where *semiosis* was far more important than *mimesis*. In his polemic and rather reductive rejection of anything too reminiscent of Barthes, Benveniste and Lacan, Raymond Tallis[1] crams together undiscerningly such diverse novelists as Barthelme, Rushdie, D.M. Thomas and Blanchot. This type of grouping does not resist rigorous critical analysis. García Márquez and Rushdie are very much concerned with creating fictional environments with a definite relevance to the world around them. And yet they too use metafictional devices. Both *One Hundred Years of Solitude* and *Midnight's Children* are 'framed' in self-reflexive plots. This appears more clearly in Rushdie's novel with the ironical device of having Saleem tell his story to the supposedly naïve Padma. But even Márquez's plot eventually shows a similar mirroring effect: Aureliano, who has at last managed to decipher Melquíades' parchments realizes that they are a prophecy of everything that happened to his family and to himself. He too is prophesized deciphering the last pages of the manuscript.

Curiously, in both novels, the protagonist with extraordinary powers is destroyed as the plot reaches its conclusion: Saleem is crushed by the multitudes he has attempted to fit into his narration. Aureliano realizes that, at the end of his reading, the parchment will coincide with the end of his life 'for it was foreseen that the city of mirrors (or mirages) would be wiped out by the wind and exiled from the memory of men' (p. 336) at that precise moment. The dénouements of both novels stress the limits of fiction and the eventual defeat of any attempt to control the world absolutely through the imagination. Far from indulging in the whimsical arbitrariness derided by Raymond Tallis, both Márquez and Rushdie reaffirm the paradox of any genuine imaginative writer intent on creating a world of make-believe which can have relevance in their readers'

---

[1] *In Defence of Realism.*

experience, while remaining acutely aware of the dangers and limits of such nearly godlike power.

In the meantime the writers have created believable and relevant fictional realities which shed an original light on the familiar world of the readers. In the hands of Rushdie or García Márquez, metafiction does not merely serve to convince others that we live in a fragmented world where only signs exist and where the only possibility left is that of juggling expertly with signifiers. Instead it becomes a particular approach which deconstructs commonly accepted views of reality: with Rushdie, the recent history of India is seen from a perspective which differs from that of the very Western 'Gandhi-mania' perceptible in film and literary representations stigmatized by the author of *Midnight's Children*. Similarly, with Márquez, Colombia takes on a reality of its own and at last escapes the colonial clichés about heavily moustached 'barbudos' or smiling natives in white dress greeting astute European coffee buyers. There remains, of course, the danger of both countries being stultified in the baroque images provided by Márquez or Rushdie. But new creators will no doubt make sure that this does not become a real menace.

Magic realist texts often contain explicit references to other works of art which they acknowledge as possible sources of inspiration. Rushdie's narrator refers to Sheherazade in the first chapter of *Midnight's Children*. Sheherazade's storytelling power has often been described as a metaphor for the creator's attempt to defer the advent of death through the special powers of art. Similarly in *One Hundred Years of Solitude*, Aureliano Segundo is discovered wholly immersed in the reading of a book which tells of a 'lamp which fulfil[s] wishes and about flying carpets' (p. 154), a reference, no doubt, to other episodes of *Arabian Nights*.

An even more devious allusion to the same text is to be found in the Canadian Robert Kroetsch's *What the Crow Said*: Rita, one of the characters, has a passion for corresponding with inmates locked up in death-row cells. Her written words, like Sheherazade, defer the advent of the dreaded encounter with the inevitable, though Lapanne, Rita's favourite correspondent, fails to escape his fate. The same novel also contains fairly obvious allusions to Edgar Allan Poe and probably to Ted Hughes' famous series of poems. Funnily enough, Hughes is also one of the inspirations behind the creation of Flapping Eagle, the hero of *Grimus*, Rushdie's first novel.

In *Midnight's Children*, other elements such as the allusion to Cyrano de Bergerac and to *Tristram Shandy*'s clock have more playful connotations aimed at the sophisticated readers who are offered riddles to check that they can see through all the narrative ploys and share the 'in-jokes' of the Oxbridge intelligentsia.

When, in the fifth chapter of *One Hundred Years of Solitude*, José Arcadio boasts about what he experienced in his voyages throughout the world, he mentions coming across Victor Hugues's ghostly ship drifting aimlessly through the Caribbean. This is a fairly obvious reference to a real-life character of West Indian history, but one who was more particularly represented in Alejo Carpentier's *El Siglo de las Luces* (1962) as a local character fascinated by the French revolution. Victor Hugues was able to bring to the New World the decree abolishing slavery on the 16. Pluviose of the year II. But, with the same energy, he also completely contradicted himself by enforcing the decree of 30. Floréal of the year X restoring the slave system. This hints at the ambiguities of providential leaders who are likely to be blinded by their success and can easily turn from liberator into tyrannical figures.

When, in *One Hundred Years of Solitude*, José Arcadio Segundo and Lorenzo Gavilán, a Mexican revolutionary, are imprisoned together by the police (p. 244), the narrator indicates that Gavilán was a companion of Artemio Cruz, a figure whom Carlos Fuentes places at the centre of his novel *The Death of Artemio Cruz* (1962). Unlike Rushdie's, Márquez's references are relatively unobtrusive. They might even go unnoticed, thus reinforcing the commonly heard (but thoroughly unfounded) prejudice that he is a spontaneous and even naïve writer. Rushdie and García Márquez should not be thought to rely mostly on 'unsophisticated' folk lore. They are highly literate practitioners of intertextuality. Consequently magic realists as we have defined them owe as much - and possibly more - to European cultures as to the 'primitive' traditions of their native countries. Their allegiance is to Rabelais, post-modernism and surrealism as much as is it to orature.

3- Comedy and the Infringement of Taboos

'Magic realists' delight in learned metatextual references, which might place their work in the category of books reserved for the knowing intellectuals. Yet they also enjoy Rabelaisian bawdiness and the transgression of taboos on sexuality, which brings them closer to the popular (some would say essentially male) tradition. In the early stages of the society described in *One Hundred Years of Solitude*, the threat of breaking the taboo of incest is vehicled by stories of people giving birth to children who might have pig-like tails or even to iguanas. José Arcadio Segundo is actually initiated to hitherto unknown sexual pleasures by his confessor who asks him whether he ever did anything with animals.

Forced to admit that he did not, he makes up for this ignorance by going secretly at night the next Tuesday with Petronio, the sickly sexton, to visit female donkeys in a neighbouring field.

Robert Kroetsch goes one step further in the breaking of taboos on zoophilia by having Vera, his character in *What the Crow Said*, impregnated by bees.[1] Because of this special relation between herself and the forces of nature, she later becomes a sort of primal 'mother' to the rest of the story, thus putting herself out of bounds as a sexual object for normal human males. Similarly, in *The Invention of the World*, Jack Hodgins rejoins the great Greek myths in which human beings could mate with gods or animals: in the novel, Donal Brendan Keneally is supposed to have been fathered in the West of Ireland by a bull copulating with a woman.

The frequency of this theme is linked with the different authors picturing societies in the early stages of their evolution, when even the concept of rules limiting the range of individual freedom and sexual choices was still supposedly vague. At the beginning of *One Hundred Years of Solitude*, no one is more than thirty years old and death has not yet made its appearance in Macondo. Man is still close to the cosmic powers and, in a hopeless attempt to reclaim this cosmic union with the universe, characters throughout the novel are fascinated by incest: José Arcadio marries Rebecca, though he suspects that she may be his sister. Arcadio wants to sleep with Pilar Ternera who (unknown to him, but is this the point?) is his mother. This lack of a most basic set of rules can also be interpreted as a combination of the old logic of myths and as a mischievous allusion to the prejudices colonizing powers entertained towards the colonized. Because post-colonial societies often pretended to be closer to the myths of foundation of their own societies, novels in the New Literatures often refer to these original events when gods or super-human heroes infringed the most basic rules of incest. In the case of García Márquez or Rushdie, one cannot accuse them of being blind believers in the unbroken chain of inheritance in relation to these mythical ancestors. So one can only conclude that they do this in a deliberately rebellious mood against all forms of authority and also as a playful way of anchoring their tales in an alternative tradition free from colonial taint. In so doing, they also ironically refer to the colonial

---

[1] Strangely enough, in *Remembering Babylon* by the Australian novelist David Malouf, Janet, one of the characters, visits some hives and she is suddenly covered by a swarm of bees. Her reaction is of a sexual nature too: 'You are our new bride, her new and separate mind told her as it drummed and swayed above the earth. Ah, so that is it! They have smelled the sickly blood-flow. They think it is honey. It is.' (p. 142)

prejudices which see the colonized people as a population which deserves to be dominated because they supposedly have revolting sexual habits. So what appears to a naïve observer as a form of essentialist discourse is actually fraught with subversive undertones which add many layers of humour to the fictional plot.

In *One Hundred Years of Solitude*, the foreigners who settle in Macondo end up changing the weather pattern, the cycle of the crops and the courses of the rivers. Nature strikes back with a vengeance and rain begins to pour down, never abating for four years, eleven months and two days. The preciseness of the notation becomes as grotesque as Rabelais' when his narrator indicates that Gargantua was so greedy as a baby that he needed seventeen thousand nine hundred and thirteen cows to feed him milk. Similarly his mother was supposed to be able to produce fourteen hundred and two barrels of milk plus two jugs from her two breasts at every feed.[1]

Saleem too, in *Midnight's Children*, proves a fairly formidable baby intent on his 'self-enlargement' scheme (see p. 124). After draining up his mother's breasts, the young baby similarly suckles dry several wet nurses and proceeds to ravage the teats of the bottles offered as a substitute. Though deprived this time of Rabelais' mathematical precision, Rushdie's hero witnesses to the same Gargantuan capacity for engulfing food.

Describing the epic card game that goes on for several weeks in the basement of the church (*What the Crow Said*, p. 119), Kroetsch similarly indicates that Liebhaber, the protagonist, had dropped out of the game on a hundred and twenty eight occasions.

Rushdie uses mathematical precision elsewhere in *Midnight's Children*. It becomes comic not because of the exaggeration involved but because the precision is unexpected and irrelevant. When envisaging his eventual falling apart, the narrator indicates that he will crumble into '(approximately) six hundred and thirty six million particles' of dust (p. 37). When the narrator of *Shame* evokes the year when the dry wind blew more than ever, he adds that 'cases of fever and madness increased by *four hundred and twenty per cent*' (p. 135 [italics mine]). Similarly, when gas fields are discovered, the tribals attack the engineers and technicians whom they consider as intruders:

---

[1] See chapter VII of *Gargantua*.

> [They] raped each member of the team *eighteen point six times* on average (of which *thirteen point nine seven* assaults were from the rear and only *four point six nine* in the mouth. (p. 91. [Italics mine])

In his clever association of the 'approximately' or the 'on an average' and the useless figures, Rushdie parodies the ludicrous thirst for precision characteristic of the Western logos. In so doing, he implicitly questions the imperialistic arrogance of 'scientific' explanations.

When Omar Khayyam, the protagonist of *Shame*, is born, one of his mothers holds him by his feet and he catches his first glimpse of the mountains with his head down, which is why, according to the narrator, '[he] was afflicted, from his earliest days, by a sense of inversion, of a world turned upside-down' (p. 21). This type of report is a parody of would-be psychoanalytical causes for disorders which supposedly date back to childhood memories - all supposing that a new-born baby can see the outside world! This image also corresponds to a literal rendering of the impression felt by many Third-World people whose reality is imposed from the outside and who thus need to invert or deconstruct it in order to substitute their own vision. The Samoan writer Albert Wendt expresses this through the image of the 'flying-fox',[1] a creature half-mammal and half-bird. His flying-foxes are trickster figures who steal in other people's gardens and are familiar with the ancient forest, the site of the old gods and the repository of tradition. Omar Khayyam Shakil too is a subversive protagonist whose exceptional powers raise questions as to the materiality of what the average people consider as the 'normal' world. Because the process of representation cannot be likened to a strict mirror reflection, the narrator of *Shame* declares: 'My story, my fictional country exist, like myself, at a slight angle to reality' (p. 29).

Another 'scientific' statement is put forward when the narrator tells of General Hyder having allegedly gone without sleep for 'four hundred and twenty hours' during the time when Muslims had to hide in the 'red fortress' for fear of being massacred (p. 66). This is given as the cause for the black pouches under Hyder's eyes - a characteristic which becomes even funnier when we think of the General's counterpart in real life. This is an example of the writer's purported exploitation of popular sayings adding to the glory of the great man who sacrificed his physique for a noble cause. The novel becomes mock-heroic in pretending to create a myth which is deflated or contradicted by other elements in the plot.

---

[1] See his volume of fiction *Flying-Fox in a Freedom Tree*.

The world of magic realists is one in which the 'realistic' world is no sooner established as such than its validity is questioned through fictional manipulation. The writers thus reassert the fact that reality is not given a priori but constructed through the novelists' perception of their material and handling of language. The apparent logic and naturalness of linear time is exposed through the numerous anachronies and 'mise en abymes' which are part of the novelists' common practice.

'Muchos años después' (Many years later), the first phrase in García Márquez's *One Hundred Years of Solitude*, recurs as a leitmotiv throughout the novel and introduces prolepses which serve to whet the reader's appetite. Behind this playful formula of anticipation lies a reminder of the fictionality of the novel, which may sometimes be forgotten because of the richness and variety of the plot.

Because of Márquez's influence on post-colonial writers, this use of time has become a frequent technique: both in *Midnight's Children* and in *Shame*, Rushdie alludes to later episodes in the early stages of his novel thus providing the readers with enigmas to be solved. In *What the Crow Said*, the Canadian novelist Robert Kroetsch (probably consciously) parodies Márquez when, talking of his heroine Vera Lang, who has been miraculously impregnated by bees, he has his narrator add: 'People, *years later* [Italics mine] blamed everything on the bees' (p. 7. See also a similar phrase p. 18).

In *Shame*, Salman Rushdie often pretends that the time of the narration coincides with the time of the characters' lives. The author cannot resist the pleasure of introducing sub-plots or of commenting at length on any particular event. Suddenly the narrator appears seized by remorse at this 'inconsistency' in the organization of his tale and declares, deliberately breaking realistic illusion: 'I must get back to my fairy-story, because things have been happening while I've been talking too much' (p. 71). Sometimes he even looks like a film-director - Rushdie was born in Bombay, the Indian cinema capital and has never concealed his interest in films, including those of the popular Indian sort - whose actors patiently wait for their turn:

> On my way back to the story, I pass Omar Khayyam Shakil, my sidelined hero, who is waiting patiently for me to get to the point at which his future bride, poor Sufiya Zinobia, can enter the narrative, head first down the birth canal.[1] He won't have to wait long; she's almost on her way (p. 71).

---

[1] A similar metaphor is used for another character emerging into a different narrative world, that of England after his drop from the explosion that destroyed his Boeing in mid-air over the Channel. Here we refer, of course to Chamcha who, in *The Satanic*

At other points, such remarks are used as clever transitions between different episodes to cover up an ellipsis in the plot, as when the narrator suddenly exclaims: 'Enough. Ten years have slipped by in my story while I've been seeing ghosts' (p. 118).

Whereas, in traditional fiction, flashbacks are usually smoothed over, Salman Rushdie at times draws the readers' attention to the rhetorical process as if to make them aware of the conventions of fiction. At the end of Chapter Nine, the narrator suddenly declares:

> Time to turn back the clock, so that Iskander rises from the grave, but recedes, as well, into the background of the tale. Other people have been living lives while Harappa rose and fell (p. 196).

All these diverse strategies show the writer as a sort of trickster, an illusionist who controls the reader's 'suspension of disbelief'.

In *Shame*, Salman Rushdie really uses all the resources which denegation can provide when he elaborates on what this novel might have become if it were a realistic piece of work. And he proceeds to quote at length all the examples of corruption or mismanagement in Pakistan. He hastens to add that such a book would have been banned and burned. With hindsight one might almost consider this as premonitory of the writer's plight after the publication of *The Satanic Verses*:

> All that effort for nothing! Realism can break a writer's heart.
> Fortunately, however, I am only telling a sort of modern fairy-tale, so that's all right; nobody need get upset, or take anything I say too seriously. No drastic action need be taken, either.
> What a relief' (p. 70)

Here Rushdie behaves in the same way as Elizabethan Fools who could question the sovereign's decisions because of their cleverness at making their remarks sound jocular. One may also add that, at the time, Rushdie's distance from Pakistan, the country whose politicians might have felt offended, also contributed to his immunity. The situation changed drastically when a wider community, that of the Muslims, thought it had been insulted by what it called the author's blaspheme.

In *Shame*, the readers are constantly kept alert by this jumping from one narrative position to another. Their place is carefully indicated and

---

Verses, went down 'head first, in the recommended position for babies entering the birth canal...' (p. 4).

controlled by the artist who never forgets that his story is addressed to someone frequently placed in the position of a confidant. The narrator sometimes remarks on his characters as if they were children who have not been up to their parents' expectations:

> I am no less disappointed in my hero than I was; not being the obsessive type, I find it difficult to comprehend his obsession (p. 198).

The readers are supposed to share his concern and sympathize with him. In exchange the narrator caters for the literate tastes of the ones who become his accomplices: addressing himself to people who are used to looking out for the possible meaning of metaphors, he offers some clues, which we must of course take with a pinch of salt, as we do with every other aspect of Salman Rushdie's work. Thus he brings to the readers' attention a chain of representations based on the idea of hanging: Omar was 'ankle-hung' at birth and Raza Hyder's baby died during the process of delivery

> An umbilical cord wound itself around a baby's neck and was transformed into a hangman's noose (in which other nooses are prefigured). (p. 82)

The readers are warned to expect more of the same kind and feel a thrill of recognition when the plot reaches the moment of Iskander Harappa's hanging.

The narrator is bent on entertaining the readers whom he loves to startle with unexpected events, phrases or words: Bariamma, the old woman who looks after the gynaeceum in Raza Hyder's family, is called 'Big Mother' though she is actually quite small. Other characters are given names which turn them into stereotypes: Raza Hyder and Bilquís produce two daughters, Sufiya Zinobia, alias Shame, and Naveed, alias Good News. The daughter of Iskander Harappa, Raza's political rival, is called Arjumand. But she is frequently referred to as the 'virgin Ironpants', an allusion to her fiercely defended virtue. The Cantonment district of the city of Q. is usually called 'Cantt', an appropriate qualification for the abode of the 'Angrez, or British, sahibs' (p. 12). Whole ethnic groups receive particularly apt and striking names such as the 'One Godly' for the Muslims and the 'Stone Washers' for the Hindus. Some of the characters have habits or obsessions which cling to them and tend to connote them systematically: Bilquís, who lost everything when her father's cinema was blown up by Hindu fanatics, cannot help dreading the hot wind which reminds her of the burning blast of the explosion which sent her flying in the street. From that point on, whenever the Loo - a name which can no doubt be taken as a pun - blows, she fears that all her stable environment might be destroyed. The mechanical repetition of the same attitude comes as an absurd and comic source of relief in the novel.

The author does not hesitate to play on words: when Zoroaster discovers Farah's pregnancy, he suddenly finds 'that his empty customs house is too full to accommodate a daughter whose belly [reveals] her adherence to other, unacceptable customs' (p. 52). Rushdie plays on the literal and the figurative sense of some phrases: Old Shakil's three daughters, once they have decided not to see the outside world again, start selling the furniture of the immense house to cover their daily expenses:

> The three mothers of the imminent Omar Khayyam Shakil were using the past, their only capital, as a means of purchasing the future (p. 19).

Salman Rushdie is adept in the art of mimicking some characters' pompous speaking habits: Eduardo Rodrigues, Omar Khayyam's first schoolmaster, always takes himself very seriously and talks in 'capital letters':

> To Succeed in Life... one must be Of the Essence. Yes, make yourself Essential, that's the Ticket... and who is most Indispensable? Why, the fellow who does the Dispensing! I mean of Advice, Diagnosis, Restricted Drugs. Be a Doctor; it is what I have seen in You (p. 49).

So Omar Khayyam's 'vocation' arises out of a pun voiced by his humourless pedagogue who later becomes his rival in love.

Humour helps to defuse the tension in the most serious moments: when it has become obvious that Sufyia Zinobia, Hyder's ferocious daughter who married to Omar Khayyam, can only disgrace the family, they decide to lock her up in the attic (possibly a reference to Charlotte Brontë's other 'mad woman in the attic') where her husband applies on her all the resources of his art:

> Omar Khayyam would go unobserved into that darkened room, that echo of other death-cells, to inject into the tiny body lying on its thin carpet the fluids of nourishment and of unconsciousness...

> The family had to be told... They were all accomplices in the matter of Sufiya Zinobia; and the secret was kept. The 'wrong miracle'... she disappeared from sight. Poof! Like so (p. 237).

The horrid conspiracy of silence that contributes to eliminate from sight a woman because she openly displays the cruelty that others veil under the reason of state is made light of by the end of the paragraph with its dialectal English and onomatopoeic finality which contrast sharply with the rest of the passage.

Hyder's chief religious adviser is called Maulana Dawood, a combination of 'Maulana' (a learned Muslim scholar) and 'Dawood', the name of the translator of the *Koran*. Rushdie turns this character into a stereotype of the religious fanatic. The author also reminds the reader that he is inspired by the old tradition of the *Arabian Nights* with his mention of an adventurous cinema owner called Sindbad. Unfortunately Sindbad's sexual pranks cause him to be butchered on the order of a jealous husband called Raza Hyder.

When the tone becomes too tragic, the author provides comic release as if to encourage the reader never to take problems too seriously or perhaps because, in an absurd world, laughter becomes the essential life force. Rushdie does not hesitate to play with various cultural references which are meant to tease the reader's taste for literary guesswork. The conversational convention and the digressions are deliberately in the style of *Tristram Shandy*. Omar Khayyam, the hero of *Shame* was born in Nishapur like the author of the *Rubaiyat* but he never wrote quatrains. In one of the passages when the author pretends to speak in his own voice, he draws a parallel between himself and the old poet:

> Omar Khayyam's position as a poet is curious. He was never very popular in his antique Persia; and he exists in the West in a translation that is really a complete reworking of his verses, in many cases very different from the spirit (to say nothing of the content) of the original. I, too, am a translated man. I have been borne across. It is generally believed that something is always lost in translation; I cling to the notion - and use, in evidence, the success of Fitzgerald-Khayyam - that something can also be gained. (p. 29)

Apart from the literal sense referring to Rushdie's success in translation, this remark might also refer to the rearranging that has taken place in the process of creation, the 'real' world of Pakistan becoming a fictional universe which is not necessarily less authentic. The translation of Rushdie may also be this uprooting from the East and this process of having to carry across material from another culture which has to be reorganized in order to be accessible to the new public. Salman Rushdie

here evokes the ambiguity which the Italian language shows so well with
its resemblance between *traduttore* (translator) and *traditore* (traitor). Is a
writer like Rushdie a proper interpreter of Pakistan's problems? Has he a
right to speak with authority on the subject? Can he, as a citizen of a
developed country, speak with authority on a nation to which he has only
limited and temporary access? These questions are left unanswered by the
author. Yet they loom large in the practice of many writers with
multicultural backgrounds.

Rushdie delights in setting riddles to the readers and in solving them
for them later on: when Omar Khayyam leaves his home town on the
train that takes him to his medical college, an ice vendor at the station
utters an enigmatic sentence: 'Such is life... one ice block returns to town
and another sets off in the opposite direction' (p. 54). We know that
Omar Khayyam has just bought a block of ice from the vendor to stop the
heat melting 'the marrow out of [his] bones' (p. 54). Yet, up to that point,
we are left in doubt concerning the other block. Then we learn that Farah,
the girl whom Omar was in love with and who had run away with
Rodrigues, their teacher, has just returned to town alone and childless.
The mystery clears when we remember that Farah was nicknamed
'Disaster' or 'the ice block': 'on account of her subzero coldness toward
her many admirers' (p. 48). The author indulges in a similar riddle when
he mentions that the story is set in the fourteenth century, only to add that
he is using the Hegiran calendar, which brings us back to the present
time. The titles of the chapters often play on enigmatic meanings. They
are contrived so as to whet the reader's appetite by giving the impression
that some essential truth will be revealed at the end, a technique
reminiscent of Dickens's in *Bleak House*. A similar effect is achieved
when the narrator anticipates on future events and stops short of
providing all the details. The readers have been given just enough to
renew their interest and to leave them expectant of more adventures to
come.

This alternation of moments of revelation and of suspense places the
readers in the position of voyeurs who wait for the narrator to show them
a reality which is all the more precious since it remains partly veiled. The
narrator himself indulges in this game of seeing inside structures which
are supposed to be hermetic to the outside world. The theme of
voyeurism is already clearly established in *Midnight's Children* where
Doctor Aadam Aziz first catches a glimpse of his beloved through a
holed sheet held by formidable matrons; the ailing lady cannot disclose

her body entirely to a stranger, even if he be a medical practitioner. So Aadam has to comply and ask for the suffering part of the girl's body to be placed near the hole, a sure way of trapping the young doctor in love's snares... In *Shame*, characters indulge in similar voyeuristic activities: Omar Khayyam falls in love with Farah after catching sight of her through a telescopic lens. His voice breaks and his testes suddenly drop into place. Seeing the object of his desire, he instantly passes from childhood to adulthood - or so he says to Farah later on. Rodrigues ponders on the role of doctors and declares:

> What's a doctor after all? - a legitimized voyeur, a stranger whom we permit to poke his fingers and even hands into places where we would not permit most people to insert so much as a finger-tip, who gazes on what we take most trouble to hide; a sitter-at-bedsides, an outsider admitted to our most intimate moments... (p. 49)

This sounds almost like a description of the way Rushdie's narrators behave: they pry into their characters' most private stories and interfere in businesses which these characters - were they true human beings - would rather keep secret. The narrator interprets episodes for the reader. He gives meaning to the chaos of experience and often soothes the anguish of the readers by offering stories which reflect on their own predicament and have a cathartic effect. Yet, in order to do so, the narrator is given full licence to see what remains hidden from most people: his ability to look through the walls of the house where the Shakil sisters have locked themselves up is a good example of this special power. The narrator plays on this supreme privilege when he retains some vital information under the pretext that he has not seen everything: the mystery that subsists concerning Omar's 'true' mother is never solved. If it were, the fantasmatic power of the boy's 'three mothers' would be deflated. Rushdie is such a clever storyteller that he succeeds in keeping the readers' interest constantly alive and in having them accept what would elsewhere appear grossly incredible.

Taking up one of the essential elements of the novel, one could read *Shame* as a story which is unveiled behind a peephole, the narrator keeping the control of the opening or closing of the orifice. The degree of enjoyment is to be measured by the rhythm of this alternate showing and hiding, this *fort-da* which Freud saw as the basis of the child's ability to perceive the world through symbols. The pleasure taken in this activity comes partly from its being prohibited; the narrator of *Shame* shows that, in the Islamic world of the characters, the eyes are the most frequent source of sin: Bariamma presides over a dormitory of women which their husbands can visit at night only once the lights have been turned off - and the narrator adds mischievously that this may be all the more enjoyable to the different partners because it allows for more or less voluntary mistaking of partners... The narrator even pretends that he shares Bariamma's prudish attitude when he alludes to Raza Hyder's call on his wife in the dormitory, a famous event which results in Bilquís's becoming pregnant.

The eyes are one of the first parts of the body to be punished: when chastisement comes at the end of the novel, when Raza is brought back to Nishapur by Omar Khayyam, the old dictator lies sick and naked in his own excreta. The three sisters force him to enter the dumbwaiter which they had built to communicate with the outside world. When he is in, they pull the lever of a mechanism which they had installed for their own self-defence:

> and the ancient spring-releases of Yakoob Balloch worked like a treat, the secret panels sprang back and the eighteen-inch stiletto blades of death drove into Raza's body, cutting him into pieces, their reddened points emerging, among other places, through his *eyeballs* [Italics mine], adam's apple, navel, groin and mouth (p. 282).

A quote from *Grimus* could serve as a definition of Salman Rushdie's fiction which is 'A Dance of Veils In Which Much That Is Wonderful Is Revealed ' (p. 250) - and hidden, one is tempted to add.

Despite the clearly political implications of *Shame*, the writer never lets himself be carried away by ideology in the reductive sense of the word. He insists on art's ability to hold at the same time entirely irreconcilable positions. He wants to be, as the narrator says, referring to Büchner's play, both Danton and Robespierre. *Midnight's Children* attempts to fuse realism and fantasy. In *Shame*, Rushdie explores the possibility of turning fiction into a fruitful dialogue between the two. The end-product is not smoothly rounded off. The author manifests his desire to entertain the reader and to display his virtuosity with words and fantasy. But he never forgets that genuine art always acknowledges its own limits.

Rushdie's discourse belongs to the rhetoric of excess also characteristic of the works of Carpentier, Asturias and García Márquez. Details are plentiful, the fictional world swarms with different characters, scenes and locales which are so many opportunities for the narration to digress, almost for its own sake. The world to be described is too large, too profuse in various colours, smells, emotions and life to be circumscribed by classical rhetoric. One feels that the characters are overflowing from the cauldron in which they have been left simmering with the lid on for too long. Post-colonial discourse has been suppressed, constricted in the strait-jacket of metropolitan speech forms. Once the liberation process starts, it is not easy to put an end to this protean outpouring of voices and peoples. Using forms which have been labelled as magic realism, the post-colonial writer seems to indulge in the same pleasure of excesses as Rabelais. It is no wonder that Bakhtin's notion of 'polyphony' was derived from his study of the author of *Gargantua*, for this work is an example of what happens when literature taps the sources of popular lore and does not let itself be hampered by social taboos. Interestingly, when post-colonial writers seek the liberation of discourse from metropolitan fetters, they frequently resort to Rabelais' example. Perhaps the iconoclastic spirit is given a freer rein because of the international climate prevailing since the 1960s. But, more probably, the silent multitudes of the Third World which were kept silent for too long cannot come to life in an ordered manner and post-colonial writers naturally turn to more baroque artistic models.

E- Magic Realism and the New Literatures

In 'Magic Realism as Post-Colonial Discourse',[1] Stephen Slemon analyzes the concept in terms of a 'dialectical struggle within the culture's language, a dialectic between 'codes of recognition' inherent within the inherited language and those imagined codes - perhaps utopian or future-oriented - that characterize a culture's 'original relations' with the world' (p. 12). His notion of 'imagined codes' is particularly important in that the so-called 'authenticity' or link between writers and their notion of the 'original culture', the 'native' tradition, is deeply influenced by ideological codes prevalent at the period when their sensitivity was formed or at the time when they started writing. Roots and origins are always imaginary, even more so when the ground of inheritance in which these roots are planted has suffered depreciation by comparison with the ruling models usually imported by the colonial or neo-colonial power. These new imagined roots may in turn be used as shallow ideological constructs by despots who exploit the nativist vein: the Duvalier clan in Haiti based their tyranny on some aspects of the Voodoo. Similarly the Negritudinists criticized by Wole Soyinka[2] tapped the sources of Africanity.

---

[1] *Canadian Literature* 116, pp. 9-24.
[2] See 'Who's Afraid of Elesin Oba?' in W. Soyinka, *Art, Dialogue and Outrage*, pp. 62-81.

Slemon's insistence on magic realism being a characteristic of conflicting codes of discourse is particularly fruitful. Perhaps one may question the validity of the term 'magic realism'. But the distinctions which Slemon derives from the term do help to define some of the New Literatures' major features. To Slemon, social relations in post-colonial literatures are thematically expressed in three ways:

> The first involves the representation of a kind of transcendent or transformational regionalism so that the site of the text, though described as familiar and local terms, becomes a metonymy of the post-colonial culture as a whole. The second is the foreshortening of history so that the time scheme of the novel metaphorically contains the long process of colonization and its aftermath. And the third involves the thematic foregrounding of those gaps, absences, and silences produced by the colonial encounter and reflected in the text's disjunctive language of narration (pp. 12-13).

The limited locale of the narration is raised to the status of a world scene. Various readers find some ways of projecting their own experience of life and their own dream landscape on Márquez's Macondo or on Jack Hodgins' recreation of Vancouver Island. Wilson Harris's *Palace of the Peacock*, despite its very particular style and language, brings together memories of the Amerindian past, the conquest and the modern exploitation of workers by large land-owners in Guyana, a limited stage which opens out onto wider concepts of the silent heritage and the resurrection of suppressed fragments of meaning in man's experience. Harris provides a very good example of Slemon's third category, with his concern for giving 'voice' to the silences, the absences in a country's past and tradition.

Yet a survey of the applicability of Slemon's use of the term 'magic realism' leads one to put together so many different types of novels that one may wonder whether the term still retains value as a tool for making distinctions. Slemon argues that it can 'provide a matrix for differing works differing widely in genre' and allow for a widely comparative method resting on a sounder basis. Basically it helps to distinguish between 'classical metropolitan literature' (itself a dubious category, because of all the various types it includes) and post-colonial literature, which, in Slemon's article, is raised to the pinnacle. In a clever twist, Slemon argues that perhaps the New Literatures provide an opportunity to give new definitions to old terms which have been for too long controlled by the metropolises. Perhaps Slemon's argument is also influenced by the prevalent climate among a group of Australian, New Zealand and Canadian academics, who are emerging as an impressive body of scholars in a new field after fighting a battle, which has raged for several decades, to gain recognition for unjustly neglected texts. Perhaps the author of this argument is also guilty of adhering to the same ideological premises, which, when placed in their historical context in a few decades, will appear sadly outdated.

The term 'magic realism' is not often used in relation to the English-speaking world, except by such critics as Jeanne Delbaere.[1] Still the term has had particular appeal to some Canadian academics and artists. For Geoff Hancock in his article 'Magic Realism, or, the Future of Fiction',[2] Canadian writers have followed after painters who attempted to juxtapose real forms and unlikely places. The presence of a strange object suddenly emerging from a familiar background or the flooding of an object in an extremely clear light suddenly adds new dimensions to the picture. Hancock sees this technique as a way of breaking the conventionality of traditional nineteenth-century fiction. Yet he draws a distinction between magic realism and surrealism or fantasy writing. For him, the former is far superior to the other two; he objects to surrealism using a linear association of ideas which dispenses with logic and to fantasy's excessive dependence on the supernatural and the absurd. For him, 'magic realists place their extraordinary feats and mysterious characters in an ordinary place, and the magic occurs from the sparks generated between the possibilities of language and the limitations of physical nature' (p. 5). It seems that, for Hancock, reality is something given *a priori* and language simply mirrors or modifies it. Yet there is no such thing as objective reality. What we know of it is always perceived and filtered through the sensitivity of a viewer; it is already fashioned by the subject's education, ideological presuppositions and by the time and place where he/she lives. Therefore Hancock's implicit conception is an oversimplification of the issue. In fiction, there is no artistic reality which is not already fashioned by a particular language as the vehicle of a specific culture. But perhaps Hancock is more interested in 'magic realism''s potential for giving added value to the Canadian writers he likes. They define themselves as different from the 'Great' British tradition identified with conventionality and seek for an alternative model in Latin American writers such as García Márquez. Canadian culture also rebelled against the domination of a metropolitan power. Hancock probably admires Latin American novelists because they provide an alternative American culture to the other imperialistic superpower to the south. Hancock's definition of magic realism therefore has nationalistic undertones which make him

---

[1] In Weisgerber, pp. 154-179.
[2] *Canadian Fiction Magazine* 24/25, 1977, pp. 4-6.

blind to the ambiguities of the term (ambiguities which also exist in common critical responses to that so-called school).

The term 'magic realism' applies best to García Márquez, who combines social concern and a free use of language. According to our more restrictive definition of the term, the magic realist aims at a basis of mimetic illusion while destroying it regularly with a strange treatment of time, space, characters, or what many people (in the Western world, at least) take as the basic rules of the physical world.[1] Magic realists usually have a definite idea of their social role and pose political problems, which beset the (post-colonial) country described.

One may wonder whether it is not preferable to abandon the term 'magic realism' altogether. An alternative is to restrict it severely in order to differenciate it from 'the fantastic', its next of kin. It may be appropriate to reserve the label to those texts that share strong similarities with García Márquez's *One Hundred Years of Solitude* and Rushdie's *Midnight's Children* or *Shame*. These novels, which have a strong realistic basis, depict large communities in the process of making their own history in the face of strong imperialistic resistance. The main characters are larger than life and veer towards the allegory. But this 'serious' concern is evoked in problematic terms which involve mock heroism as well as heroism. 'Magic realists' are clearly sophisticated in the use they make of metafiction, intertextual references, an interweaving of the 'realistic' and 'fantastic' modes but also of an implicit questioning of the polarity on which such terms are based. This restrictive definition excludes texts such as most of Borges' and Cortázar's works which do not have this broad allegorical framework and concern limited environments and a relatively small number of characters and are best fitted within the category of the fantastic. Magic realists create multitudes and delight in profusion and variety. They willingly use the grotesque and the picaresque. Their purpose is not that of intellectual theorizing, although their particular approach of reality contains an implicit questioning of simplistic conceptions of the relationship between art and language.

After so many quarrels concerning definitions, it may be wise to remember that even more sharply focussed generic terms than 'magic realism' are to be envisaged in their specific context. It would be intellectually satisfying if such categories could have a universal and unvarying value. But any serious examination forces one to admit that such is not the case. In *Qu'est-ce qu'un genre littéraire?*, Jean-Marie

---

[1] This, of course, depends very much on the cultural references of the viewer or reader.

Schaeffer argues that one cannot conceive of literature as a super-organism whose organs could be the different genres. A work of art can and does belong to several genres at the same time. Any classification depends on an arbitrary sense of ordering whose logic is to be found mainly in the goals which the classifier seeks to reach. Todorov's interest in the fantastic at the end of the sixties is not foreign to the questioning concerning the intellectual and material preconceptions of the 'affluent society' which led to the various 'student uprisings' in the years around 1968.

The different terms devised by Carpentier and Asturias were part of a general movement towards the redefinition of the cultural relationships between Europe and its former colonies, not to mention the often conflictual links between Latin America and its giant northern neighbour. It cannot be separated from the Third-World ideology prevalent in intellectual circles at the time. Because of its anchoring in First-World criticism, it is tainted by the 'cosmopolitan' spirit denounced by Timothy Brennan in *Salman Rushdie and the Third World*. Its success at the time may be linked with the Western fashion for alternative 'minority' societies, liberation heroes of the Che Guevara type and ecology.

The term 'magic realism' has many acceptations, in fact so many that various authors include a spectrum of radically different works under a name whose mere evocation has at times 'magic' value too. This characteristic may indicate that its validity may not be purely generic but may have other more commercial connotations which have to do with the desirability of certain literary labels at particular moments in the history of publishing.

The 'boom' was made saleable to European readers because they had become aware of the limits of a merely Eurocentric conception of literature. The traumas of decolonisation and the intellectual debates surrounding this troubled period led many people to re-examine their vision of the 'Third World'. Thus such strikingly innovative novels as those of Carpentier, Asturias and García Márquez found a receptive audience. Their success had been prepared by the personal links these different writers had with the publishing circles of Barcelona and Paris.

At present, because Europe is going through a radical questioning of its own identity, writers expressing themselves in this mode do not appear to generate so much interest on the old continent. And yet, here and there, on the 'margins',[1] in Canada, in the West Indies or in Belgium, 'magic realism' is represented. Weisgerber argues that this presence outside the main centres of 'culture' can be accounted for by the

---

[1] The term 'margin' is not used here in a derogatory sense. On the contrary...

'margins'' search for their own roots and identity. Through 'marginal' modes of expression, writers are rediscovering those myths which might help them to transcend their marginal position.

Besides the polarities which separate the colonizer and the colonized, the metropolitan and the indigenous artist, a number of post-colonial writers are developing aesthetic theories based on certain aspects sometimes related to 'magic realism' in order to define their hybrid cultures. These are to be found especially in the English-speaking and French-speaking world and constitute a theoretical basis for a practise of literature which differs from the old imperialistic binary opposition between 'them' and 'us'. These literatures are deliberately cross-cultural and practise what is called *métissage* in the French West Indies.

With their different sensibilities, Edouard Glissant and Wilson Harris both attempt to go beyond the post-colonial division so often stigmatized by outside observers and sometimes implicitly adopted by artists such as L.S. Senghor. The resolution of the polarity involves an exploration of the concept of hybridity discussed by Homi K. Bhabha in relation to the apparent opposition between theory and politics:

> The challenge lies in opening up a space that can accept and regulate the differential structure of the moment of intervention without rushing to produce a unity of the social antagonism or contradiction.... When I talk of *negotiation* rather than of *negation*, it is to convey a temporality that makes it possible to conceive of the articulation of antagonistic or contradictory elements: a dialectic without the emergence of a teleological or transcendent History.... In such a discursive temporality, the event of theory becomes the *negotiation* of contradictory and antagonistic instances that open up hybrid sites and objectives of struggle, and destroy those negative polarities between knowledge and its object, and between theory and practical-political reason.[1]

The term 'hybridity' has been questioned by some critics who feel that it contains definitely negative connotations and smacks too much of the half-caste or mongrel syndrome. It need not be so however if one uses 'hybrid' in the dynamic sense of a representation which goes beyond the initial polarity of its component elements. While one may understand the reservations of intellectuals originating in countries where people 'of mixed blood' were traditionally sneered at by both the native and the white population, the term 'hybrid' still contains enough positive potential to be used as description of a major post-colonial characteristic.

---

[1] Homi K. Bhabha, *The Location of Culture*, p. 25.

IV - TOWARDS HYBRID AESTHETICS

A- Definitions of 'Culture':

In order to avoid limiting hybridity to sterile 'racial' considerations, it needs to be placed firmly in its cultural context. Cultures and civilisations have often been taken as synonyms. For E.B. Tylor in *Primitive Culture*, words such as 'culture' or 'civilization' refer to the body of sciences, arts, beliefs, moral principles, laws, customs, in short all the habits and faculties acquired by human beings as part of their social life. Tylor draws a distinction between three stages in the evolution of societies: the savage, the barbarian and the civilised. He thus reintroduces a hierarchy between 'civilisation', which is reserved for the highest point on his evolutionary scale, and 'culture', which can apply to the so-called 'primitive'. This eminently questionable hierarchy has been queried by anthropologists such as Sapir who distinguishes between 'authentic' and 'spurious' cultures, categories which one also has difficulty accepting.

In a post-colonial context, does genuine multiculturalism, with no one culture dominating the other, exist? Is there such a thing as a hard core of culture which the individual will refuse to give up and which constitutes the limit of the multicultural play in which he/she frequently indulges?

The word 'acculturation' has been in common use since the 1880s especially in North American anthropological literature. This term refers to the phenomena resulting from the contacts between several civilisations: elements are borrowed from other sources and integrated into the original culture.

Nineteenth-century theorists such as Gobineau were fascinated by the notion of race which has since proved so dangerous. In *Essai sur l'inégalité des races humaines* (1853-55), Gobineau mythified the notion of original purity: the Aryans, the 'noblest race', were supposed to have migrated from Central Asia and become 'bastardized' during their progression westwards through mating with yellow and black people. The mixture of different 'bloods' was supposed to have made the 'best' regress to the stage at which the 'worst races' were. Gobineau's time corresponded to the imperialistic and chauvinistic phase of colonial history (between 1880 and the turn of the century) which saw the generalization of a belief in the scientific validity of such racial distinctions. From that point on it was easy to assimilate the biological and the cultural and to set up a hierarchy of races and cultures. It thus became the 'duty' of the 'superior' race to bring light to the darker races, hence the notion of the white man's burden, popularized by Rudyard Kipling, which associated this racist premise and a good measure of paternalism. Later on the criterion used to reassert the supposed superiority of Western cultures was the more advanced state of its technological and scientific knowledge. What Gobineau saw as the 'natural' hierarchy of races with white Europeans at the top and blacks at the bottom could not be questioned or reversed by positive action. These theories have since served to justify tyranny, discrimination and genocides in many parts of the world. We now know that the concept of race is purely ideological and a pretext to exclude so-called 'inferior' peoples. Since then differences between groups of population have been attributed to cultural factors. Such a vision of society is radically different from any ideology of cultural purity or authenticity. It is based on dynamic interchange, for there is no culture without history and without its own counter-culture(s).

In Europe, questions concerning multiculturalism or cross-culturalism have been increasingly discussed since immigration from the Third-World to the former metropolises has become a major political issue. This problem has been abundantly debated in the USA.[1] In his study entitled *L'Interculturel*, Claude Clanet defines culture as this network of meaningful representations characteristic of a group or of a sub-group which are considered as values et produce rules and norms which the said group endeavours to transmit and through which it distinguishes itself from neighbouring groups.[2]

'Interculturality' is thus defined as this complex of processes - psychic, relational,... institutional - generated by the interaction of cultures within the framework of mutual exchanges and with a view to preserving the relative cultural identity of the partners in this relation.

Cross-culturalism or multiculturalism becomes relevant when, in an individual or in a given group, several systems of reference cohabit. And this is frequently encountered in societies affected by the processes of conquest or colonisation. But this question did not emerge only with nineteenth-century imperialism. Apart from very few exceptions, each culture has always been enriched by exchanges with the outside world.

---

[1] See in particular 'White Terror and Oppositional Agency: towards a Critical Multiculturalism' in David Theo Goldberg, ed., *Multiculturalism: a Critical Reader*.

[2] Définition de la culture proposée par Claude Clanet (*L'Interculturel*): 'ensemble de significations prépondérantes propres à un groupe ou à un sous-groupe qui apparaissent comme valeurs et donnent naissance à des règles et à des normes que le groupe s'efforce de transmettre et par lesquelles il se différencie de ses groupes voisins.' (pp. 15-16).

Roman culture was based on its Latin references with a strong admixture of Greek influences. Then, in its distant provinces, borrowings from the Celts and Germans led to various processes of hybridization.

Needless to say, very few cultures remained 'pure' for a prolonged period, except perhaps in the case of remote Amazonian or New Guinea forest dwellers. And, even then, these populations generally saw their values change as they interacted with other neighbouring social groups.

Unlike what some early anthropologists nostalgic of a mythic idea of cultural 'purity' would have us believe, most cultures have been cross-fertilized by others. The richest and most complex have generally been those which have been able to synthesize elements imported from outside. As Claude Lévi-Strauss wrote, 'the chance that a culture has to put together this complex totality of inventions of all orders which we call a civilization is a function of the number of the cultures with which it participates in the elaboration - most often involuntary - of a common strategy'.[1] He goes on to add that 'the exclusive fatality, the unique fault which can affect a human group and prevent it from completely fulfilling its nature, is to be alone'.[2] For Lévi-Strauss, the preservation of this diversity is necessary throughout the world, for it conditions the permanent process of cross-fertilization generated by exchanges. This plurality is threatened by the hegemonic propensity of some dominating cultures which tend to crush others. Even if, to follow McLuhan's analysis, the creation of a 'global village' is a feature of contemporary society, it remains desirable to preserve diversity which is the very essence of life. Forms of art such as the theatre practised by Peter Brook, who directed a stage adaptation of the *Mahabharata*, are models of this new drama enacted by actors originating from several continents, each contributing his/her own sensibility to the interpretation of the work.

The adoption of multiculturalism requires the questioning of dominating ideologies and may in turn lead to generalized relativism and its extreme form which involves the loss of any permanent ruling code and system of reference. Such a recomposition of the sytem of values is positive when it leads people or whole groups to abandon their ethnocentrism and endeavour to understand how different populations

---

[1] *Structural Anthropology*, Vol. II, p. 355. 'La chance qu'a une culture de totaliser cet ensemble complexe d'inventions de tous ordres que nous appelons une civilisation est fonction du nombre et de la diversité des cultures avec lesquelles elle participe à l'élaboration — le plus souvent involontaire — d'une commune stratégie' (*Anthropologie Structurale Deux*, p. 414).
[2] *Structural Anthropology*, Vol. II, p. 356. 'L'exclusive fatalité, l'unique tare qui puissent affliger un groupe humain et l'empêcher de réaliser pleinement sa nature, c'est d'être seul' (p. 415).

react without necessarily condemning them because they behave in unexpected ways. But when the gap widens and individuals in turn lose the sense of a stable axis around which their own system of values revolves, there are risks of disruption and conflict.

One must also be wary of the uses to which the term 'multiculturalism' is sometimes submitted. In New Zealand, it was favoured in official government terminology to refer to a form of unspoken assimilation. It looked as though the only 'ethnic' people were the Maori, while the Pakeha represented 'normality'. The original inhabitants of the country ran the risk of becoming folkloric creatures, which led them to advocate biculturalism, a practice whose advantage was to give equal status to the two communities, at least in theory. There are infinite variations between the two extremes of assimilation and separation leading to the formation of physical and/or cultural ghettoes. Although this may be an almost impossible task, we use the term 'multicultural' in the creative sense of the genuine interaction between several cultural forms considered equally worthy of being preserved, developed and respected as ways of structuring social relations.

B- *Post-colonial Literatures and Hybridization*

In the New Literatures in particular, popular cultures have played a major role in the re-definition of 'culture'. This phenomenon echoes the processes evoked by Mikhail Bakhtin when he commented on the 'dialogism' at work in Rabelais. In the Caribbean, E.K. Brathwaite's experience,[1] with the introduction of the rhythms of jazz and calypso into poetry, forms part of a similar endeavour. George Lamming's integration of West Indian peasant culture into the mainstream of fiction also shows his desire to repossess a native heritage as opposed to the overwhelming prestige of the Anglo-classic culture inculcated by the school institution in the Caribbean until the 1960s. Though apparently concerned with recovering peasant roots, such a vein of inspiration cannot be confused with European 'regionalist' fiction which is often nostalgic, escapist and politically conservative. For Lamming and Brathwaite, writers cannot merely opt for an alternative culture; they practise a 'dialogue' between the colonial culture and those forms which have been salvaged from the old slave tradition. Such a dialogue has often involved a privileging of

---

[1] See E.K. Brathwaite's poems included in his volume *The Arrivants*. See also his theorization of 'nation language' in *History of the Voice: the Development of Nation Language in Anglophone Caribbean Poetry*.

orality, not merely as a model to be reproduced but as a means of expression which could be integrated into literature.

One of the most current approaches has been the elaboration of a hybrid genre on the borderline between the novel and the folktale. In *The Palm Wine Drinkard*, the Nigerian Amos Tutuola created a fantasy world where ghosts and city dwellers live side by side. Ben Okri, the author of *The Famished Road*, followed in the footsteps of the author of *The Palm Wine Drinkard* and in those of Wole Soyinka.

When it is practised by writers from formerly colonized countries, multiculturalism asserts a model of national identity different from that imposed by the 'dominant culture'. In this sense the strategies of multiculturalism sometimes coincide with those of nationalism. They are always complex, paradoxical and hybrid. They integrate diverse elements and partly synthesize them. These sometimes deliberately confrontational positions are not always devoid of ambiguities. Ngugi's recent novels (*Devil on the Cross* and *Matigari*), though apparently 'revolutionary' in a Fanonian sense, take up rhetorical images inspired directly from the Bible. Whether they follow nationalistic objectives or whether, like Wilson Harris, they search for this common heirloom of humanity, post-colonial writers cannot evade facing the complexities of a modern world whose cultures are all engaged in complex interaction.

Most post-colonial cultures are now the result of hybridization. The New Literatures show that it is difficult and even dangerous to locate artists too systematically within one environment. In *Orientalism*, Said raises this point when he writes:

> Can one divide human reality, as indeed human reality seems to be genuinely divided, into clearly different cultures, histories, traditions, societies, races, and survive the consequences humanly?.... When one uses categories like Oriental and Western as both the starting and the end points of analysis, research, public policy... the result is usually to polarize the distinction - the Oriental becomes more Oriental, the Western more Western...[1]

A lucid examination of the New Literatures shows that it is impossible to classify influences and traits as strictly referring to one culture or another. Any representation is always the result of unstable, imperfect mergers whose validity stems from their transformational potential rather than from any spurious sense of 'purity' which Said stigmatizes when he evokes excessive reactions to what had become a largely imaginary enemy in the post-colonial period. He talks of these people obsessed with 'Africanizing the Africans, Orientalizing the Oriental, Westernizing the

---

[1] *Orientalism*, pp. 45-46.

Western'.[1] Their desire to find solutions in religious absolutes where the political and the religious will become one are doomed to failure because they ignore the fundamentally metamorphic nature of cultures in the contemporary world of mass media and satellite communication. Said stresses the fact that post-colonial literatures are 'hybrid and encumbered, or entangled with a lot of what used to be regarded as extraneous elements'.[2] And these features result from the historical and political reality of the countries in which the writers are deeply involved.

In a provocative article entitled 'Post-modernism and Post-colonialism',[3] Simon During defines post-modernism as a love of the 'simulacrum'. 'The post-modern society is dominated by replication.... pastiche replaces expressivism and realism as the dominant mode of cultural production' (p. 367). For During, post-modern society, which in his mind can be identified as Western society (including the old and the neo-imperialists) has become so centred that it has ceased to realize it, thus leaving no place for emergent post-colonial identities. Post-colonials speak through the medium of representations which have been imposed on them as universals and yet remain somehow strange. They 'hear themselves speak', thus implicitly distancing themselves - but not enough - from these signifiers given to them as absolutes. Unlike other critics, Simon During insists on the basic diversity of the post-colonial experience: 'Obviously New Zealand post-colonialism is not the same as Australian post-colonialism, is not the same as Nigerian, is not the same as Indian and so on' (p. 369). His article has the merit of showing that the fight for genuine originality cannot be wholly separated from the tendency on the part of many writers to be absorbed in what he calls the post-modern condition, a dangerous universalizing concept which constitutes a new form of essentialization of culture.

Post-colonial writers pursue their art through the adoption of hybrid and often problematic forms. In Africa, such syntheses were the result of missionary education and of urbanization. In the Anglophone parts of the continent, because of the colonialists' emphasis on indirect rule and the transposition of a British-type class-system, the 'old gods' remained alive and influential. Consequently, with the first generation of African university graduates, a spate of written literature soon emerged, with deep roots in the African past and cultures. In Francophone Africa, on the contrary, there was no such radical class-separation; if a young person

---

[1] Said, 'Figures, Configurations, Transfigurations' in Anna Rutherford, ed., *From Commonwealth to Post-colonial*, p. 11.

[2] *Ibid*, p. 15.

[3] In *Landfall* 155 (Sept. 1985), pp. 366-80.

could successfully pass all the many hurdles of the highly competitive French educational system, he or she was considered (almost) like other French people - with the difference that he or she was led to believe that 'our ancestors are the Gauls'. These particular conditions account for the rise of the Negritude movement, with all its negative 'Noble Savage' aspects exemplified by some of L.S. Senghor's poems, which describe the world in terms of a duality between black and white, body and *logos*. Though the *métissage* theme does temper the excesses of such a view, this dichotomy remains based on classic colonial stereotypes of the black man who is good at dancing and music, a marvellous sportsman, a generally happy and smiling fellow, but not really the equal of the white man in more intellectual matters. Soyinka was prompt to denounce some of these excesses.[1] But the rift between contemporary African cultures remains deep, because, besides the extreme original diversity of social and linguistic practices in this immense continent, one cannot wholly erase the various syntheses which resulted from radically different colonial organizations. If anything - this is a paradox, when one thinks of all the destructive aspects of the process - colonization and the levelling effect of world technology have done more than any other factor to bring the educated layers of the population closer together culturally speaking. Such ideologies as Pan-Africanism, Marxism - and its Fanonian version in particular - and the united stance against apartheid have strengthened this sense of belonging to one single continent with more common interests than rivalries. All these have become determining factors in the building of rich literary syntheses.

The 'White [euphemistically referred to as 'Old'] Commonwealth', with the addition of South Africa, is a specific case; it is made up of Canada, Australia and New Zealand, three areas with a population of predominantly European origins (though the influence of the Caribbean or Asian elements has become increasingly important in Canada, while Australia has begun to acknowledge the cultural impact of the Asian components of its population).

Among this group of nations, Canada has probably paved the way for a synthesis arising out of confrontation, in this case that of the Francophone Québecois and Acadiens v. the majority of Anglophone people. So far there has been more confrontation than synthesis, despite attempts by different enlightened writers to overcome this rift. For all its limitations, Hugh MacLennan's *Two Solitudes* (1945) may be a first step towards acknowledgement of a dual heritage. But a more interesting form

---

[1] See, in particular, 'Ideology and the Social Vision' in Soyinka, *Myth, Literature and the African World*.

of imaginary synthesis, that of the European and the Métis, is to be found in Margaret Laurence's *The Diviners* and *A Bird in the House*. Much literature in the 'Old Commonwealth' has been concerned with exploring the fragile umbilical chord still linking the colonials with the 'Mother-country'. In recent decades, liberal guilt towards the fate reserved for the native populations, which were pushed aside in the process of colonization - not to mention the genocide of the Tasmanians and the cultural and physical disasters that have affected the Australian Aborigines - has led a number of novelists to re-examine decisive moments in the white settlement of their countries. These have attempted to revise history and sought to redress in terms of fictional representation some of the wrongs inflicted by their ancestors. Quite naturally, this has led to a rejuvenation of the genre of the historical novel or to the recreation of an archetypal world where the drama of conquest and oppression are re-played in a more distanced way, as we see in the novels of J.M. Coetzee.

When the conquered people finally summed up enough courage to speak and write about their experiences openly, they aimed at giving their own version of what happened to their people. This does not mean that they 'reclaimed their past', as some over-simplifications would lead us to believe. This cannot be done. But at least they sought to re-possess it in imaginative terms, to articulate the trauma of conquest and deprivation so that at least that part of their collective memory be not confiscated entirely. They reclaimed the tragic history as their own, in their own terms, and not through stereotyped representations vehicled by colonial propaganda. But when they chose to do so in the language of the colonizer, they knew the risks they were taking, in terms of their initial readership. Using a language is never completely innocent because the linguistic fabric and the organization of the world it carries with it determine the way the experience is perceived. Meanwhile, their 'white' education had opened up their outlook to foreign models, which, in turn, also became part of themselves.

All these factors have contributed to a diverse, but definitely 'post-colonial' attitude to literature - and to fiction in particular. The urgent need to build imaginary syntheses, which is inherent in any artistic activity, has taken on particular forms and importance in the New Literatures. Language can less than elsewhere be taken for granted. A particular urgency in dismantling stereotypes as part of the national effort towards self-definition has made the artistic enterprise more of a challenge than elsewhere. And, quite naturally, the writers have tended to turn towards variations of the realistic tradition to build their own syntheses. What they have achieved cannot leave the European or North American reader indifferent. The trauma of cultures dismantled and reconstituted, though fragmentarily at first, may well be what the 'First World' is about to experience, torn as it is by a radical re-appraisal of its values. The present debates about multiculturalism are no longer limited to post-colonial societies. Yet the cultural establishment has not yet really taken stock of this. After centuries of the old world influencing the new, we may well be in the initial stages of a movement in reverse. This makes the examination of the post-colonial experience more urgent, even for people who believe they can ignore it.

In the early stages of the New Literatures and because the new nations wished to build their own sense of identity, every effort was made to give new value to the old traditions, which had sometimes been almost erased by the colonizers. In the case of the Caribbean, where massive transplantation of population had made it difficult to even define which old traditions should be resurrected, the problem was still more dramatic. The new leaders laid the emphasis on what remained of the African and Indian past. But this search for 'authenticity' too often led critics to ignore that part of the cultural heritage which came from the 'old continent'. It may be a sign of the times that writers in the New Literatures are now confident enough to acknowledge all the diverse components of their inspiration.

A good example of this new awareness is to be found in the special link between Salman Rushdie and Günter Grass. *The Tin Drum*, no doubt a model for Rushdie when he wrote *Midnight's Children*, has been described as a piece of magic realism. Rushdie wrote a very interesting introduction to the English translation of Günter Grass's *On Writing and Politics*. After acknowledging the influence of Buñuel, Godard, Wajda, Welles, Bergman, Kurosawa, Bob Dylan, Mick Jagger, Marcuse, 'Marxengels', Borges, Ted Hughes and Ionesco (a rather long display of name dropping!), Rushdie stresses the importance of what he calls the 'literature of migration' in the twentieth century. For him, 'a full migrant suffers, traditionally, a triple disruption: he loses his place, he enters into an alien language, and he finds himself surrounded by beings whose social behaviour and code is very unlike and sometimes even offensive to his own' (p. ix). Rushdies sees Grass as something of a migrant because he came from a Kashubian background, which means a certain dialect and specific cultural traditions. Grass also had to migrate linguistically because he had to make a conscious effort to grow out of the 'Nazi-infected' language of his youth to fashion a rejuvenated idiom which could again serve in a meaningful and creative way. Grass had to move into a new country after the defeat of Hitler's armies. After such an experience, a writer can no longer take reality for granted. Like the artists in the New Literatures, Grass understood the problematic nature of reality and had to 'enter the process of making it', as Rushdie puts it (p. xii). Grass's position and that of the artists in the New Literatures may be a prefiguration of our human condition in a world where ideologies, concepts of identity and even nationhood are becoming far less clear-cut than they were twenty years ago. With his incredible optimism, Rushdie may be offering his own utopian version of the new cosmopolitan man.

Writers such as Salman Rushdie or Patrick Chamoiseau, the Martinican author of the novel *Texaco*, seem to indulge in a playful combination of different influences and reader-expectations. Both associate classical novelistic narration with adaptations of the oral tale. The effect is that the voices speaking through the text are multiplied so as to give the illusion that one is listening to a whole community whose many stories are collected in the mouth of a single storyteller.

One cannot seriously believe that either Rushdie or Chamoiseau is unaware of the transformations that traditional oral narration have undergone in the process. The conditions of enunciation are fundamentally different in writing. Tellers of tales are no longer physically surrounded by groups of avid listeners ready to respond to certain passages of the story. They cannot supplement their speech with attitudes or gestures which serve to stress certain key moments or to verify that attention is not flagging.

The nature of the audience has also been radically modified. Rushdie and Chamoiseau cannot frankly believe that they are addressing themselves to a traditional (often uneducated audience). What then do they recreate in terms of literary performance? Rather than reproduce conditions of enunciation which have changed, they insert a semblance of multiple voices by leaving the story to be told by different members of the community.

Moreover, because the reader's expectations cannot be taken for granted, because the references shared between writer and reader are problematic, because the reader frequently belongs to a culture foreign to the cultural references of the oral tales contained in the text, the writer is tempted to be more didactic, to flatter the reader's taste or to titillate him/her with details or attitudes foreign to the original culture's code of behaviour.

Both Rushdie and Chamoiseau create characters who refer to several codes of behaviour, basically one which belongs to a traditional culture and another one which is shared by most modern Western readers. Can these writers be said to be truly multicultural in the sense that these different cultural references are blended? Or, on the contrary, does one code impinge on the other?

In a given culture, a code is a set of - often unwritten - precepts to which people refer for the smooth functioning of their social lives. When Rushdie or other similar writers play the game of cultural relativism, juxtaposing fragments from different cultures as though they were simply representations which could be re-shuffled freely, they may encounter violent reactions from people who feel threatened in their most basic beliefs. The responses are even more violent when the foundations of these cultures are shaky because they have been threatened by colonialism or because the world is changing too fast for people to adapt.

The so-called Rushdie affair is an example of the limits of cultural relativity. The freedom of expression remains a basic ideal to be defended unreservedly. But just as some very weak patients are not ready to hear the truth about their illness, some people cannot bear to see all their values parodied because they are not quite sure that they have anything firm to hold on to.

A clear example of this is provided by the absence of reaction - even on the part of integrist Christian minorities - when the Canadian novelist Timothy Findley parodied Noah's adventures and represented Yahweh as a rather wheezy, shabbily dressed figure who sucks lozenges in *Not Wanted on the Voyage* (1984). Here the readers are obviously American or European and do not feel threatened in the basic pillars of their culture. Some critics have argued that Salman Rushdie may have misjudged the potentially explosive value of *The Satanic Verses* for people who, because they perceive themselves as a vulnerable community in their own sub-continent, feel seriously affected by the parodies contained in the book. This applies even more to the Muslim minorities in Britain - who, had they read the book properly, would have realized that it is a defence of their humanity.

Why has the term 'magic realism' - independently from its vague definition - enjoyed such success among sophisticated international readers? More than a question of fashion, which can be exploited by publishers for only a limited number of years, this new genre may well have provided a new mode of expression whose potential has not been fully explored. The lasting popularity of a new genre usually corresponds to a specific type of readers' expectations. The rise of a transnational public for major works by creators from the former colonies reflects a change in tastes. One may suspect that part of the interest possibly stems from a taste for exoticism on the part of European or North American readers. But, far from flattering this tendency, such creators as Wole Soyinka, Salman Rushdie and Wilson Harris plunge their audience into a complex world where the marvellous exists side by side with horror, where clichés are exposed and more questions are raised than answered.

The popularity of the New Literatures and of new genres such as magic realism may well appear as the latest stage in a series of radical changes in human perception of the universe over the last 150 years. Since the second half of the nineteenth century, several epistemological revolutions have taken place. The probing of unconscious desires found in the works of Virginia Woolf, in Henry James and also in Conrad corresponded to an age in which Freud's discoveries had proved that there were many different layers of reality beneath the visible surface. Ferdinand De Saussure's linguistic exploration of the radical break between the signifier and the signified made James Joyce's parodic constructions possible. Since then the experiments of García Márquez, Amos Tutuola, Wilson Harris, Salman Rushdie and Ben Okri have shown the revolutionary potential of the multicultural imagination and the importance of a re-evaluation of storytelling, a welcome change after the narcissistic introspective excesses of some of their predecessors. But, unlike the makers of 'popular' fiction who tend to use the recipes and clichés of social stereotypes or situations, post-colonial novelists people their works with a profusion of diverse characters whose lives coincide with decisive historical moments in their societies. For many of them, playfulness and fantasy serve to deflate the seriousness of their purpose. But one cannot confuse their fiction with fairy tales. Even when their implied readers are children - such is the case of Rushdie's *Haroun and the Sea of Stories*[1] - only sophisticated adults can make full sense of the stories.

Most of these writers have been 'translated', as Rushdie says, using the term in its etymological sense of 'transferred', 'carried over' from one culture to another. In *Salman Rushdie and the Third World*, Timothy Brennan argues that the success of writers he calls 'cosmopolitan' stems from the fact that they mould their local cultures into Europe's images of them. 'Propelled and defined by media and market' (p. 33), they supposedly provide exoticism in the negative Orientalist sense developed by Edward Said. For Brennan, they form 'a creative community,

---

[1] I have commented on this in my essay ''The Gardener of Stories': Salman Rushdie's *Haroun and the Sea of Stories*', *Journal of Commonwealth Literature*, XXIX, 1, 1993.

international in scope, that the publishing industries have actually unified in the minds of the Western public' (p. 35). This type of argument is based on a refusal to acknowledge the ambiguities of the new international culture being born, not only to flatter the exotic taste of 'First-World' readers, but also to take stock of the general recomposition of cultures in most former European or North American metropolises.

The American 'melting-pot' cliché is now exposed for what it always was, a cover-up for juxtaposed ghettos. The world of culture may be in the process of achieving what will be a much slower process in the rest of society, the formation of a community wide open to all sorts of influences and plastic enough to develop instead of merely absorbing the new into the old. Brennan's analysis is inspired by a brand of Third-World rhetoric which suspects the active intervention of First-World imperialism whenever writers from the New Literatures gain rapid success in the media. This may be truer in North America than in Europe where the old colonial centres are increasingly aware of their weaknesses. In North America, the distribution of books and their promotion in the media is concentrated - more than in some European countries such as France - in the hands of capitalistic empires whose logic is that of supply and demand and has little to do with literary quality, unless it happens to bring back financial returns. Fortunately courageous small (and not so small) publishers and discerning editors and critics exist the world over and their enthusiasm, added to their influence in key reviewing newspapers, in cultural programmes and in official funding institutions can do much to break the monopoly of levelling mediocrity.

There may be a threat of our (far from complete) 'global village' being fashioned by CNN or the main broadcasting and publishing networks. Still there remains enough vitality in writers from the New Literatures to resist the sirens of the international media and strike back at the centres when they prove hegemonic. Eighteenth-century Europe saw the creation of a European culture, at least among the moneyed classes. We may well witness the birth of a new world culture in which the emphasis is laid not so much on synthesis but on creative diversity and the refusal of cultural barriers.

The breakdown of the colonial empires and of the East block have led to the destructive resurgence of forms of nationalism based on the finding of scapegoats and the exclusion of anybody considered as different. Some nations in the Islamic world are tempted to replace the flawed values offered by the West by 'pure' ethical principles supposedly provided by the local tradition. To a lesser degree, the forces of intolerance are also at work through the different European 'National Fronts' or through some religious sects in Europe and America. In a fast-changing world, these new-found certainties are likely to become irrelevant as people discover how tyrannically imposed stability can easily be confiscated by an elite minority.

Literary creation has so far escaped these pitfalls. Far from supporting the new regimes based on exclusion of otherness, major writers have delighted in offering a multi-faceted reality rich in its diversity. Far from imposing a centre-oriented angle of vision, they adopt several viewpoints simultaneously and delight in presenting the richness and variety of the world. In this sense such novelists as Gabriel Garcìa Márquez, Salman Rushdie, Wole Soyinka and Wilson Harris can perhaps be considered as the founding fathers of a new truly multicultural artistic reality.

C- *Edouard Glissant's Aesthetic Theories*

Among the most productive hybrid aesthetics developed by post-colonial artists, Edouard Glissant's study entitled *Le Discours antillais* (Caribbean Discourse) occupies a prominent position. This volume, with its mixture of theory, poetic passages and meditations in prose sets out to reflect the radically diverse and unmonolithic nature of Caribbean identity. The book can be compared in its scope to E.K. Brathwaite's *History of the Voice*. But it is more ambitious, more philosophical and less elliptic. Glissant's unique position may stem from the variety of his talents; starting with volumes of poetry such as *Un Champ d'îles*, *La Terre Inquiète* and *Les Indes* the author moved on to *Soleil de la Conscience*, a book of essays in the form of poems in prose. Already at this early stage Glissant manifested his fondness for forms which break down accepted categories. In 1958, *La Lézarde* won the 'Prix Renaudot', a major French literary award. Since then Glissant has alternated different genres with *Le Sel Noir*, *Le Sang Rivé*, *Monsieur Toussaint*, *Le Quatrième Siècle*, *L'Intention Poétique*, *Malemort*, *Boises* and *La Case du commandeur*. Born in Martinique in 1928, Glissant was strongly marked by the social and cultural conditions of the surrounding islands which were so dependent on the plantation system and colonialist structures described by Fanon. Educated partly in Martinique and partly in France, Glissant was influenced by Surrealism, Marxism, Freudian theories, Césaire, Barthes, Sollers, Deleuze... His poetry and epic inspiration also owe a lot to Saint-John Perse, the poet born in Guadeloupe in a planter family whose ancestors had settled in the West Indies at the end of the seventeenth century. The variety of these sources witness to Glissant's eclectic tastes.

In *Le Discours antillais,* Glissant collected a number of essays which he did not try to rewrite in a logical sequence. The volume expresses a diversity of approaches to such burning Caribbean problems as dispossession, massive emigration, alienated history, culture and language. The exploration associates argumentation, interviews as well as elliptic and highly imaginative interpretations. The reader meanders through chapters which evoke multiplicity and profusion rather than monolithic clarity. The writer claims the right to be 'opaque'. Logic and clear-cut distinctions belong to the realm of colonial ideology. For Glissant, transparency is to be linked with the so-called 'universality' which the West has always used as a pretext for not recognizing the originality of other peoples.

Le Discours antillais explicitly uses accumulative techniques for 'accumulation is the most appropriate technique to unveil a scattering reality'.[1] Repetition marks the traces of problematic flaws which the Caribbean artist attempts to probe. He cannot go about it in a straightforward manner because his reality has been so obfuscated that his only alternative to the universalist pretensions of colonialist discourse is the 'unspoken multiplicity of the Diverse'.[2]

Glissant believes that the West Indian is used to the 'Detour' (*le Détour*). For him, Creole is a response to and a protest against the master's desire to reduce the slave to stuttering, to a child's prattle. Faced with this situation, the West Indian systematizes stuttering and the reduplication of syllables is a symptom of this. But Creole is rich with its wordplay and double meanings. For Glissant, syncretism and the very spectacular ritual of Voodoo correspond to this strategy of 'Detour'. Starting from negative impulses, the West Indian seeks to give them a positive value. 'The Detour is a profitable strategy only if the Return comes to fertilize it: not a return to the dream of origin, to the motionless unicity of Being, but a return to this nexus which one had been compelled to neglect; it is there that one must activate the components of Relation, or succumb'.[3] Faced with the colonizers' greed and their universalizing

---

[1] 'L'accumulation est la technique la plus appropriée de dévoilement d'une réalité qui elle-même s'éparpille' (*Le Discours Antillais*, p. 13). All the English translations from Glissant's works are mine.
[2] 'l'élan des peuples néantisés qui opposent aujourd'hui à l'universel de la transparence, imposé par l'Occident, la multiplicité sourde du Divers' (*Le Discours Antillais*, pp. 11-12).
[3] 'Le Détour n'est ruse profitable que si le Retour le féconde: non pas retour au rêve d'origine, à l'Un immobile de l'Etre, mais retour au point d'intrication, dont on s'était détourné par force; c'est là qu'il faut enfin mettre en oeuvre les composantes de la Relation, ou périr' (*Le Discours Antillais*, p. 36).

discourse, Glissant opposes the necessary diversity (*le Divers*). 'Diversity which is neither chaotic nor sterile but which corresponds to the human spirit's striving towards a transversal relationship which shuns all universalist forms of transcendence.... The Same requires Being, Diversity sets up the Relation'.[1] Glissant favours 'rhizomatous thinking' (*la pensée rhizomatique*) which forms part of this search for Relation.

Starting from the realization that the relationship between the different layers of the Caribbean population is marked by paralysis and a hardening of antagonism, Glissant explores the reality of the islands which, to him, have been mentally colonized from the outside. Their reality was confiscated under the guise of transparent representations of themselves fashioned by the French and imposed under the pretext of adopting universalist values. Faced with this 'scattered reality', he adopts a discursive position which shuns homogeneity and prefers to accumulate diverse modes of expression rather than impose a unique rhetoric which would be a duplication of the colonial voice.

Like Fanon, he denounces the servile imitation of French models practised by so many West Indians of his time. He also stigmatizes some people's desire to replace the tyranny of European culture by that of African roots. For him, this obsession with the 'One' should make way for the necessity of the 'Relation' with the Other. The Caribbean people have no reason to deny their African origins but they must not claim them as exclusive. For him, the inhabitants of Martinique are torn between this irreversible and gaping wound of their separation from Africa and this painful feeling of being cut off from their idealized image of French identity. He suggests a synthetic approach as the only way out of this predicament and condemns any interpretation of such a composite nature as a process of bastardization. He believes that each component of this greater body of identity can only enrich the other in the process.

Glissant underlines the dangers inherent in the Third-World writer's unquestioning adoption of the realistic genre. For him there is a serious risk of reality being flattened out in the process since 'mimesis presupposes that what is represented is 'true reality'. When it is linked with two realities with one bound to reproduce the other, the participants in this experience can only consider themselves as living in a permanently unreal world. Such is our situation'.[2] In order to avoid the

---

[1] 'Le Divers, qui n'est pas le chaotique ni le stérile, signifie l'effort de l'esprit humain vers une relation transversale, sans transcendance universaliste.... Le Même requiert l'Etre, le Divers établit la Relation' (*Le Discours Antillais*, p. 190).

[2] 'Toute mimésis suppose que ce qui est représenté est le 'vrai réel'. Quand elle porte sur deux réalités dont l'une est vouée à reproduire l'autre, il ne peut manquer que les

risk of Caribbean reality being reduced to its folkloric component, Glissant prefers the approach adopted by the Haitian Jacques Stephen Alexis, the author of *Compère Général Soleil* (1955), who developed the theory of 'marvellous realism', or that of García Márquez.

In the recovery of his reality, the Caribbean man cannot follow one single strand of his origins only. Glissant insists on the presence of Africa and the overwhelming weight of the slave trade in that history. But he is also conscious of the mixed heritage which he sees as an element of richness opposed to the tyranny of unification. One is reminded here of the poem 'A Far Cry from Africa' in which Derek Walcott writes:

> I who am poisoned with the blood of both,
> Where shall I turn, divided to the vein?
> I who have cursed
> The drunken officer of British rule, how choose
> Between this Africa and the English tongue I love?
> Betray them both, or give back what they give?[1]

Unlike Walcott who, at that point, still sees his diverse origins as a schizoid element, Glissant immediately envisages the possibility of what he calls *la relation*. He stigmatizes people's tendency to glorify unified roots. To him, asserting that peoples are all *métis* (of mixed blood) is a 'deconstruction of the *métis* category as an intermediary between two 'pure' extremes':

> As a proposition, *métissage* does not primarily consist in the exaltation of the composite structure of a people: indeed no people has ever been preserved from interracial breeding. As a proposition, *métissage* implies that it is from now on unnecessary to glorify a single origin whose guardian and perpetuator race might be.... Stating that people are métis means that one deconstructs the category called 'métis' which might be a middle term between two 'pure' extremes.[2]

The breaking down of such illusion of unity means that the West Indians of Martinique and Guadeloupe must repossess their own history which can only be recovered through a patient exploration in depth of the

---

tenants de l'opération se considèrent comme vivant un irréel permanent. C'est notre cas' (*Le Discours Antillais*, p. 449).
[1] Derek Walcott, *Collected Poems 1948-1984*, p. 18.
[2] 'Le métissage en tant que proposition n'est pas d'abord l'exaltation de la formation composite d'un peuple: aucun peuple n'a en effet été préservé des croisements raciaux. Le métissage comme proposition souligne qu'il est désormais inopérant de glorifier une origine 'unique' dont la race serait gardienne et continuatrice.... Affirmer que les peuples sont métissés... c'est déconstruire aussi une catégorie 'métis' qui serait intermédiaire... entre deux extrêmes 'purs'' (*Le Discours Antillais*, p. 250).

Caribbean landscape. For the people's history lies buried under the surface. Here one is reminded of Wilson Harris's similar attempt to bring back to the surface the hidden Amerindian past of oppression and eradication. One also thinks of E.K. Brathwaite's poem 'Coral'[1] in which the meditation starts from the apparent lifelessness of the mineral reef and gradually draws the whole history of the Caribbean out of this oxymoronic object which is seemingly dead yet contains the seeds of multiple living creatures.

For Glissant, the recovery of Caribbean history runs counter to the force that seeks to impose a ready-made structure provided by the metropolis. Instead of dividing the past following the major periods of French history (as most have done so far), the West Indians must first become aware of all the '*occasions ratées*' (aborted opportunities): the maroons failed to be perceived as figures of resistance and dignity and became werewolves instead, according to the interpretation of the colonizers. The 'liberation' of the slaves in 1848 was recuperated by the dominant ideology. Ideals of belonging to France came to relay dreams of Mother Africa. The 1946 Bill which instituted Martinique and Guadeloupe as '*Départements d'Outre-Mer*' (French overseas territories) marked for Glissant the extreme limit of alienation. As an alternative to purely French landmarks, Glissant suggests that Martinican history be re-written with reference to the slave trade, the plantation system, the emergence of the local elites, the victory of beetroot - a metropolitan rival to the main West Indian cash crop - over sugar cane, the law of assimila-tion and the threat of cultural nothingness which characterizes the present time. In his analysis, the artist reflects on the relationship between history and literature. The primary link between the two is, in his opinion, to be found sketched out in myths, these problematic representations which need to be explored in depth. Literature cannot be content with flat imitation or with pure subjectivity.

Glissant believes that the West Indian writer must combine two discourses, the epic and the political, which, in Western culture, correspond to two different phases. The Caribbean artist must fulfil a political role, a 'function of desacralisation, of heresy, of intellectual analysis, which means exposing the working of a given system... demystifying. It also has a function of sacralisation, the bringing together of the community around its myths, its belief, its imaginary

---

[1] In *The Arrivants*, pp. 232-234.

representations'.¹ The second role corresponds to the mythic preoccupation evoked before.

For Glissant, the Caribbean people must reclaim their roots in the soil, even if this land was imposed upon them by the massive deportation of their ancestors. His poetry is elemental and only through the soil, the lava, the volcanoes, the trees and the sea can images be born. This approach has nothing to do with a romantic escape into the past. Art must help the people to recapture a land which is in the process of being colonized in their own imagination. 'Our landscape is its own monument: the trace it signifies can be spotted underneath. All is history'.² Glissant feels he has a special responsibility in the creation of a national literature which must 'name' the new peoples and signify their rootedness. If it fails to do so, it can only dabble in regionalism and folklore. Thus literature has an epic, almost sacred mission which the poet fully assumes in such heroic poems as *Les Indes*. Here again, the writer is not only a mouthpiece or a demagogue. His language must question as much as explain. Glissant asserts in *Soleil de la Conscience* that 'prose orders what is given elsewhere' yet he also adds that failure to signify may also be the lot of the speaker who places too much trust in this new-born word which 'skids on its own surface'. But people must also know themselves before they be rid of the burden of their being. This problem, as far as Glissant is concerned, cannot be separated from the relationship between what he calls the *I* and the *We*. In *Le Discours Antillais*, he opposes different types of society defined according to the articulation between these two poles: in Socrates or Jesus Christ, both revolutionaries in their own ways, an *I* opposes the *We* to refashion it. In fascism or extreme nationalism, the *We* tyrannizes the *I*. The *I* is diluted in an illusory *We* in pseudo-collectivist systems. For Martinique, the question 'Who am I?' remains meaningless so long as 'Who are *We*?' has not found an answer. Glissant does not pretend to recapture some legitimate filiation which he sees as a false sense of unification. His *We* is a scattering of diverse 'islands' which can be made to communicate on a more genuine basis. In those terms, one's identity becomes a questioning in which the relationship with the other defines human beings. In his examination of the Caribbean situation, Edouard Glissant resorts to the idea of *relation*

---

¹ 'fonction de désacralisation, fonction d'hérésie, d'analyse intellectuelle, qui est de démonter les rouages d'un système donné... de démystifier. Il a aussi une fonction de sacralisation, fonction de rassemblement de la communauté autour de ses mythes, de ses croyances, de son imaginaire...' (*Le Discours Antillais*, p. 192).
² 'Notre paysage est son propre monument: la trace qu'il signifie est repérable pardessous. C'est tout l'histoire' (*Le Discours Antillais*, p. 21).

('relation' and 'relationship' as well as the process of relating). He opposes *le Même* (the Same) - which corresponds in his opinion to the universalizing power of the West - to *le Divers* (Diversity), a conception which has to be fought for by nations that have wrenched their right to be present in the world. This process knows occasional tragedies such as the war in Viet-Nam or South African apartheid. But the 'naming' of the peoples originally suppressed by the major powers has made it possible to save traditional oral literatures in Africa or Haiti. A national literature must demystify tyrannical systems and bring together the members of the community round its myths and its beliefs. This dual process desacralizes false idols and sacralizes more meaningful representations. This cannot be effected peacefully and harmoniously for the new nations must at the same time fight while searching for their roots. They must be militant and clear-sighted while keeping a critical eye on their own actions and positions.

The poet is not naturally the mouthpiece of his own people. It is his duty to anchor his speech, though imperfect, in the 'immense chanting of the world'. In *L'Intention Poétique*, Glissant explores the nature of language. To him it is not only 'this cry which I have chosen... Not only the cry but the throbbing *absence* inside it'.[1] So far he sees Martinican people as prisoners of discourses which denote their alienation: they tend to use a 'baroque' variety of French, ornate, highly rhetorical and interspersed with flowery clichés. This type of speech aims at asserting the user's French citizenship and his distance in relation to Creole. Glissant opposes the Spanish-inspired baroque of South America to what he calls the 'flamboyant emptiness' of Martinique. The fundamentally imitative and caricatural nature of such utterances precludes all creativity. Glissant distinguishes between this 'elitist discourse', the 'traditional oral discourse' of the plantations which is now broken and tainted with folklore and the 'delirious discourse' which originates in an exacerbation of the other two. 'Literary discourse' wanders from flawed tradition to tragic delirium in an attempt to synthesize them and overcome their weaknesses. Yet Glissant clearly admits that it sometimes inherits the faults while remaining unable to extract their meaning.

The written text must be rejuvenated by the oral tradition and languages. Creole remains unsure of itself. It must assert its originality in relation to French and become 'opaque' to it. Glissant also admits that his French has been fertilized by Creole ever since his childhood. The

---

[1] 'Non pas seulement le cri, mais l'*absence* qui au cri palpite' (*L'Intention poétique*, p. 43).

question is not to eliminate one language in favour of another. On the contrary, whenever possible, there must be a dialogue between the different languages at one's disposal. This type of exchange will only prove fruitful if it rests on an equal basis which is very different from the traditional hierarchy of languages.

Using a paradox, Glissant, who handles the written word so wonderfully, declares: 'I would be almost tempted to say that the written medium is the universalizing trace of the Same, whereas the oral might be the organised gesture of Diversity'.[1] For him this orality corresponds to the return to a mother tongue which was 'constrained or crushed by the official language'.[2]

Finally *Le Discours Antillais* explores various directions and remains open. It is anything but a system in the static sense of the word. Glissant advocates a non-essentialist aesthetic conception based on a non-universalizing diversity. To him, this possibility is linked with the emergence of an orality which cannot be reduced to the triumph of audio-visual material. This orality merely sums up and amplifies the voices of new, sadly neglected peoples. He claims that Martinican reality can only be understood as a collection of all its diverse potentialities which he does not wish to unify.[3]

For Glissant, the first characteristic of the *Relation* is *métissage*. This goes side by side with multilingualism, which is incompatible with the hegemonic practise of French, in colonial times, and of English now. This *métissage* also means for the West Indian a need to combine music, gesture and dancing which are also original means of communication. It is necessary to 'conciliate at last the values of the civilisations which possessed writing with the long depreciated traditions of the peoples of orality'.[4]

Perhaps Glissant's reflection heralds the future of writing in post-colonial countries.

---

[1] 'Je ne serai pas loin de penser que l'écrit est la trace universalisante du Même là où l'oral serait le geste organisé du Divers' (*Le Discours Antillais*, p. 192).
[2] 'La langue maternelle orale est contrainte ou écrasée par la langue officielle' (*Le Discours Antillais*, p. 194).
[3] '... le réel martiniquais ne se comprend qu'à partir de tous les possibles, avortés ou non, de cette Relation, et du dépassement qu'on en réalise, de même les poétiques multipliées du monde ne se proposent qu'à ceux-là seuls qui tentent de les ramasser dans des équivalences qui *n'unifient* pas' (*Le Discours Antillais*, pp. 465-466).
[4] 'Il s'agit pour nous de concilier enfin les valeurs des civilisations de l'écrit et les traditions longtemps inférioriséees des peuples de l'oralité' (*Le Discours Antillais*, p. 462).

Let us, West Indians, not refrain from learning about and claiming the virtues and traditions of negroes, Indians and Europeans which have come to us; but let us not hesitate to readjust them. This warm rediscovery of oneself must not lead us to fruitlessly implore an exclusive notion of the past. This vocation looks towards the future. The clash of cultures means a dynamic passion of cultures.

By turns, language beats the negro rhythm, fuses within the ample flow of Spanish prose. The quick-flowing design of Caribbean storytellers and the newest form of picaresque irony. Realism inherited from the West flows smoothly into semi-ritual chanting.... We are at the crossroads of Cultures, at another watershed, faced with a new measure of knowledge and life.[1]

In their study *Lettres Créoles*,[2] Patrick Chamoiseau et Raphaël Confiant take up notions very close to those developed by Glissant. They add the importance of 'Créolité'. For them, 'Literature sees the convergence of wild diversity. The whole world is beginning to echo in each of its particular corners. We must from now on attempt to apprehend it, far from the reductive dream of Universality, in its broken richness which bears the harmony of Diversality'.[3] This literature which 'was born here, in the Americas... has known the process of creolisation which, in the melting pot of the open islands, has mingled all the diversity in the world. Approach it in French and in Creole: two languages but the same goal'.[4]

---

[1] 'Ne reculons pas, Antillais, à connaître et à revendiquer les vertus et les traditions tant nègres qu'indiennes qu'européennes venues jusqu'à nous; mais n'hésitons pas à les rajuster. Que cette chaude redécouverte de soi n'incline pas à une imploration stérile et exclusive du passé. Cette vocation est projetante: le choc des cultures est une passion dynamique des cultures.
Tour à tour le langage bat le rythme nègre, se coule en l'ampleur de la prose espagnole. Le tracé alerte des conteurs antillais, et l'ironie picaresque la plus neuve. A un réalisme hérité de l'Occident... succède sans discontinuer la mélopée semi-rituelle.... Nous voici au carrefour des Cultures, à un autre partage des eaux, face à une nouvelle mesure de la connaissance et de la vie' (*L'Intention poétique*, p. 142).
[2] *Lettres Créoles: tracées antillaises et continentales de la littérature 1635-1975*, Hatier (Paris, 1991). Translations from *Lettres Créoles* mine.
[3] 'La littérature voit converger ses diversités folles. Le monde se met à résonner de sa totalité dans chacun de ses lieux particuliers. Il nous faut désormais tenter de l'appréhender, loin du risque appauvrissant de l'Universalité, dans sa richesse éclatée, mais harmonieuse d'une Diversalité' (p. 204).
[4] 'née ici, aux Amériques, [la littérature créole]... a connu la créolisation qui, dans le creuset des îles ouvertes, a mélangé tout le Divers monde. Aborde-la en français et en créole: deux langues mais une même trajectoire...' (p. 13).

D- *Wilson Harris and* Palace of the Peacock

For the Guyanese writer Wilson Harris,[1] homogeneity is a dangerous cultural model usually imposed by the dominant ethnic group which inevitably seeks to eliminate or rule over the others. To this Harris opposes 'the paradox of cultural heterogeneity, or cross-cultural capacity [which] lies in the evolutionary thrust it restores to orders of the imagination...' Harris also talks of 'the ceaseless dialogue it inserts between hardened conventions and eclipsed or half-eclipsed otherness...'[2] He advocates 'cross-cultural imaginations that bear upon the future through mutations of the monolithic character of conquistadorial legacies of civilisation'.[3] For him, 'the unity or density of original expression, in a work of profound imagination, is paradox; it is both a cloak for, and a dialogue with, eclipses of live 'otherness' that seek to break through in a new light and tone expressive of layers of reality'.[4] In novels such as *Palace of the Peacock*, Harris initiates a dialogue between myths belonging to diverse and traditionally antagonistic cultures (those of the conquistadores who searched for the Eldorado and those of the Amerindians who were almost wiped out by the newcomers) without allowing one to subjugate the other. He too is preoccupied by this need to establish a relation and a constructive dialogue, the only way for him to build up a feeling of community and mutual compassion between people who have been enemies, and this without forgetting the lessons of history.

Through a radical use of language, through a revisioning of fictional conventions, through an entirely original treatment of time and place, Wilson Harris attempts to take stock of the radically novel reality of the post-colonial experience.

His vision was deeply influenced by his colonial education first in New Amsterdam and then in Georgetown, the capital of his native Guyana. His early short stories and poems published privately or in *Kyk-over-al*, a local journal, reflect this traditional conception of the literary artefact. The influence of the Greek and Roman classics filters through the young man's interpretation of the world around. The heroes of his poems[5] are Tiresias, Agamemnon, Heracles, Achilles, Anticleia... Yet,

---

[1] For a comprehensive examination of the works of Wilson Harris until 1980, see Hena Maes-Jelinek, *Wilson Harris*. See also Hena Maes-Jelinek, ed., *Wilson Harris: the Uncompromising Imagination*. Michael Gilkes, ed., *The Literate Imagination: Essays on the Novels of Wilson Harris*.

[2] *The Womb of Space*, p. xviii.

[3] *Ibid.*, p. xv.

[4] *Ibid.*, p. xvii.

[5] Republished by New Beacon Books in London as *Eternity to Season* in 1978.

even at that point, their figures serve to translate a reality fundamentally different from that of classical scholars. 'Troy', a poem, heralds the themes which Harris developed later in his novels. Living as he did in a world where local representations, native culture and history were considered unworthy of interest, he already probed what to others seemed an uninteresting *tabula rasa*. Starting from the reality of destruction, from the apparently negative character of life in the colony, the author bravely assumed that what others describe as this vacant surface cannot be all there is to reality. Though Harris's use of language in 'Troy' did not yet match the boldness of expression found in subsequent novels, the ideas that were to prove so fruitful later on are already visible. Using the image of the fallen leaves through which the life of the tree renews itself, the poet writes:

> ... On the gravel and the dry earth
> each dry leaf is powder under the wheels
> of war. But each brown root has protection
> from the spike of flame. Each branch
> tunnels to meet a well or inscrutable
> history.[1]

For Harris, history before the European conquest is not absent as the colonizers would like one to believe; it simply lies dormant under the guise of apparently dead objects or representations which require a visionary eye to restore them to life. And this is the task which the young aspiring writer sets himself. Relentlessly and despite the incomprehension and indifference with which his early writing was met, Wilson Harris proceeded to re-evaluate history, language and fictional conventions through an increasingly revolutionary approach to fiction.

Many of his works are at the same time creative and philosophical since the writer does not believe that a separation should be made between these genres. What matters to him is a thorough exploration of this reality which was confiscated, creatively speaking, by people who saw no creative potential in the West Indies. Accounts of the slave society in the nineteenth century stressed the void and degeneracy of the plantocracy, a vision which led even twentieth-century novelists such as V.S. Naipaul to seek an escape into the 'real' world of England, where literary-minded people had a right to exist. Naipaul views the West Indies as philistine societies where nothing beautiful was ever created because

---

[1] *Ibid.*, p. 11.

the islands were only used and abused to make money for absentee landlords whatever the cost in human terms.

For Harris, Naipaul is an example of these adept and even at times brilliant Caribbean intellectuals who merely adopted the conventions of Western intellectuals without questioning their premises and gained success through facile means by flattering the ready-made image that the Western world has of the West Indies. This criticism was particularly aimed at Naipaul's relatively conventional handling of language which contrasts sharply with Harris's radical experiments. For Harris, Naipaul is just an example of what he calls the 'comedy of manners', a form of expression which adopts fashionable clichés and expresses them competently but unimaginatively. In *Tradition, the Writer and Society*,[1] Harris stigmatizes what he calls a conventional view of the West Indian 'which sees him in crowds - an underprivileged crowd, a happy-go-lucky crowd, a political or a cricketing crowd, a calypso crowd'. This conception satisfies the lovers of clichés and all those who seek for easy generalizations, but it fails to account for a feature which the author sees as generally submerged under the other surface appearances. 'What in my view is remarkable about the West Indian in depth is a sense of subtle links, the series of subtle and nebulous links which are latent within him, the latent ground of old and new personalities'.[2]

For Harris, V.S. Naipaul's 'comedy of manners' novels turn their backs on the rich world of reality which lies under superficial appearances. They merely 'consolidate' fashionable visions or prejudices and fail to question them in depth. This genre which Harris also calls the 'novel of persuasion rests on grounds of apparent common sense'[3] but in fact corresponds to 'an acceptable plane of reality'[4] which masks more profound layers of existence:

the novel which consolidates situations to depict protest or affirmation is consistent with most kinds of overriding advertisement and persuasion upon the writer for him to make national and political and social simplifications of experience in the world at large today. Therefore the West Indian novel - so called - in the main - is inclined to suffer in depth... and may be properly assessed in nearly every case in terms of surface tension and realism.[5]

---

[1] New Beacon Books (London, 1973 [1967]), p. 28.
[2] *Ibid.*
[3] *Ibid.*, p. 29.
[4] *Ibid.*
[5] *Ibid.*, p. 30.

Unlike this type of fiction, Harris advocates the pursuit of a subtle thread of tradition which runs in depth and which it is the writer's duty to reveal. Artists cannot be content with expressing politically correct feelings and views. They have to dig under the surface of reality and search for this web of hidden relationships which give meaning to the world. This necessity is even more pressing in the West Indies where minorities were excluded not only from political power but also from literary representation other than stereotypical. Unlike other writers, Harris believes that such an approach cannot be made without a radical questioning of conventional uses of language. For him nineteenth-century realism can only yield fashionable judgements. He advocates a use of language which serves a 'vision of consciousness... because the concept of language is one which continuously transforms inner and outer formal categories of experience, earlier and representative modes of speech itself'.[1] Figures of speech become an integral part of this search in which the writer uses 'a momentous logic of potent explosive images.... Such a capacity for language is a real and necessary one in a world where the inarticulate person is continuouly frozen or legislated for in mass'.[2] Taking up a cliché to refer to the Americas, Harris then talks of the necessity for a development of the 'melting pot' which he relates to the necessary dialogue between people who, like the first slaves on the plantations, who could not speak to one another because they lacked a common tongue, had to search for a common ground of dialogue.

Harris's novels are regularly called 'difficult' or 'hermetic' by readers who cannot resolve themselves to acknowledging the profound exploration of perspectives which is an integral part of the author's purpose. One of the appeals of novels such as *Palace of the Peacock* or *The Secret Ladder* is that, unlike later works by Harris, they can also be enjoyed for the storyline which, on the surface, develops in a fairly linear manner. More recent Harris novels cannot be read for their purely diegetic qualities. They explore older traditions, 'rehearse'[3] visions of reality and reflect on memory or the art of creation.

In the different units composing the '*Guyana Quartet*'[4] as well as *Heartland* (1964), a sadly neglected masterpiece, Guyanese locations and social realities, the flora and fauna of the Amazonian forest can easily be recognized by readers familiar with the context. Occasionally in more

[1] *Ibid.*, p. 32.
[2] *Ibid.*, p. 32.
[3] See *The Infinite Rehearsal*, the title of Harris's novel published in 1987.
[4] *Palace of the Peacock* (1960), *The Far Journey of Oudin* (1961), *The Whole Armour* (1962) and *The Secret Ladder* (1963).

recent works such as *Carnival* (1985) or *The Four Banks of the River of Space* (1990), Guyanese settings reappear very distinctly. However the author's distance with his native South American country since he settled in England in the late 1950s has led to more geographical abstraction in his reference to Guyana.

In *Palace of the Peacock*, the crew's voyage upriver takes them to places fraught with allegorical meanings: the Straits of Memory, a dangerous passage on the river, echoes the topography of *The Pilgrim's Progress* and serves to remind the men of the necessity to acknowledge suppressed history. Most critics have stressed the allegory implicit in the composition of the crew which includes members of most ethnic groups in Guyana. This issue was particularly topical at the time of writing when the two major parties vying for political prominence in the new country about to emerge after independence were largely split along racial lines with the 'East Indian' descendants of indentured workers siding with the 'communist' Jagan and the people of African origin opposing them. The characters in *Palace of the Peacock* are shown to be part of a single family of human beings; their submerged family links are revealed as they advance. This large community cannot exclude the Amerindians allegorized in Mariella, the woman used and abused by the plantocrat Donne.

The first stage of the voyage takes the crew to the Mission of Mariella, a toponym which can be read in two ways: it is Mariella's home-village, a settlement possibly linked with a local mission. The 'mission' of Mariella can also be understood as her role, the part she plays in the process of conscience raising. The novel opens with the narrator's dream that Mariella is shooting down a galloping horseman who represents the dominating conquistador and colonial master. Through this act, she symbolically destroys not only the oppressive system but also the totalitarian prejudices, the blind ignorance of true reality on which this system was based. The figure of Mariella blends with that of the old Arawak woman forced to accompany the crew as a guide and interpreter with the local populations. Later on in Donne's vision through the window in the cliff (p. 106), she merges with the nativity image of the woman holding the child. These various female characters possess powers of perception, creation and redemption far superior to those of their male counterparts in the early stages of their adventure. The apparent helplessness and subaltern position of women in colonial society is transmuted into a superior sense of vision, which opens onto possible solutions to the deadlock of polarized social structures. Like women,

Amerindians are used and abused whenever the planters feel the need for cheap manpower.

Faced with the prevailing ideology which would lead him to adopt the party of the 'mulattoes' who always held a privileged position in the West Indies, the author, who has European, African and Amerindian forebears, indicates his preference for a definitely cross-cultural identity.

In *Palace of the Peacock*, the Amerindians are called 'the folk'. This suggests that they represent the forgotten heritage which every Guyanese must acknowledge before reaching the vision at the end of the journey. They occupy the 'heartland', the land of the heart, the heart of the country's vital forces. But the choice of a particular population must not be mistaken for racial prejudice on the part of Wilson Harris. In *The Secret Ladder*, a similar role is played by Poseidon, the leader of the bush negroes whose interests are ignored by the Georgetown decision-makers when they plan to drown Poseidon's land under a reservoir designed to bring supplies of fresh water to the coastal planters. Poseidon is not chosen because of his racial origins but because he represents a forgotten part of the country's heritage. The author chooses types of characters who are ignored, unacknowledged, or despised. Yet such figures also have their failings. Poseidon himself is tempted to pursue a disastrous course of action when he captures Bryant and Catalena and proceeds to torture them, an initiative radically at variance with Harris's belief in dialogue and mutuality.

On the surface, *Palace of the Peacock*[1] could be summed up as a linear succession of narratological units such as departure, testing of characters, near-destruction, death and rebirth to the possibility of vision. The division of *Palace of the Peacock* into four 'books' which are themselves subdivided into three chapters of roughly equal volume suggests a carefully planned progression. After the 'dream' about the shot horseman evoked above,[2] the first chapter continues with scenes whose status as dream or 'reality' cannot be clearly ascertained. The narrator and his brother Donne leave on a boat expedition upriver to chase Amerindian workers who fled to escape Donne's ruthlessness. In Book Two, the crew's arrival at the Mission of Mariella causes confusion and awe in the people who remember that a similar crew was recently drowned in the rapids nearby. The latest 'ghostly' crew begin a process of self-

---

[1] All references to *Palace of the Peacock* correspond to the edition of *The Guyana Quarter*, Faber and Faber (London, 1985).
[2] For an alternative reading of the same scene, see Sandra Drake, *Wilson Harris and the Modern Tradition*.

examination which leads them to the reassess their relations with the 'folk'.

In Book Three several members of the crew suffer fatal accidents. The men's experience of deprivation and destruction prepares them for the climax at the beginning of Book Four in which they meet their own nothingness. Yet, gradually, from this despair emerge a series of visions leading to the final apotheosis in which the now returned 'I' narrator contemplates savannahs reminiscent of the landscape in the first chapter. Though initially empty, this grassland soon becomes peopled. A tree sheds its leaves and metamorphoses into a peacock which suggests a vision of perfection through diversity and symphonic interplay. Music and dance complete this metamorphic tableau which constitutes the climax of the novel.

The journey theme can be interpreted on several levels: beyond the superficial one alluded to above, this is also a voyage into the self, into the relations between self and other, a discovery of death and transmutation, an alchemical enterprise - alchemical notions[1] fuse notions borrowed from Carl Jung's *Psychology and Alchemy* and echoes of the myth of the Eldorado. It is also an Orphean quest, an Odyssey, a plunge into Dante's Inferno and an experience of the heart of darkness (Conradian evocations abound).

Spatially speaking the crew travel from the savannahs to the interior and, in the final vision, back to a transformed image of the savannahs. This apparently cyclic movement which brings the voyagers back to the place of their departure can be analyzed in terms of Wole Soyinka's image of the Möbius strip.[2] The return to the origin is no mere repetition

---

[1] The novel was analyzed in Jungian terms by Michael Gilkes in *Wilson Harris*.

[2] Soyinka's use of the Möbius strip in section VI ('Recessional') of his poem 'Idanre' gives an indication of the dramatist's conception of this possibility of escaping from the infernal cycle of repetition, which seems to be the destiny of history. According to Soyinka, Atunda, the slave who rebelled against the first deity, rolled a rock on his master and smashed him to bits, thus creating the multiple godhead. In his note to the poem, Soyinka comments of the motif of the self-devouring snake which Ogun sometimes wears around his neck and which symbolizes the doom of repetition. For him, the Möbius strip, a mathematical figure, might symbolize 'a possible escape from the eternal cycle of karmas that has become the evil history of man. Only an illusion but a poetic one, for the Möbius strip is a very simple figure of aesthetic truths and contradictions.' Further on in the same note, Soyinka talks of the 'evolutionary kink' suggested by this figure. The poem itself reads:

> Evolution of self-devouring snake to spatials
> New in symbol, banked loop of the 'Mobius strip'
> And interlock of re-creative rings, one surface
> Yet full comb of angles, uni-plane, yet sensuous with

of a routine pattern. The starting point has been transformed through a deepening of the watcher's sense of perception. The material part of the journey is 'framed' by a 'dream' scene at the beginning and a visionary tableau at the end, thus reversing the expected order in a realistic novel where any oneiric element is always firmly planted in a recognizable reality.

Despite these unexpected features, it is possible to follow the succession of days of the journey: the crew who set off upriver led by Donne soon meet dangerous rapids which force them to carry their boat through the forest round the falls. The narrator indicates that it takes them three days to reach the water again. Yet the narrator's counting of days only starts when they set off from the Mission of Mariella. The reader is occasionally given landmarks such as 'the second day's journey into the nameless rapids above Mariella' (p. 79), 'the sun rose on the third day of their setting out from Mariella' (p. 84), 'the fantasy of the fourth day dawned - the fourth day of creation - the fourth day since they had all set out from Mariella' (p. 92), or 'the dawn of the sixth day of creation' (p. 108). The chronology of the journey starts from the Mission at Mariella possibly because that is where the men discover the story of their 'double' crew who died in the rapids not so long ago, a realization which adds a new dimension to their quest. The end of Chapter III also gives an indication of the possible significance of this surprising chronology: after the first test undergone by the crew in the rapids and among dangerous submerged rocks in the river, the narrator suddenly sees his companions on the boat under another form:

> In this remarkable filtered light it was not men of vain flesh and blood I saw toiling laboriously and meaninglessly, but active ghosts whose labour was indeed a flitting shadow over their shoulders as living men would don raiment and cast it off in order to fulfil the simplest necessity of being. (p. 33)

The narrator suddenly envisions the material reality of these people as if duplicated by another human envelope, 'ghostly' because it is not perceptible immediately but part and parcel of their multifarious identity. And the narrator adds: 'In this light it was as if the light of all past days and nights on earth had vanished. It was the first breaking dawn of the light of our soul' (p. 33). After this experience, all previous events belong to another reality which is not included by the narrator in the chronology of creation.

Complexities of mind and passion (*Idanre*, p. 83).

This dimension which, in other contexts, might be called fantastic, must be examined differently here since fantasy presupposes a system in which the primary level of reality can be assessed fairly clearly, which is not the case in Harris's works. So it seems preferable to examine the author's complex notion of reality and to outline the various levels of representation which make up this rich artistic vision.

The addition of the term 'creation' to the chronology of the crew's progression suggests that their journey has to be interpreted not only in material terms but also in terms of a quest, of a personal experience which will change them radically. Their journey spans across seven days like the creation of the world in Genesis. But it is also the creation of themselves as fuller individuals who are getting rid of their simplistic prejudices. It is characteristic that the last scene should be one in which the music and dancing hints at a possible harmony which they had been estranged from in their former existence. The evocation of their ghostly double leads the crew to face their own physical destruction and that of their own prejudices in order to achieve a fuller sense of identity.

The materiality of history is duplicated by the power of myths. In *Palace of the Peacock*, the term 'myth' often serves to question the absoluteness of borders ('every boundary line is a myth' [p. 22]) and the strict separation between concepts. Myth is opposed to superficial reality in the narrator's remark concerning colonial conventions which are 'an actual stage, a presence, however mythical they seemed to the universal and spiritual eye' (p. 24). Far from corresponding to delusion or falseness, myth is also a set of representations in which the members of the crew can project their most secret longings.[1] The narrator erases the difference between myth and substance while clearly linking myth with the submerged layers of history inscribed in the landscape when he evokes the high cliffs which bar the crew's way upriver.[2] Myth and substance are complementary aspects of the same reality which has to do with time and history.[3]

Myth and dreams both provide privileged access to a deeper reality under the surface of appearances. This is not to mean that 'dream' is

[1] See the way they react to Wishrop's narration of how he murdered his wife and her lover: 'They could not conceive of him as a real murderer. They preferred to accept his story as *myth* (italics mine). He was an inspired vessel in whom they poured not only the longing for deathless obedience and constancy... but the cutting desperate secret ambition he swore he had once nourished' (p. 56).
[2] 'The precipitous cliffs were of volcanic *myth* (italics mine) and substance he dreamed far older than the river's bed and stream' (p. 82).
[3] See Vigilance's perception of 'the span and gulf of dead and dying ages and myth' (p. 83).

never taken in its sense of 'unreality'; Wilson Harris fully uses the resources of polysemy. Yet the whole novel is overshadowed by a reversal of the usual relationship between solid reality on one hand and insubstantial dreams on the other. Like the other novels in the *Guyana Quartet*, *Palace of the Peacock* resorts to apparently realistic elements and conventions in order to subvert them. The deep interweaving of 'dream' and 'reality' at the beginning of *Palace of the Peacock* illustrates the writer's warning to the reader not to take the materiality of events at face value. The initial chapter tells of a dream from which the narrator thinks he is waking, but which is actually another form of dreaming. This laborious process of waking up eventually leads the reader to wonder what the real significance of this opposition between dreams and reality, between life and death, really is. Dreams are linked with metamorphosis and with the characters' attempt to reach essences. Through this privileged activity the characters discover the existence of a hitherto unsuspected network of subterranean relations between previously antagonistic elements or people.

In *Palace of the Peacock*, people, but also elements of the landscape such as the sky, trees, rock or water can dream[1] when they are vivified by the imagination of the onlooker. Dreams are linked with moments of archetypal history which, like the Arawak woman's recollection of the 'Siberian unconscious pilgrimage' (p. 61) lead the characters to reflect on the parodox of origins. On the surface, the Amerindians are a conquered and defeated race. Yet the dreaming memory of this first journey across the Strait of Behring leads them to discover that the near-extinction and extreme vulnerability of their 'race' is an illusion. The author suggests that their survival will depend on their not using the same strategy of conquest as their colonial masters. Only the realization of their genuine potential can lead them to the 'miracle of spirit which the world of appearances had never truly known' (p. 62). Paradoxically the memory of dreams can resurrect moments before one's birth.[2]

The root 'mus-' contained in the words 'musing' and 'muse' provides an occasion for associations of images: both Mariella and the old Arawak evoke Dante's guide, companion and inspirer. These 'muses' are 'conscripted', abused and possibly violated. Yet they are mediators between the tyrannical figure of the rulers and the fleeing Amerindians.

---

[1] See daSilva's assertion: 'The impossible start happen I tell you. Water start dream, rock and stone start dream, tree trunk and tree root dreaming, bird and beast dreaming' (p. 87).
[2] daSilva wonders: 'Ah been dreaming far far back before anybody know he born. is how a man can dream so far back before he know he born?' (p. 86).

The muse reveals the blindness in Donne, the conqueror, who thinks he now possesses these women and, through them, the native population, the 'folk'. But, for Harris, muses cannot be conscripted. They fight back and kill the conqueror, as is exemplified in the initial dream, or they leave him helpless, without a translator, in a foreign world which he mistakenly believes he can dominate with his own naked strength. Thus the muse becomes a materialization of the object of man's desire which cannot be possessed and which leaves man alone with his own powerlessness so long as he does not realize that possession, mastery and conquest are only superficial notions which only lead to deadlock.

Another interesting linguistic association of the word 'muse' is the importance of 'music'[1] as a representation of this web of relations which unite the elements of creation under the surface of polarized reality. What could appear as just a feeble pun is supported by the association of dreams, musing, vision and music in the final scene of the novel where Carroll's whistling introduces a scene of transcendence and potential harmony.

To use geometrical metaphors, time and space in this novel can be read horizontally (the linear story) or vertically (the echoes of other times or other similar incidents). This conception reflects the author's desire to probe beyond the surface of realism in order to uncover unique hidden layers of meaning. Their discovery can unblock the sterile polarizations present in the contemporary world. The piercing of the surface of time goes together with a questioning of space envisaged as circumscribed by strict borders and limits. At the beginning of Chapter II, the narrator declares: 'The map of the savannahs was a dream. The names Brazil and Guyana were colonial conventions I had known from childhood' (p. 24). Here the verb 'dream' is probably to be taken in the sense of fictitious, imagined by man. These frontiers outlined on a sheet of paper are purely conventions which correspond to colonial prejudices but not to the deep reality of a continent which was carved up by the conquerors. The original inhabitants obeyed another logic of place, that of semi-nomadic people who cleared a section of the forest, cultivated it for a few years and then moved on until the fertility of the soil was regenerated. Borders are man-made and the only genuine ones separate basic elements such as land and water. In Harris's novels, frontiers are areas of transition rather than limits. Many crucial passages are set in transitional spaces, not quite

---

[1] Russell McDougall has a long development on the radical 'dream' and talks of the novel as a 'metaphoric symphony' in his perceptive article "'Corporeal Music': the Scale of Myth and Adjectival Insistence in *Palace of the Peacock*' in Hena Maes-Jelinek, *Wilson Harris: the Uncompromising Imagination*, pp. 92-105.

land and not yet water such as beaches whose contour is modified by the cycles of tides. The spot on which the protagonist stands one day may well have been one which was for a long time under water. Many scenes of revelation or of initiation see the characters plunging into a borderline element. The beach at the beginning of *Heartland* and the meeting with Poseidon in the swamp in *The Secret Ladder* are examples of this.

Harris probes the inner layers of reality through his exploration of images but also through his particular use of syntax. Hena Maes-Jelinek has perceptively remarked on the author's idiosyncratic handling of the conjunction 'and'.[1] When it links two verbs, rather than refer to a succession, 'and' suggests that the action evoked by the first verb is inaccurately rendered and the narrator ventures another signifier. This particular feature stresses the lack of correspondence between language, which is always approximate, and essential ideas, which remain basically inaccessible. It may also indicate that reality cannot be reduced to one single feature. So the second (or third) verb evokes another undiscovered facet. In this case, the use of 'and' can be related to the fading effect in cinema when one representation melts into another as in the first page of the novel when the narrator talks of the wind which 'had been stretched *and* torn and had started coiling *and* running in an instant' (p. 19 [italics mine]). This syntactic idiosyncrasy serves to dynamize the meaning of words, to force them into a dialogue. The passage from the first term to the second indicates a progression from the more manifest to a hidden dimension when the narrator, disturbed by Mariella's 'black hypnotic eyes', evokes 'a watching muse *and phantom*' (p. 21 [italics mine]). A second layer of reality hidden under a superficial one can be evoked through this device, as we see in 'There was a curious edge of mockery *and interest* in Donne's voice' (p. 22 [italics mine]). It may also correspond to the union of apparently incompatible opposites as in 'a shot rang out suddenly, near *and yet far*' (p. 19 [italics mine). It may mark the passage from a literal to a metaphorical dimension as in 'The sun blinded *and ruled* my living sight' (p. 19 [italics mine]). In this case one may strip the sentence of the second element and the disturbing aspect of the vision disappears, which shows the important metamorphic possibilities introduced by the author with this type of construction. The unveiling of hidden possibilities is suggested in 'I awoke in full and in earnest with the sun's blinding light *and muse* in my eye' (p. 21 [italics mine]). Sometimes - less often than the other way round in this novel - Wilson

---

[1] In *Wilson Harris*, p. 14: 'Harris's use of 'and' is a distinctive feature of his style: it often links a series of varied images in an attempt to grasp an undefinable reality...'

Harris starts with a metaphor and ends with a literal representation as in 'Someone rapped on the door of my cell *and room*' (p. 19 [italics mine]).

All these lexical and syntactical characteristics show that Harris's works possess an important dimension of dialogue or *heteroglossia* in the Bakhtinian sense of the word. *Palace of the Peacock* and *The Secret Ladder* contain moments when various social classes express themselves in their own language, each presenting its own version of truth. Yet dialogue is even more fundamental in the sense that Harrissian philosophy owes a lot to the *I* and *Thou* articulated in the philosophy of Martin Buber. Reality in the *Guyana Quartet* is basically double-faced, like Janus. Harris would argue that most readers prefer to stay on the superficial level which many unquestioning people consider as the palpable real. The quest undergone by the characters leads them first into a second dimension, that in which the characters are placed face to face with their doubles. The first stage in their crisis of perception leads them to the Mission of Mariella where they discover that, not so long ago, a crew with the same names was wrecked with all hands lost on the same river. This 'coincidence' helps them to discover that they possess within themselves a dimension of otherness which must be revealed and developed. The death of the previous crew, their 'doubles', prefigures what will happen to them but it also signifies the creative potential inherent in the destruction of their old conception of themselves. The discovery of the first crew's predicament serves as a stage of revelation on which they see themselves 'rehearsing' their future fate, thus providing them with a sense of distance and the possibility of reflecting upon their plight.

This process of duplication does not merely concern characters; it also affects nature. This is clearly represented by the dual world of the river along which the crew travels: the water reflects what lies above the surface; it also divides liquid reality into what lies above the surface and what lies under. The narrator's use of 'half-' becomes a ruling device for drawing the readers' attention to the limited character of their perception of reality. But such a mathematical division must not be mistaken for a purely binary conception of the world by the author. Instead, the 'half-' serves to break the monolithic appearance of representations seen from a positivist point of view. The 'half-' is a wound in the corporeal integrity of this object, a door open onto other dimensions which escape any possibility of reduction to some fixed notion of meaning. Considered from a 'post-colonial' perspective, this might appear as an attempt to liberate language from the shackles of meaning imposed from the outside by the metropolis. But Harris goes further than this simple 'decolonization' of signs: he also questions purely oppositional stances which, he argues, can be just as fossilized as those of the colonizers. Harris's enterprise consists in exploring the possible ground of dialogue which, according to him, exists beyond a polarized conception of relations between colonizer and colonized.

Perhaps Harris's text might be viewed in terms of Roland Barthes' evocation of reading pleasure. According to the French theoretician, evoking Sade, 'the pleasure of reading... clearly proceeds from certain breaks (or certain collisions).... The language is redistributed. Now *such redistribution is always achieved by cutting.* Two edges are created: an obedient, conformist, plagiarizing edge (the language is to be copied in its canonical state, as it has been established by schooling, good usage, literature, culture), and another edge, mobile, blank (ready to assume any contours), which is never anything but the site of its effect: the place where one has intimations of the death of language. These two edges, *the compromise they bring about,* are necessary; it is the seam between them, the fault, the flaw, which becomes so'.[1] Barthes uses this distinction to privilege texts in which language runs wild, becomes a pure flow of words which make little case of syntax, privileging instead continuous jubilation. Harris's works never attain such a level of 'aestheticism'. For the Guyanese writer, the novel is an occasion to discuss issues of burning relevance to societies and human beings. Still one might take some liberties with Barthes' context and say that, in Harris's works, the presence of the 'other side' predominates, increasingly so in the later novels. Language tends to 'die' in the sense that words and sentences

---

[1] Barthes, pp. 6-7. 'Le plaisir de la lecture vient évidemment de certaines ruptures (ou de certaines collisions).... le langage est redistribué. *Or cette redistribution se fait toujours par coupure.* Deux bords sont tracés: un bord sage, conform, plagiaire (il s'agit de copier la langue dans son état canonique, tel qu'il a été fixé par l'école, le bon usage, la littérature, la culture) *et un autre bord,* mobile, vide (apte à prendre n'importe quels contours), qui n'est jamais que le lieu de son effet: là où s'entrevoit la mort du langage. Ces deux bords, *le compromis qu'ils mettent en scène,* sont nécessaires' (Barthes, *Le Plaisir du texte,* pp. 14-15).

cease to have any definite meaning clearly identifiable by purely rational methods. The reader needs to work in depth, along the paradigmatic axis as well as along the more traditional syntagmatic one. He/she will be led to fill the numerous gaps in the text with representations which always remain partial steps along a progression which is constantly resumed and never completed.

CONCLUSION

Imperialistic powers deprived the colonized people not only of their territories and wealth but also of their imagination. The first task of writers seeking for alternatives to these de-realized representations of themselves involved building up a strong sense of identity in their independent nations. Consequently any grid such as mimesis which offered an articulation of this new awareness was favoured. Initially formalist questioning about the nature of reality smacked too much of the old colonialist sense of alienation. Genres such as the utopia were shunned because what set out to be 'ideal' systems were always imposed on the conquered people from the outside by a Prospero wishing to manipulate all these potential Calibans. The construction of unshackled identities often involved a recourse to orality, the use of the allegory and the creation of national epics which need not be overly didactic since, so often, heroism and mock-heroism are represented in equal proportions. The surface of mimesis, with its appeal to the metropolitan logos and its mirage of objective reality was frequently undermined by subterranean native layers of perception. One may debate how much of this 'tradition' was indigenous or reflected the influence of European currents such as surrealism. The rich body of post-colonial literature distinguishes itself through its definitely hybrid nature

By implicitly offering a reshuffling of generic classification, post-colonial literatures raise questions concerning genres and their relation to reality. Metropolitan novelists have been more concerned with depicting the traumas of private worlds and the gaps and fissures within individuals. In the process, post-colonial reality is shown to include more than people's conscious perception of it. Writers offer counter-discourses to the dominant logos of the metropolises. This does not mean that they necessarily reject all of the colonizer's perception but that they consider it to be at best relative and approximate and at worst alienating for the colonized person. Reality is shown to be the sum of the different components of their hybrid identity. Far from conceiving of this as a bastardized alternative to the 'full' metropolitan version of reality, post-colonial artists build temporary syntheses and are acutely conscious of the relativity of their visions anchored in a certain history and context. Because reality is multiple and contradictory to them, they feel the need to approach it from several - sometimes widely differing - angles, hence the 'mixed' genres that they use. Magic realism is one of the best-known forms of this generic hybridity. 'Magic realism' may owe as much to surrealism and to the European learned traditions than to 'traditional cultures'. It may pander to the tastes of Westerners eager to read about quaint exotic worlds. But it also serves another much more important purpose. In the form illustrated by García Márquez, it constitutes a counter-discourse which uses fantasy in a manner reminiscent of indigenist literature while subverting its premises. Where primitivists provide a vision of a magic world which is organic and unproblematic, rooted in a made-up authenticity, García Márquez confronts the logic of fantasy to that of the positivist conception of realism. The presence of the two radically antithetic - but nevertheless equally essentialist - discourses in the same fictional structure results in a mutual questioning of each one's pretensions to totality and unproblematic sense. The seriousness of political discourse is duplicated and somewhat undermined by the equally serious - at least on the surface - conventions of magic. Implicit irony results from the simultaneous presence of these two apparently incompatible logics in one single fictional *locale*. Perhaps García Márquez's use of magic realism matters less as a (problematic) genre than as a trope for the radically disturbing nature of cross-culturalism.

The very frailty and temporariness of magic realism is proportional to the writers' fast-recomposing artistic universe. The assertiveness and success of these hybrid aesthetics is a measure of the vitality of the post-colonial movement. The old colonial sense of inferiority has all but disappeared and the new writers proudly assert their differences. They also draw the metropolitan readers' attention to the multifarious aspect of their reality which can no longer be envisaged in simple ethnocentric terms. The new syntheses do not always go without traumas or divisions. But the vitality of the metamorphosis augurs well for the future.

Any comparative study or theoretical generalization about post-coloniality exposes its author to the risk of implicitly looking for essences, fixed definitions in what remains an extremely varied field of exploration. Advocating the destruction of the old dominating colonial viewpoint may lead to the sacralization of the 'Other' or the 'Margins' of Empire, a dangerous task if it results in the consolidation of polarities legitimately denounced by Edward Said when he stigmatizes the Orientalist's obsession with the difference between 'us' and 'them'. Wilson Harris's critical and fictional discourse rests on this denunciation of post-colonial polarization which prevents the discovery of hidden layers of reality which the partisan outlook refuses to acknowledge because such an approach questions ready-made oppositions and reassuring ideological canons. The works studied here constitute only one part of an infinitely varied field. We have chosen to privilege fiction, poetry or theory which revitalize the readers' vision of reality. This task seems all the more urgent in a period when laissez-faire theories and the gospel of free trade have led to the apparent destruction of ideologies and a general tendency to privilege individualism. This means the triumph of the dominating economic powers over the weakest, a newer and more dangerous form of imperialism because it applies worldwide and does not even extend its mesh under the pretence of a moral or sacred mission. The study of the New Literatures shows that this process is not ineluctable. Voices can be raised to defend the idea of new post-colonial identities, not in the form of absolutes but as positive representations which structure and give meaning to the people's experience. Literature need not succumb to the tyranny of post-modernist correctness. The questioning of the imperialistic logos does not necessarily result in the endless fragmentation of experience. Patricia Grace, Albert Wendt, Wilson Harris, Salman Rushdie, Edouard Glissant and García Márquez, with their different sensibilities, contribute to this reassertion of literature's relevance as a provider of convincing interpretations of the world. They can use all the post-modernist devices when they serve their purpose. But they rarely succumb to the solipsistic vertigo of a purely formalist universe of fiction.

Post-colonial writers have brought a major contribution to the revitalization of outdated genres such as realism. They have demonstrated with much authority that reality can be multifarious. The hybrid experience of most post-colonial writers does not place them in a no man's land between two cultures. It forms the basis of their questioning of the fixed terms that such a polarity implies.

Referring to Wilson Harris, Homi K. Bhabha suggests directions which the new international culture might take. He advocates 'an *inter*national culture, based not on the exoticism of multiculturalism or the *diversity* of cultures, but on the inscription and articulation of culture's *hybridity*. To that end we should remember that it is the 'inter' - the cutting edge of translation and renegotation, the *in-between* space - that carries the burden of the meaning of culture'.[1] This points towards a new definition of culture which does not favour nationalism, fixed identities or polarities. Cross-culturalism might then serve as a useful reminder of the very nature of identity and culture, two notions which are far more problematic than common stereotypes might lead us to believe.

Art need not choose between consecrated versions of metropolitan forms and reified representations of revolutionary alternatives. The most powerful novels to have come out of the New Literatures hint at the possibility of a profound dialogue between different conceptions of

[1] Homi K. Bhabha, *The Location of Culture*, p. 38.

reality. One may choose to define these works thanks to the label 'magic realism'. I have advocated a narrowing of the definition if this term is to have any generic validity instead of merely serving temporary marketing strategies. But perhaps the merit of the phrase 'magic realism' is to suggest a field of possibilities in which the term will no longer be an oxymoron. The post-colonial creative potential truly possesses a magic reality...

BIBLIOGRAPHY

Achebe, Chinua. *Things Fall Apart*. London: Heinemann, 1958.
Achebe, Chinua. *Girls at War*. London: Heinemann, 1972.
Achebe, Chinua. *Arrow of God*. London: Heinemann, 1974.
Achebe, Chinua. *Morning yet on Creation Day*. London: Heinemann, 1975.
Achebe, Chinua. *Anthills of the Savannah*. London: Heinemann, 1987.
Adam, Ian and Helen Tiffin, eds. *Past the Last Post: Theorizing Post-Colonialism and Post-Modernism*. Hemel Hempstead: Harvester Wheatsheaf, 1991.
Ahmad, Aijaz. *In Theory: Classes, Nations, Literatures*. London: Verso 1994 (1992).
Alexis, Jacques Stephen. 'Du Réalisme fantastique chez les Haïtiens', *Présence Africaine* (1956) pp. 8-10.
Allende, Isabel. *The House of the Spirits*, London: Black Swan, 1990 (1985).
Amado, Jorge. *Tocaia Grande*. Rio de Janeiro: Distribuidora Record, 1984.
Anand, Mulk Raj. *Coolie*. London: Bodley Head, 1972 (1936).
Aristotle, Horace, Longinus. *Classical Literary Criticism*. Harmondsworth: Penguin, 1979.
Armah, Ayi Kwei. *Two Thousand Seasons*, London: Heinemann, 1979 (1973).
Ashcroft, Bill, Gareth Griffiths and Helen Tiffin. *The Empire Writes Back: Theory and Practice in Post-Colonial Literatures*. London/New York: Routledge, 1989.
Ashcroft, Bill, Gareth Griffiths and Helen Tiffin, eds. *The Post-Colonial Studies Reader*. London: Routledge, 1995.
Asturias, Miguel Angel. *Hombres de Maíz*. Madrid: Alianza Editorial, 1986 (1972).
Bakhtin, Mikhail: Michael Holquist, ed. *The Dialogic Imagination: Four Essays by M.M. Bakhtin*. Austin: U of Texas Press, 1994.
Bardolph, Jacqueline. *Ngugi wa Thiong'o, l'homme et l'oeuvre*. Paris: Présence Africaine, 1991.
Barthes, Roland. *Le Plaisir du texte*. Paris: Seuil, 1973. Translated by Richard Miller: *The Pleasure of the Text*. London: Jonathan Cape, 1976.
Barthes, Roland, L. Bersani, Ph. Hamon, M. Riffaterre, I. Watt. *Littérature et réalité*. Paris: Seuil, 1982.

Bessière, Irène. *Le Récit fantastique: la poétique de l'incertain*. Paris: Larousse, 1974.

Bhabha, Homi K. *The Location of Culture*. London: Routledge, 1994.

Billington, Rosamund, Sheelagh Strawbridge, Lenore Greensides and Annette Fitzsimons. *Culture and Society*. London: Macmillan, 1991.

Bock, Hedwig and Albert Wertheim, eds. *Essays on Contemporary Post-Colonial Fiction*. Munich: Max Hueber Verlag, 1986.

Brathwaite, E.K. *The Arrivants*. Oxford: Oxford UP, 1986 (1967, 1968, 1969, 1973).

Brathwaite, E.K. *History of the Voice*. London: New Beacon,1984.

Brennan, Timothy. *Salman Rushdie and the Third World: Myths of the Nation*. London: Macmillan, 1989.

Brydon, Diana. 'The Myths that Write Us: Decolonizing the Mind'. *Commonwealth* 10-1 (1987) pp. 1-14.

Caillois, Roger. *Anthologie du fantastique*. Paris: Gallimard, 1966.

Carpentier, Alejo. *The Kingdom of this World*. Harmondsworth: Penguin, 1975 (1949).

Carpentier, Alejo. *Razon de ser*. La Habana: Editorial Letras Cubanas, 1980 (1976).

Carpentier, Alejo. *Los Pasos perdidos*, Madrid: Catedra, 1985 (1953).

Recopilación de textos sobre Alejo Carpentier. La Habana: Casa de la Americas, 1977.

Carrillo, German D. *La narrativa de Gabriel García Márquez*. Madrid: Editorial Castalia,1975.

Chamoiseau, Patrick. *Texaco*. London: Granta, 1997 [Paris: Seuil, 1992].

Chamoiseau, Patrick et Raphaël Confiant. *Lettres Créoles: tracées antillaises et continentales de la littérature 1635-1975*. Paris: Hatier, 1991.

Chanady, Amaryll Beatrice. *Magical Realism and the Fantastic: Resolved versus Unresolved Antinomies*. New York: Garland Press, 1985.

Clanet, Claude. *L'Interculturel*. Toulouse: Presses Universitaires de Toulouse, 1990.

Combe, Dominique. *Les Genres littéraires*. Paris: Hachette, 1992.

Communication 8 (1966).

Couffon, Claude. *Asturias*. Paris: Seghers 1970.

Coussy, Denise. *L'Oeuvre de Chinua Achebe*. Paris: Présence Africaine, 1985.

Craig, David, ed. *Marxists on Literature*. Harmondsworth: Penguin, 1975.

Dash, Michael. 'Marvellous Realism: the Way out of Négritude'. *Caribbean Studies* 13-4 (1974) pp. 57-70.

Dash, Michael. *Edouard Glissant*. Cambridge: Cambridge UP, 1995.

Dirlik, Arif. 'The Post-Colonial Aura: Third-World Criticism in the Age of Global Capitalism'. *Critical Enquiry* 20-2 (1994) pp. 328-356.

Drake, Sandra. *Wilson Harris and the Modern Tradition*. Westport: Greenwood, 1986.

During, Simon. 'Post-modernism or Post-colonialism'. *Landfall* 39-3 (1987) pp. 32-47.

During, Simon. 'Post-modernism or Post-colonialism Today'. *Textual Practice* (1-1) pp. 32-47.

Durix, Carole and Jean-Pierre Durix. *An Introduction to the New Literatures in English*. Paris: Longman France, 1993.

Durix, Jean-Pierre. *The Writer Written: The Artist and Creation in the New Literatures in English*. Wesport, Ct.: Greenwood Press, 1987.

Earle, Peter, ed. *Gabriel García Márquez*. Madrid: Taurus, 1981.

Ellison, Ralph. *Invisible Man*. Harmondsworth: Penguin, 1982 (1952).

Eri, Vincent. *The Crocodile*. Ringwood, Vic.: Penguin, 1973 (1970).

Fanon, Frantz. *Black Skin, White Masks*. London: MacGibbon & Kee, 1968 (1952).

Finnegan, Ruth. *Oral Literature in Africa*. Nairobi: Oxford UP, 1976 (1970).

Fletcher, D.M., ed. *Reading Rushdie*. Amsterdam/Atlanta: Rodopi, 1994.

Flores, Angel. 'Magical Realism in Spanish American Fiction'. *Hispania*, XXXVIII (2nd May 1955) pp. 157-192.

Fowler, Alastair. *Kinds of Literature: an Introduction to the Theory of Genres and Modes*. Oxford: Clarendon Press, 1982.

Fuentes, Carlos. *Cristóbal Nonato*. Mexico: Fondo de Cultura Economica, 1987.

García Márquez, Gabriel. *One Hundred Years of Solitude*. London: Picador, 1978 (1967).

Recopilación de textos sobre Gabriel García Márquez. La Habana: Casa de las Americas, 1969.

Gates, Henry Louis, ed. *Black Literature and Literary Theory*. New York: Methuen,1984.

Genette, Gérard. *Introduction à l'architexte*. Paris: Seuil, 1979. Translated by Jane E. Lewin: *The Architext: an Introduction*. Berkeley, Los Angeles, Oxford: University of California Press, 1992.

Genette, Gérard et al. *Théorie des genres*. Paris: Seuil, 1986.

Gilkes, Michael. *Wilson Harris*. London: Longman, 1975.

Gilkes, Michael, ed. *The Literate Imagination: Essays on the Novels of Wilson Harris*. London: Macmillan, 1989.

Glissant, Edouard. *La Lézarde*. Paris: Seuil, 1958. Translated by Michael Dash: *The Ripening*, London: Heinemann,1985.

Glissant, Edouard. *Le Quatrième siècle*. Paris: Seuil, 1964.

Glissant, Edouard. *L'Intention poétique*. Paris: Seuil, 1969.

Glissant, Edouard. *Malemort*. Paris: Seuil, 1975.

Glissant, Edouard. *La Case du commandeur*. Paris: Seuil, 1981.

Glissant, Edouard. *Le Discours Antillais*. Paris: Seuil, 1981. Translated and with an introduction by J. Michael Dash: *Caribbean Discourse*. Charlottesville: University Press of Virginia, 1989.

Glissant, Edouard. *Poétique de la relation*. Paris: Gallimard, 1990. Translated by Betsy Wing: *Poetics of Relation*. Ann Arbor: Michigan University Press, 1997.

Glissant, Edouard. *Poèmes complets*. Paris: Seuil, 1994.

Glissant, Edouard. *Introduction à une poétique du divers*. Paris: Gallimard, 1996.

Goldberg, David Theo, ed. *Multiculturalism*. Oxford: Blackwell,1994.

Goldie, Terry. *Fear and Temptation: The Image of the Indigene in Canadian, Australian and New Zealand Literature*. Kingston: McGill-Queen's UP, 1989.

Gordimer, Nadine. *July's People*. Harmondsworth: Penguin, 1982 (1981).

Gordimer, Nadine. *Selected Stories*. Harmondsworth: Penguin, 1975.

Grace, Patricia. *Potiki*. Auckland: Penguin, 1986.

Grace, Patricia. *Electric City*. Auckland: Penguin, 1987.

Grant, Damian. *Realism*. London: Methuen, 1970.

Grass, Günter. *On Writing and Politics*. Harmondsworth: Penguin, 1985.

Gray, Stephen, ed. *The Penguin Book of Southern African Stories*. Harmondsworth: Penguin, 1985.

Griffiths, Gareth. *A Double Exile: African and West Indian Writing Between Two Cultures*. London: Marion Boyars,1978.

Gunew, Sneja and Fazal Rizvi, eds. *Culture, Difference and the Arts*. St Leonards, Australia: Allen & Unwin, 1994.

Hamburger, Käte. *Logique des genres littéraires*. Paris: Seuil, 1986 (first German edition: *Die Logik der Dichtung*. Stuttgart: Ernst Kett, 1977).

Hamner, Robert D., ed. *Critical Perspectives on V.S. Naipaul*. London: Heinemann, 1979 (1977).

Hancock, Geoff. *Magic Realism*. Toronto: Aya Press, 1980.

Hankin, Cherry, ed. *Critical Essays on the New Zealand Short Story.* Auckland: Heinemann, 1982.

Harris, Wilson. *The Guiana Quartet.* London: Faber and Faber, 1985 (includes *Palace of the* Peacock [1960], *The Far Journey of Oudin* [1961], *The Whole Armour* [1962], *The Secret Ladder* [1963]).

Harris, Wilson. *Heartland.* London: Faber and Faber, 1964.

Harris, Wilson. *The Infinite Rehearsal.* London: Faber and Faber, 1987).

Harris, Wilson. *Tradition, the Writer and* Society. London: New Beacon, 1967.

Harris, Wilson. *Eternity to Season.* London: New Beacon, 1978 (1954).

Harris, Wilson. *Explorations.* ed. by Hena Maes-Jelinek. Mundelstrup: Dangaroo Press, 1981.

Harris, Wilson. *The Womb of Space.* Westport, Ct.: Greenwood Press, 1983.

Hernández, Ana Maria, ed. *En el punto de mira: Gabriel García Márquez.* Madrid: Editorial Pliegos,1985.

Hodgins, Jack. *The Invention of the World.* Toronto: Macmillan, 1977.

Huggan, Graham. 'Decolonizing the Map: Post-Colonialism, Post-Structuralism and the Cartographic Connection'. *Ariel,* (20-4) pp. 115-129.

Hutcheon, Linda. *Narcissistic Narrative.* London: Methuen, 1984.

Ihimaera, Witi. *Pounamu Pounamu.* Auckland: Heinemann, 1972.

Ihimaera, Witi. *Tangi.* Auckland: Heinemann, 1973.

Ihimaera, Witi. *Whanau.* Auckland: Heinemann, 1974.

Ihimaera, Witi. *The New Net Goes Fishing.* Auckland: Heinemann, 1977.

Ihimaera, Witi. *The Matriarch.* Auckland: Heinemann, 1986.

Jackson, Rosemary. *Fantasy, The Literature of Subversion.* London: Methuen, 1981.

James, C.L.R. *Minty Alley.* London: New Beacon 1971 (1936).

JanMohamed, Abdul R., *Manichaean Aesthetics: the Politics of Literature in Colonial Africa.* Amherst: U of Massachusetts Press, 1985.

JanMohamed, Abdul R. 'The Economy of Manichaean Allegory': The Function of Racial Difference in Colonialist Literature'. *Critical Inquiry,* 12-1 (1985).

Jauss, Hans Robert. *Towards an Aesthetic of Reception.* Brighton: Harvester, 1982.

Jenks, Chris. *Culture.* London: Routledge, 1993.

Karp, Eliane. 'Transposicion del Surrealismo Francés al 'Real Maravilloso' Latinamericano: El Caso de Miguel Ángel Asturias con *Hombres de Maiz'*. *Lexis*, VI-1 (1982) pp. 99-116.

Killam, G.D. *The Novels of Chinua Achebe*. London: Heinemann, 1969.

King, Bruce. *The New English Literatures*. London: Macmillan, 1980.

La Licorne, 22: La Logique des genres (Poitiers, 1992).

Kroetsch, Robert. *What the Crow Said*. Toronto: New Press, 1983 (1978).

Kunene, Mazisi. *Emperor Shaka the Great*. London: Heinemann, 1979.

Laurence, Margaret. *A Bird in the House*. Toronto: McClelland and Stewart, 1963.

Laurence, Margaret. *The Diviners*. Toronto: Knopf, 1974.

Lawson, Henry, Colin Roderick, ed. *The Master Story Teller*. Sydney: Angus and Robertson, 1984.

Leal, Luis. 'El Realismo mágico en la literatura hispanoamericana', *Cuadernos Americanos*, 4 (July-August 1967) pp. 230-235.

Le Cam, Georges-Goulven. *Mythe et stratégie identitaire chez les Maoris de Nouvelle-Zélande*. Paris: L'Harmattan, 1992.

Lee, John A. *Children of the Poor*. Christchurch: Whitcombe and Tombs, 1974 (1934).

Leiris, Michel. *Cinq études d'ethnologie*. Paris: Denoël, 1969.

Lejeune, Philippe. *Le Pacte autobiographique*. Paris: Seuil, 1975. Translated by Katherine Leary: *On Autobiography*. Minneapolis: University of Minnesota Press, 1989.

Lévi-Strauss, Claude. *Anthropologie Structurale Deux*. Paris: Plon, 1973. Translated by Monique Layton: *Structural Anthropology*, Vol. II. London: Allen Lane, 1977.

Lukács, Georg. *The Theory of the Novel*. translated from German by Anna Bostock. London: The Merlin Press, 1971.

McGregor and Mark Williams, eds. *Dirty Silence: Aspects of Language and Literature in New Zealand*. Auckland: Oxford UP, 1991.

Macherey, Pierre. *Pour une théorie de la production littéraire*. Paris: Maspero, 1974. Translated by Geoffrey Wall: *A Theory of Literary Production*. London, Henley, Boston: Routledge and Kegan Paul, 1978.

Maes-Jelinek, Hena. *Wilson Harris*. Boston: Twayne, 1982.

Maes-Jelinek, Hena, ed. *Wilson Harris: The Uncompromising Imagination*. Aarhus: Dangaroo, 1991.

Malouf, David. *Remembering Babylon*. London: Chatto & Windus, 1993.

Mannoni, Octave. *Prospero and Caliban: the Psychology of Colonization*. New York: Praeger, 1964 (1950).

Mannoni, Octave. *Clefs pour l'imaginaire ou l'autre scène*. Paris: Seuil, 1969.

Márquez Rodríguez, Alexis. *Lo Barroco y lo real-maravilloso en la obra de Alejo Carpentier*. Mexico: Siglo Veintiuno Editores, 1982.

Merchant, Paul. *The Epic*. London: Methuen, 1971.

Milner, Max. *La Fantásmagorie*. Paris: Presses Universitaires de France, 1982.

Minta, Stephen. *Gabriel García Márquez, Writer of Colombia*. London: Cape, 1987.

Naipaul, V.S. *A House for Mr Biswas*. Harmondsworth: Penguin, 1973 (1961).

Naipaul, V.S. *The Middle Passage*. London: A. Deutsch, 1962.

New, W.H. *Among Worlds*. Erin, Ontario: Press Porcepic, 1975.

New, W.H. *Dreams of Speech and Violence, The Art of the Short Story in Canada and New Zealand*. Toronto: U. of Toronto Press, 1987.

Newman, Judie. *The Ballistic Bard: Post-colonial Fiction*. London: Arnold, 1995.

Ngugi wa Thiong'o. *The River Between*. London: Heinemann,1965.

Ngugi wa Thiong'o. *A Grain of Wheat*. London: Heinemann,1967.

Ngugi wa Thiong'o. *Homecoming*. London: Heinemann,1972.

Ngugi wa Thiong'o. *Petals of Blood*. London: Heinemann,1977.

Ngugi wa Thiong'o. *Devil on the Cross*. London: Heinemann,1980.

Ngugi wa Thiong'o. *Writers in Politics*. London: Heinemann,1981.

Ngugi wa Thiong'o. *Matigari*. London: Heinemann,1987.

Nuttall, A.D. *A New Mimesis: Shakespeare and the Representation of Reality*. London: Methuen, 1983.

Okara, Gabriel. *The Voice*. London: Heinemann,1963.

Okri, Ben. *The Famished Road*. London: Cape, 1991.

Parry, Benita. 'Problems in Current Theories of Colonial Discourse'. *Oxford Literary Review*, 9-1 & 2 (1987) pp. 27-58.

Pearson, Bill. *Fretful Sleepers and Other Essays*. Auckland: Heinemann, 1974.

Radford, Daniel. *Edouard Glissant*. Paris: Seghers, 1982.

Roh, Franz, *Nach Expressionismus. Magischer Realismus. Probleme der Neuesten Europäischen Malerei*. Leipzig: Kinkhardt & Biermann, 1925.

Rulfo, Juan. *Pedro Páramo*. London: Serpent's Tail,1994 (1955).

Rushdie, Salman. *Grimus*. London: Gollancz, 1975.

Rushdie, Salman. *Midnight's Children*. London: Picador, 1982 (1981).

Rushdie, Salman. *Shame*. London: Cape, 1983.

Rushdie, Salman. *The Satanic Verses*. London: Cape, 1988.

Rushdie, Salman. *Haroun and the Sea of Stories*. London: Granta, 1990.

Rushdie, Salman. *Imaginary Homelands*. London: Granta, 1991.

Rushdie, Salman. *East, West*. London: Cape, 1994.

Rushdie, Salman. *The Moor's Last Sigh*. London: Cape, 1995.

Rutherford, Anna, ed. *Commonwealth Short Stories*. London: Macmillan, 1979.

Rutherford, Anna, ed. *From Commonwealth to Post-Colonial*. Mundelstrup: Dangaroo, 1992.

Said, Edward. *Orientalism*. Harmondsworth: Penguin, 1991 (1978).

Said, Edward. *Culture and Imperialism*, London: Vintage, 1994 (1993).

Sargeson, Frank. *The Stories of Frank Sargeson*. Auckland: Penguin, 1982 (1964).

De Saussure, Ferdinand. *Cours de linguistique générale*. Paris: Payot, 1972.

Schaeffer, Jean-Marie. *Qu'est ce qu'un genre littéraire?* Paris: Seuil, 1989.

Scorza, Manuel. *Garabombo, el Invisible*. Caracas: Monte Avila Editores, 1978 (1977).

Shadbolt, Maurice. *Season of the Jew*. London: Hodder and Stoughton, 1986.

Sharrad, Paul, ed. *Readings in Pacific Literature*. Wollongong: NLRC, U of Wollongong, 1993.

Shohat, Ella. 'Notes on the 'Post-Colonial''. *Social Text* 31/32 (1992) pp. 99-113.

Slemon, Stephen. 'Monuments of Empire: Allegory/Counter-Discourse/Post-Colonial Writing'. *Kunapipi* 9-3 (1987) pp. 1-16.

Slemon, Stephen. 'Magic Realism as Post-Colonial Discourse'. *Canadian Literature* 116 (1988) pp. 9-23.

Slemon, Stephen. 'Post-Colonial Allegory and the Transformation of History'. *Journal of Commonwealth Literature* 23-1 (1988) pp. 157-168.

Sontag, Susan, ed. *A Barthes Reader*. London: Jonathan Cape, 1982.

Soyinka Wole, *A Dance of the Forests* in *Collected Plays 1*. Oxford: Oxford UP, 1973 (1963).

Soyinka, Wole. *Idanre and Other Poems*. London: Eyre Methuen, 1974 (1967).

Soyinka, Wole. *Myth, Literature and the African World*. Cambridge: Cambridge UP, 1976.

Soyinka, Wole. *Aké, the Years of Childhood*. London: Rex Collings, 1981.

Soyinka, Wole. *Art, Dialogue and Outrage*. London: Methuen, 1993.

Spivak, Gayatri Chakravorty. *In Other Worlds: Essays in Cultural Politics*. New York: Methuen, 1987.

Stead, C.K. *Smith's Dream*. Auckland: Longman Paul, 1971.

Stead, C.K. *Answering to the Language*. Auckland: Auckland UP, 1989.

Sturm, Terry, ed. *The Oxford History of New Zealand Literature*. Auckland: Oxford UP, 1991.

Tallis, Raymond. *In Defence of Realism*. London: Arnold, 1988.

Tiffin, Chris and Alan Lawson, eds. *De-Scribing Empire: Post-Colonialism and Textuality*. London: Routledge, 1994.

Tiffin, Helen. 'Post-Colonial Literatures and Counter-Discourse'. *Kunapipi*, 9-3 (1987) pp. 17-34.

Tiffin, Helen. 'Post-Colonialism, Post-Modernism and the Rehabilitation of Post-Colonial History'. *Journal of Commonwealth Literature* 23-1 (1988) pp. 169-181.

Todorov, Tzvetan. *Introduction à la littérature fantastique*. Paris: Seuil, 1970. Translated by Richard Howard: *The Fantastic: a Structural Approach to a Literary Genre*. Ithaca, NY: Cornell UP, 1975.

Todorov, Tzvetan. *Les Genres du discours*. Paris: Seuil, 1978. Translated by Catherine Porter: *Genres in Discourse*. Cambridge: Cambridge UP, 1990.

Todorov, Tzvetan. *Michael Bakhtin, le principe dialogique*. Paris: Seuil, 1981.

Todorov, Tvetan. *The Conquest of America: The Question of the Other*, trans. Richard Howard. Ithaca: Cornell UP, 1982.

Trinh T. Minh-ha. *Woman, Native, Other: Writing Post-coloniality and Feminism*. Bloomington: Indiana UP, 1989.

Tutuola, Amos. *The Palm Wine Drinkard*. London: Faber and Faber, 1952.

Vax, Louis. *L'Art et la littérature fantastique*. Paris: Que Sais-je?, 1974.

Walcott, Derek. *Collected Poems 1948-1984*. New York: Noonday Press, 1986.

Wedde, Ian. *Symmes Hole*. Auckland: Penguin, 1986.

Weisgerber, Jean, ed. *Le Réalisme magique*. Paris: L'Age d'Homme, 1987.

Wendt, Albert. *Flying-Fox in a Freedom Tree*. Auckland: Longman Paul, 1974.

Wendt, Albert. *Inside Us the Dead*. Auckland: Longman Paul, 1976.

Wendt, Albert. *Pouliuli*. Auckland: Longman Paul, 1976.

Wendt, Albert. *Leaves of the Banyan Tree*. Harmondsworth: Penguin,1981 (1979).

Wendt, Albert. *The Birth and Death of the Miracle Man*. Harmondsworth: Viking, 1986.

Wendt, Albert. *Ola*. Auckland: Penguin, 1991.

Wendt, Albert. *Black Rainbow*. Auckland: Penguin, 1992.

Williams, Mark. *Leaving the Highway: Six Contemporary New Zealand Novelists*. Auckland: Auckland UP, 1990.

Williams, Raymond. *Marxism and Literature*. Oxford: Oxford UP, 1977.

Zabus, Chantal. *The African Palimpsest: Indigenization of Language in the West African Europhone Novel*. Amsterdam/Atlanta: Rodopi, 1991.

INDEX

—A—

aboriginal 93

acculturation 149

Achebe, Chinua vii; 6; 16; 21; 22; 26; 27; 46; 63; 67; 69; 70; 83; 84; 86; 87; 102; 191; 192; 196

agenda 59; 61

Agitprop 21; 33; 64

Ahmad, Aijaz 4; 191

Aké 83; 199

Alexis, Jacques Stephen 62; 72; 73; 115; 165; 191; 197

alienation 9; 62; 76; 77; 107; 166; 168; 187

allegorical 12; 25; 35; 36; 37; 42; 94; 114; 146; 175

allegory vii; 15; 18; 24; 35; 36; 37; 41; 42; 59; 84; 115; 116; 120; 146; 175; 187; 195; 198

Amado, Jorge 35; 120; 191

Anand, Mulk Raj 23; 60; 191

anchoring 2; 17; 21; 32; 66; 72; 91; 100; 132; 147

Anthills of the Savannah 191

anthropologist 6; 69

anthropology 6; 151; 196

anti utopia vii; 26

anticolonialist 109

apartheid 21; 29; 38; 155; 168

Arabian Nights 130; 139

Ariosto 106

Aristotle 16; 45; 46; 191

Armah, Ayi Kwei 33; 34; 36; 191

Arrow of God 6; 46; 63; 191

Ashcroft, Bill 1; 7; 37; 59; 62; 72; 191

Asturias, Miguel Angel 104; 107; 108; 109; 110; 111; 112; 116; 142; 147; 191; 192; 196

Auerbach, Erich 58

Austen, Jane 75

authentic 10; 60; 61; 103; 109; 139; 149

authenticity 10; 11; 63; 95; 143; 150; 157; 188

autobiographical 9; 60; 75; 83

—B—

Bakhtin, Mikhail 35; 81; 143; 152; 191; 199

Balzac, Honoré de 45; 52; 63; 120

Bardolph, Jacqueline v; 64; 191

baroque 105; 106; 107; 110; 130; 143; 168

Barthelme, Donald 129

Barthes, Roland 54; 55; 56; 58; 129; 162; 184; 191; 198

bastardization 164

believable 45; 62; 63; 84; 130

Ben Jelloun, Tahar 4

Benveniste, Emile 129

Bessière, Irène 81; 192

Bhabha, Homi 1; 11; 66; 148; 189; 192

Bioy Casares, Adolfo 104

Birth and Death of the Miracle Man (The) 87; 200

Blanchot, Maurice 129

Boldrewood, Rolf 4

bone people (the) 36; 87

Boom 79; 102

Borges, Jorge Luis 102; 104; 146; 157

Bradbury, Malcolm 20

Brathwaite, Edward Kamau 67; 152; 162; 166; 192

Brecht, Bertold 22; 33; 50; 51

Brennan, Timothy 147; 160

Breton, André 109

Buber, Martin 183

—C—

Caillois, Roger 79; 81; 82; 192

canonical 9; 19; 59; 184

carnivalesque 81; 115

Carpentier, Alejo vii; 67; 68; 79; 104; 105; 106; 107; 108; 109; 110; 112; 116; 124; 131; 142; 147; 192; 197

Cary, Joyce 68; 74

Cervantes, Miguel de 31

Chamoiseau, Patrick 158; 170; 192

Chandra, Vikram 77

Clanet, Claude 150; 192

Coetzee, J.M. 36; 156

colonial vii; viii; 1; 2; 3; 4; 6; 7; 8; 9; 10; 11; 16; 18; 19; 21; 22; 23; 24; 25; 26; 30; 31; 32; 33; 34; 35; 37; 42; 43; 45; 46; 47; 48; 49; 51; 55; 57; 59; 60; 61; 62; 63; 65; 66; 67; 68; 69; 71; 74; 77; 80; 81; 82; 84; 104; 106; 107; 108; 111; 120; 121; 124; 125; 127; 128; 130; 132; 135; 143; 144; 146; 148; 149; 152; 153; 154; 156; 160; 161; 162; 163; 164; 169; 171; 175; 179; 180; 181; 183; 187; 188; 189; 190; 191; 192; 193; 195; 197; 198; 199